The Nature Process is a personal invitation from Gaia her~ ~port you at the deepest level possible in order to experience ~' ~ossible growth. It is an invitation to trust Life in ways yo~ ~ther than "anthropomorphizing Earth" Tabitha ~ ~rtant journey in how we can become more Ea~ ~ critical if we are to fully reconnect, heal, and evo~ ~ature Process is pure genius because it outlines a 'natu~ ~ dependent on our intellects, experts, or facilitators. Tabitha illu~ ~ow we can all tap into Nature's wisdom and follow where it leads. If you long to go beyond ecological theory and into loving partnership with Nature – as you transform your life – this is the field guide for you.

- TreeSisters
www.treesisters.org

"I feel like I am walking away with an amazing tool that I can use for the rest of my life."

~ Peggy W.

"For me the Nature Process is a form of prayer."

~ Holly B.

The Nature Process
(2nd Edition)

The Nature Process
(2nd Edition)

DISCOVER THE POWER AND
POTENTIAL OF YOUR NATURAL SELF
AND IMPROVE YOUR WELL-BEING

❧ ❧ ❧

Tabitha Jayne

ISBN: 099569446X
ISBN: 9780995694460

For J.

Oh Earth, Wait for Me
Return me, oh sun,
to my wild destiny,
rain of the ancient wood,
bring me back the aroma and the swords
that fall from the sky,
the solitary peace of pasture and rock,
the damp at the river-margins,
the smell of the larch tree,
the wind alive like a heart
beating in the crowded restlessness
of the towering araucaria.

Earth, give me back your pure gifts,
the towers of silence which rose
from the solemnity of their roots.
I want to go back to being what I have not been,
and learn to go back from such deeps
that among all natural things
I could live or not live; it does not matter
to be one stone more, the dark stone,
the pure stone which the river bears away.

Pablo Neruda

Contents

Preface

※　※　※

I NEVER EXPECTED THE NATURE Process to take off the way it did. In just over two short years, hundreds of people from over twelve countries around the world have taken part in the online program while over a hundred people have taken part in The Nature Process Director of Training & Development, Sami Aaron's talks, workshops and retreats in the United States. Six more people are on their way to become The Nature Process Facilitators and Coaches while the waiting list for the facilitator training program continues to grow. The program was so successful that we've had to spend the last eighteen months developing the infrastructure to support The Nature Process reach its full potential.

Most importantly, through our unique business model that enables us to give 100% of the profits of our online program to selected non-profits, we've raised nearly £16,000 ($21,000 US) to help reforest the tropics within ten years by calling forth the unique gifts, generosity and leadership of women everywhere and focusing it towards that goal through the work of the non-profit organisation, TreeSisters. And that's only the beginning.

This book was originally written from the first online program's course content. Since its publication nearly two years ago, there has been a lot of developments, both within The Nature Process and the research that accompanies it. In order to do the book justice, and make it a more valuable resource for you to read, these developments needed to be included.

Part of this is including stories of people who have used The Nature Process and offering more detailed practical exercises that can help you apply the five principles of The Nature Process, both separately and together, into your daily life. I've also included chapter summaries to help you remember the key points along with questions for reflection while you're out experiencing the beauty and wonder of the natural world.

There are two types of exercises included within the book. The first type of exercises are practical outdoors activities that can help you experience the principles/steps of The Nature Process and are suited to those who aren't familiar with meditation and prefer a more dynamic, interactive way of connecting to nature. The second are guided meditative exercises that were used in the second The Nature Process online program. These exercises are ideal if you already have a meditation practice that you're looking to deepen and you'll find them at the back of the book with the page referenced in the specific chapter associated with the exercise. This is so not to distract from the main content of the book.

As the number of people interested in facilitating and coaching The Nature Process continues to grow, I've also written this book with the awareness that you may be reading this as part of attending a workshop or training run by one of them. I wanted to provide them with the best possible book to support their work so that they can do what they do best, facilitating/coaching the experiential side of The Nature Process, and leaving the science and understanding of The Nature Process to me.

It's important to stress here that The Nature Process is all of its five principles, either practiced together in a specific order, or in an order of your choosing, or even separately. There has been some confusion about this possibility so I want to reinforce that here and will do so again throughout the book.

Also, there's a lot of language that I've wanted to amend to make the book clearer and more concise. As a result, I've re-written some of the sections and chapters of the book entirely. The online course was originally presented to a woman-only audience. With the number of men interested in The Nature Process growing I wanted to ensure they were not put off with some of the overtly female content, especially in the chapter on Natural Attractions!

In the last chapter of the first edition of this book I mentioned not knowing where The Nature Process has the potential to take you. Since that book was released, and as a result of my own journey exploring what comes after

The Nature Process, I wanted to expand upon this and give an inkling of what comes through continued practice with The Nature Process.

For me, one of the results of creating and teaching The Nature Process is that I decided to return to university to undertake my second masters in Consciousness, Spirituality and Transpersonal Psychology. These are big words that basically mean the study of people's subjective experiences with something more than their human self, and of the potential humans have when they become a 'whole being.'

It's truly humbling to see how The Nature Process has grown – and how it wants to continue growing. There have been many times, when I've been out in nature, that I've asked what I can do to contribute to the challenges of our current world and of how I could be of service. Through The Nature Process I've found one way to help make this world a better place for all life on Earth.

Introduction

❧   ❧   ❧

Our world faces a crisis as yet unperceived by those possessing
power to make great decisions for good or evil.

- ALBERT EINSTEIN

THERE'S SOMETHING WRONG WITH THE world we live in. You've felt it your entire life. At first you didn't know exactly what it was. You couldn't explain it. Yet no matter what's happened in your life it's been there, like a splinter in your mind.

Over the years, you've watched as the existing political, financial, educational, societal, and environmental structures have begun to crumble. We are in the middle of a global crisis. Civilisation as we know it is breaking down.

Yet with every crisis comes the opportunity for growth. Even though there's a wave of fear and uncertainty currently sweeping the planet, deep down within you is a seed of hope. You hope that the changes we're currently experiencing are the birth pangs of a new world being born. You hope that humanity can evolve, repair the damage that we've inflicted on the world and ourselves and create a better a future for all.

It's this hope that drives you forward. You not only believe in a better future, you are inspired to take action to help create this better future.

In this future, business puts the planet before profits.

Leaders put people before power.

Success is measured by how much positive impact you make.

Individually, we let go of the stories that keep us stuck and step into the complete awesomeness of who we are born to be.

Collectively, we bring the impossible into reality. We step beyond the limitations of ego and self.

Peace reigns. Equality exists for all.

The world is whole.

Balanced.

Now I have no idea *how* this will happen, and maybe neither do you.

I only know that it *will*.

Why?

I believe in nature.

The nature around us.

The nature within me and within you.

Together we are one.

And together we're changing the world.

When I forget that we can change the world, I go back to nature.

I am reminded.

The next step is revealed.

I take action.

I'm helping to make the world a better place.

The time is *now*.

Are you in?

I'm offering you a choice just like Morpheus did with Neo in the *The Matrix*.

You can put down this book, take the blue pill, and continue on with your life as it is. Believe whatever you want.

Or you can take the red pill. Access your forgotten childhood experiences of joy and wonder in nature. Follow the white rabbit into its hole and discover just how deep it connects you to the Earth.

The choice is yours.

When you spend time in nature, let go of your stress and anxiety and deepen your connection to nature, you discover a new way of being. You step into a state of flow and creativity that allows you to innovate both in life and in business.

You can't help but change how you view this world. You no longer see yourself as separate from it. You see yourself as part of it. When you see yourself as a part of the Earth, you can't help but make different choices in how you live your life.

You'll be inspired to step up into your full potential – both personally and professionally. You'll no longer just be getting through the daily grind struggling to find meaning and purpose. You'll wake up feeling truly alive, full of enthusiasm and energy.

Your relationships with your loved ones will improve. You'll start to view your life from a new perspective that helps you discover what's important and gives you the courage to take action towards making your dreams a reality.

As you do you'll help create the world that we all want to live in. We all have a part to play no matter how big or small. Everything in nature has a role, a purpose. You are no different.

Deep down you already know this is possible. It's this knowledge that has brought you to this book. It's this knowledge that has led me to write this book.

You see, my childhood was traumatic. Severe ill health. Bullying. Domestic violence. Rape. For peace, I turned to books, nature, and magic. As I grew into a young adult, I found drugs and alcohol masked the pain.

Then, when I was twenty-two, my younger brother, Peter, died in a car accident.

My whole world turned upside down. I saw how I was living my life and knew I had to find a new path. I started spending more time outdoors in woods like I'd done as a child. It gave me a sense of clarity and peace about what I needed to do.

The next five years were spent trying to turn the worst thing that ever happened to me into the best. I devoted my time and energy to healing, spiritual growth, work, university, and the charity I was inspired to found to help young adults affected by bereavement.

Instead of truly healing, I ended up tired, stressed, and burnt out. I felt empty inside.

I needed a change. When I saw the opportunity to volunteer in Northern Spain I took it because of my brother Peter's nickname—Pedro. The natural landscape there was amazing: vivid, green and so alive. Inspired by this, I decided to move there and teach English.

Throwing myself into a country, language, and culture that I knew nothing about ended up being a time of powerful self-development. Finally, I started to heal from my brother's death and my traumatic childhood.

A couple of years later, I challenged myself to do a weekend retreat in Spanish in rural Galicia. That weekend I was forced to face parts of me that I wasn't fully comfortable with. You see, I'd always been able to sense things that weren't there. I had trained as a psychic and medium for a few years after my brother died but had never been able to accept the idea that I wasn't making some of it up – even when I'd do a reading for someone and be able to give them really accurate information.

At this retreat there was an old oak tree standing alone at the corner of a field. It was one of the most incredible trees I'd ever seen, with a wide trunk and full branches filled with green leaves. The power emanating from this tree was incredible. I couldn't take my eyes off it and kept feeling a physical pull to return again and again to the tree. As crazy as it sounds, it felt like the tree was speaking to me.

On the last day of the retreat, I approached the tree early in the morning. There was a sense of reverence within me as if I were approaching a wise and holy man. Stopping close to the tree, I put my hand on its trunk and was inspired to ask its permission to climb it.

That's when something really weird happened. I felt as if the tree was speaking to me in my head. It told me the best way to climb up into its branches. Once there, the tree told me to climb out to the edge of its branches to remove some trapped plastic, then slide down the branch to the Earth. My heart was pounding and I thought I was mad. It looked dangerous.

I sat up there in the tree's branches with my mind racing. Should I do this? What if I fell and hurt myself? What if the tree was really speaking to me?

What if it was all in my head? I didn't know what to do. Finally, I decided I had to do what the tree had asked me to. It was the only way I'd know the truth.

I followed the tree's instructions on where to place my feet and hands as I slowly climbed out towards the branches where the plastic was. The exhilaration I felt as I managed to pull the plastic free without falling was intense. Then, there was the panic as I looked at the branch the tree told me to slide down.

I tried to climb back up the way I'd come but almost slipped and fell as the tree told me it wasn't possible. Slowly, I climbed out onto the branch. Halfway along, I stopped and perched on the branch like a bird. The branch swayed gently hidden high amongst the leaves as I looked out over the field.

A sense of peace filled my entire being. I thought of my brother and felt fully connected to him. I remembered when we'd scattered Peter's ashes in the woodland area, as he'd requested. We'd gone back a few days later to find bright red flowers carpeting the Earth where his ashes had fallen.

As fast as the memory came to mind, it hit me like a bolt of lightning. Nature and my brother were one. I hadn't lost my brother. Peter was everywhere. Just as I was. We were all one. Like magic, with a click of my fingers, the remaining pain over his death melted away to be replaced by the most immense feeling of love and connection that remains with me to this day.

Climbing down from that tree I felt like a totally different person. My life was never the same again. I started spending even more time outdoors and began a masters in applied ecopsychology (the study of the human-nature relationship) to help me understand how to deepen my connection to nature. As I did, I connected deeper to myself too.

Yet there was one area of my life to which I had never thought to apply this connection with nature. That was my business. I was using nature to help support the stress and anxiety of setting up my own company but I had never thought to use it as a tool to grow my business. The last two and half years have been incredible. I went from a struggling and frustrated solopreneur to the director of two companies with a growing team of people. I also now host

'Sustainable: The Podcast' which features inspiring interviews with leaders in the field of sustainability sharing best practice and tips to help organisations become more sustainable. My work with The Nature Process led me to return to university with a scholarship to study more about the extraordinary experiences people have when connected to nature and the potential they have for transforming their lives – and the world.

What started initially as a short course to promote my work and get me more clients has turned into the start of a global movement to help humanity reconnect with the natural world. I currently have facilitators and coaches of The Nature Process in the United Kingdom, United States, Germany and Australia while hundreds of people from over thirteen countries around the world have gone through The Nature Process.

When I wrote the first edition of this book I focused heavily on how much my revenue had increased from bringing nature into my business. I've removed that from this edition because as great as it was The Nature Process is not about teaching someone how to make more money. Its real power lies in being able to help people reduce stress and anxiety in any situation while deepening their connection to nature – both inside and out. It is a therapeutic tool that has helped my clients improve their well-being and change their lives.

One of my favourite client stories is of a seventy-two-year-old woman who had lived with anxiety her whole life. She'd tried many things, some of which had helped, but she'd never been able to fully get rid of her anxiety. She felt unsafe when outside and struggled being around lots of people.

Using The Nature Process this client was able to feel non-anxious for the first time in her life. Through connecting with trees and other aspects of nature she began to feel safe outside. Then, during Hallowe'en she was able to go outside and enjoy the trick or treating in her city for the first time. This event is so big in her city that parts of it get cordoned off as there are thousands of children taking part.

It's stories like these from my clients that I'm most proud of. They are what inspire me to keep going with what I do. Who knows what The Nature Process is going to do for you?

The Nature Process comes from nature itself. I am merely the conduit that allows it to appear in this world. Its gift to me is to allow me to show what happens by creating a business that is truly nature-centred. This is still a work in progress. To allow The Nature Process to become what it wants to become is one of the most exciting things I've ever done. Its success, and those of my business clients, inspired me to create another business, EarthSelf Ltd (www.EarthSelf.org), which offers a nature-centred approach to organisational management.

I am a woman on a mission. Through using The Nature Process myself I have such clarity of purpose and sense of direction that I know exactly what I'll be doing with the rest of my life. Putting planet and profit together in a truly sustainable way while helping others to do the same and also helping people tap into the healing power of nature is my life's dream. Thanks to The Nature Process it's becoming a reality.

I'm able to dream big because I know that nature will support me to release the stress, anxiety – and fear – that comes from doing so. This is what I want for you.

In the first edition of the book I wrote about how nature was helping me live the life that I want with, living in Ibiza and travelling to Scotland, France, Andorra, Barcelona, New York and London. Now I'm back living in Scotland because my passion for the work I do is more important than travelling and having the freedom to live my life any way I want. I know I'll still travel and have adventures but they'll be related to the work I do.

The intention of sharing all this was to give you a bit of background about my journey so that you'd connect and relate to me more. However, this book is not about me and my story. It's about you and your life.

To paraphrase John Lennon, some might say that you're a dreamer. You're naturally drawn to find the positive in any situation, even when life gives you lemons.

You've always had an appreciation for nature and the gifts you've received from spending time in it. This appreciation may or may not have been shared by those around you. You might have struggled to put your experiences with nature into words or maybe you've just never felt the need. After all, nature has traditionally been seen as belonging to tree-hugging hippies, die-hard wilderness adventurers or save the planet environmentalists.

With The Nature Process, there needn't be tree-hugging, living off bugs and building natural shelters in the wood or environmental activism – unless you're attracted to doing it!

I've spent the last five years figuring out how to teach this in a way that's accessible to everyone. At first I worked with people individually, tailoring the exercises and my approach to their specific needs. Then, I developed a way to teach a group of people the same process in a far quicker and more powerful way, which allowed them to experience the benefits of connecting with nature immediately.

This book comes from this work. It takes the concepts I teach and expands them so that you're able to start reducing stress and anxiety by aligning your psyche with nature's wisdom.

Chapter One will get you to start thinking differently about nature by expanding your understanding of what nature is. You'll explore the essence and consciousness of nature, and also consider the fundamental problem with referring to our planet as "Mother Earth". You'll learn how Aristotle's hierarchy of nature helped create a split between nature and humans in Western beliefs. Then you'll explore how our expanding knowledge of the universe through scientific developments can help us see that the nature around us is a reflection of our inner nature, and how this can encourage us into a new way of sensing the world. You'll also discover more about the growing field of ecopsychology and get an overview of the scientific evidence that shows why we need to spend more time outdoors. I'll also reveal more about my own personal journey with nature.

In Chapter Two, you get an introduction to each of the five principles/steps of The Nature Process along with how the five principles/steps work together as an entire process. This allows you to gain an overview of each part of the process and why it's important before reading an example of The Nature Process in action. This will prepare you for diving deep into each principle/step in the subsequent chapters.

Chapter Three sees us diving into an explanation of natural presence. You'll discover how meditation and nature are connected along with how the Earth connects to our brains. You'll learn about connecting to different aspects of nature and what Daniel Kish, a blind human echolocation expert, can teach us about our senses. You'll explore the reality of our sensory nature, discover how we have not five senses but fifty-four. As you dive deep into understanding more about theses senses, you'll learn how you can start exploring these senses for yourself. Then, you'll learn how to experience the fifty-four senses with different brainwave states and how you can experience them anywhere - in the city and the country, indoors and out.

In Chapter Four you'll build upon your knowledge of natural presence with learning all about your natural body. You'll learn how your body responds to stress and how your mind and your body are one and the same. You'll discover what horses have to teach us about body awareness and how our bodies naturally release energy, along with understanding how emotions affect the body and how trauma and stress are stored within the body if it's not released. You'll then be guided to discover, experience, and connect to your own natural body and how to adapt this exploration should you have a physical disability. Finally, you'll understand how to connect your natural body to your natural presence.

Chapter Five leads you to discover the truth about natural attractions and why it's so important to follow them, along with the challenges of doing so. Exercise, work and death will be considered through the lenses of natural attractions. We'll touch upon the insanity of civilisation and how the stories and beliefs it creates can make it difficult to follow your natural attractions. Following this, you'll discover how to discover your natural attractions and how nature can help you explore them.

In Chapter Six you'll start an exploration of natural communication, both as part of The Nature Process and by itself. You'll learn all about the Gaia hypothesis and how this facilitates communication between us and the Earth, along with the story of Tilly Smith and how, through listening to her natural senses, she was able to save peoples' lives during the 2004 tsunami. You'll discover how to communicate with nature and make natural communication work for you no matter the beliefs you have. You'll discover the power of asking permission from nature to connect with it and a simple way in which to do so. There are also tips for starting to explore communication with nature along with an exploration of the differences in natural communication with animals, plants, trees, stones, water, and even stars – whether you believe this is possible or not. You'll then learn how you can consolidate natural communication fully into The Nature Process itself.

Chapter Seven takes you into the last part of The Nature Process and shows you how to experience a natural release. You'll discover why it's important to bring yourself back into balance and how the heart's power can help you do this. The power of your imagination and how it can help support a natural release is also explored before you discover how you can use your breath in order to achieve a successful natural release. You'll then be taken through a real-time account and analysis of my own experience with The Nature Process from natural presence right to natural release. You'll learn why it's important to take action after using The Nature Process as a tool to reduce stress and anxiety. You'll discover how to use the Natural Systems Thinking Process (NSTP) to help you integrate your experience of The Nature Process before receiving guidelines on how to use The Nature Process as a therapeutic tool. Finally, you'll explore how you can integrate The Nature Process into your daily life.

In Chapter Eight you'll focus on the potential obstacles that may stop you from fully engaging with The Nature Process. This chapter is slightly different from the others in that, for every challenge explored, there's also a suggested exercise to help you explore it. The obstacles explored in this chapter start with looking at how you can distract yourself from practicing The Nature Process and how your emotions and beliefs about nature may prevent you from getting outside and connecting to nature. You'll look at how the language you use about nature and the Earth offer clues for what you really think about nature and how this may influence how you interpret the insights you receive from connecting to nature. You'll also explore the trap of 'green' marketing and how your desire to do things that are good for the Earth can be manipulated before exploring how to stop yourself from getting caught up in the perceived 'negative' aspects of nature. I'll encourage you to be sceptical when we explore what both science and alternative approaches say about what is natural, and help you to stay in an open mindset that allows you to ask "what if?" as you consciously connect to nature. Lastly, you'll learn how to avoid accidentally disconnecting yourself from nature while falling into the trap of still thinking that you're connected.

Chapter Nine reminds you of the importance of doing the exercises in the book and experiencing The Nature Process for yourself. It also looks at inspirational historical figures who were truly connected to nature and the legacy they left upon the world. You'll also discover what it means to commit to practising The Nature Process daily and what can happen when you do. I'll then introduce you to the concept of the Earth Self and how it relates to you as a human. Lastly, I'll share how you can develop the Earth Self and what it's like to experience it through first-hand accounts.

I can't stress this enough:

This is a book that's designed not just to be read, but to be experienced.

If you do, it's going to be one "heaven" of a journey.

CHAPTER 1

Think Differently About Nature

❧　❧　❧

A human being is a part of the whole, called by us "Universe," a
part limited in time and space. He experiences himself, his thoughts
and feelings as something separated from the rest — a kind of
optical delusion of his consciousness. This delusion is a kind of
prison for us, restricting us to our personal desires and to affection
for a few persons nearest to us. Our task must be to free ourselves
from this prison by widening our circle of compassion to embrace
all living creatures and the whole of nature in its beauty.

- ALBERT EINSTEIN

WHEN YOU THINK OF NATURE, what comes to mind? Maybe you think of
aspects of the natural world such as mountains, trees, animals, and rivers.
Maybe you think of a beautiful landscape or a world that exists independent
of humanity and our civilisation. Maybe you even think of nature as wild and
savage, or something that is far simpler than the complexities of modern life.

Nature is all this and more. Nature is the universe with all its incredible
phenomena including stars, galaxies, black holes, and planets. It's also the
magic at work that holds the universe together and the reality of our existence.

It's also within us, our character and personality – our own personal
nature. It's the things we create such as cities and technology and experiences

we have such as love-making and childbirth. In essence, everything is nature. However, that means that things like war, poverty and famine are also nature.

Humanity has known that we've been part of nature for a very long time and it's something that we've not been comfortable with. One of the fundamental reasons that we created civilisation was to separate us from nature and the aspects of it that scared us, not realising that no matter what we can do we can never truly separate ourselves from nature.

As humanity has evolved, we have forgotten the meaning of nature. We have reduced it to nothing more than a resource available to us to use as we see fit with no respect or regard for the consequences.

We are now waking up to just how badly we have treated nature. Growing concern about global warming and climate change has put humanity's focus back on nature and our relationship to it.

Our main problem is that we view nature from an anthropocentric viewpoint, i.e. the human perspective. In the past, we studied nature as a way to achieve domination over it. Today we study global warming and climate change mainly in terms of the impact that it has on human activity. Whilst we talk about the changes we can make to prevent further damage to the Earth, we study the natural environment mainly in terms of how it can benefit humanity. It's all about us.

By adopting an anthropocentric viewpoint, we've forgotten a fundamental truth of our existence.

We are part of nature.

To be in harmony with nature, we don't need to study it to find out how we can control it for our own benefit. We merely need to psychologically reconnect ourselves to nature and align our thinking with nature's wisdom.

The Problem with Mother Earth

For thousands of years, the Earth and nature have both been personified as a woman. The earliest evidence of this dates back to around 22,000 BCE in the form of the Venus of Willendorf. This small female statuette discovered in

1908 in Austria has voluptuous breasts and hips, and a protruding vulva. The statue has no feet and its head is covered by circular bands.

Nothing is known about where the statue comes from, why it was made, or what its significance is. While it's speculated that this figure and others like it represent fertility goddesses, we really have no idea what they mean and if in fact they were intended to represent nature as a woman.

But perhaps not coincidentally, throughout many different cultures and mythologies nature has long been personified as a life-giving and nurturing mother from which all life sprang.

For example, in Greek mythology Gaia was great mother of the Earth and all the universe. In Roman mythology, she was known as Terra. Sumerian mythology refers to Ki as the Earth goddess, and in Egyptian mythology we had Mut, the primal mother of all who was born of none. The Māoris from New Zealand call the Earth mother Papatuanuku, while in Incan mythology Mother Earth is known as Pachamama, whose literal translation would actually be "Mother Universe."

The earliest written literal references to nature as a mother are found in ancient Greek going back to the 12th century BCE. In the English language, the first recorded use of the term was in 1266, with evidence suggesting it was popular between the 5th and 15th centuries to personify nature.

As a way of understanding nature, medieval Christian thinkers narrowed their understanding of nature to mean something that had been created by God. They didn't class her as a goddess, merely a personification of the middle zone between heaven and hell.

This idea continued and was developed during the time of the Enlightenment in the 17th and 18th centuries. Reason and logic were the foundational beliefs of the Enlightenment. The previous ideas of the medieval thinkers linked nature to God, which made it impossible to examine. In order to study nature, it had to become *separate* from God. What better way to do this than feminise nature, when women were seen as unequal to men?

This has led some people to argue that how we treat women and how we treat the planet are inter-linked. It's a branch of feminism known as eco-feminism. However, the dark side to this is that it then becomes too easy to argue that women are more connected to nature than men, when in truth men and women are both equally as connected to nature as the other.

There is a growing call to return to the ancient feminine viewpoint of the Earth as a sacred giver of life. The challenge with this perspective is that its roots lie in anthropocentrism. We refer to nature as a mother to help us understand nature better.

Stop for a moment and think about what the word mother means to you. Then think of how society defines a mother and what society expects of one. Through the identification of nature as a mother, we exclude aspects of nature that don't fit with our understanding of what a mother is.

More Than a Mother

Nature is so much more than a mother. It's more than feminine. It's more than human. The truth is that nature pushes the boundaries of what our mind can understand.

It is neither masculine nor feminine. It just *is*. It both gives life and destroys life, and it does both without conscience.

Nature engages in a complex, chaotic dance as it maintains itself in harmony. This dance is beyond what we as humans with our minds are capable of understanding. Despite hundreds of years of scientific investigation, we are not even close to having the secrets of nature fully revealed to us.

We can't understand nature intellectually. We have to become nature in order to truly understand it. We have to heal the split within our psyche and allow body and mind to experience the beauty and magnificence of nature beyond Mother Earth.

For in truth, we are not just *part* of nature. We *are* nature.

Through connecting deeply to nature we connect to ourselves and discover the truth of what it means to be fully human.

THE CONSCIOUSNESS OF NATURE

Within some philosophical, religious and spiritual approaches there is the belief that there is no separation between the spiritual and material world. They are one and the same.

Some of these approaches also believe that it's not just humans who have a spirit. All manifestations of the natural environment—such as animals, trees, plants, rocks, mountains, rivers, thunder, and wind—have souls or spirits too.

Not only is this idea present in Buddhism, Hinduism, Paganism, Jainism, Shinto, and Serer religions, along with many traditional Native American religions, but Plato, the ancient Greek philosopher, developed this with the idea of the *anima mundi* or world soul.

In his written dialogue *Timaeus*, Plato put forth the argument that, "This world is indeed a living being endowed with a soul and intelligence... a single visible living entity containing all other living entities, which by their nature are all related." For over two thousand years, this notion has continued to flourish in the philosophy and religion of the Western world.

This has also caused great debate throughout the centuries that still continues to this day. Modern science came to reject this notion, believing that sentient awareness was something only humans were capable of.

It was Rene Descartes, the 17th century philosopher, who created the split between the spiritual and physical world that we still see reflected in current mainstream Western ideology. He did this by making the distinction that the mind, along with consciousness and self-awareness, was something different from the physical brain. Descartes argued that the mental components of the mind cannot exist in space and that physical objects are incapable of thought. His work served as validation for studying nature as something separate from God.

Yet evidence is increasing that contradicts both the idea of a split between mind and body, and that consciousness exists only in humans.

We are now discovering that animals such as dolphins, elephants, pigs, chimpanzees, gorillas, bonobos, and orangutans display awareness of themselves as being separate from their environment.

The standard measurement for this is through what's known as the mirror test devised by Gordon G. Gallup, a North American psychologist, whereby a part of the animal's skin is marked in a way that's only visible in a mirror. Awareness of self is assumed when the animal directs grooming behaviour towards the mark.

Furthermore, animal cognition scientist Irene Pepperberg's work with captive African grey parrots has shown they possess near human-like levels of consciousness. They are able to use human language with meaning and perform abstract cognitive tasks related to shape, colour, and number on a level equalling that of human toddlers.

There's even research emerging that shows that plants and trees have a form of intelligence that allows them to sense, learn, remember, and react in ways which we humans would recognise.

In 2005, The Society for Plant Neurobiology was created after the first international symposium on plant intelligence was held in Florence. The society points out that plants exhibit behaviour that is just as sophisticated as animals. Because this behaviour occurs at a much slower rate than in animals, science has been unable to properly see it until now. Yet if we truly want to understand the world around us, we need to learn to see plants as dynamic and highly sensitive organisms.

In 2014, a couple of amazing conferences took place. In Ibiza, for the first time ever, there was a scientific conference on the research into Ayahuasca, a psychoactive plant medicine from the Amazon jungle. In London, a conference on plant consciousness blended together the values of plant neurobiology, permaculture, deep-ecology, eco-psychology, shamanism, and herbalism.

Plant consciousness is no longer just in the realm of philosophical, religious, and spiritual traditions. It is now firmly placed in the sphere of science, and interest and research in the field continues to grow, along with scepticism over these ideas.

We are currently in the midst of a paradigm shift within science where many of the theories we've accepted as fact are being challenged. This creates controversy about many of these new ideas with many of them being ridiculed as not possible. Thomas Kuhn talks about this in his book, *The Structure of*

Scientific Revolutions, where he states that before a new idea can be accepted as the norm it first is ignored, then discredited, before gaining momentum and becoming the new normal.

Nevertheless, evidence shows that the mind-body split as identified by Descartes was wrong, and that there was some truth in ancient philosophy, religion and spirituality after all. Within neuropsychology, there is strong evidence that shows that mental processes such as attention, memory, reasoning, language, etc., have a physical basis in the brain and body. Research into the neurobiology of plants is finding that their intelligent behaviour has a physical basis in the form of chemical reactions too. This is even as more research continues to support the idea that we are all interconnected in ways we've previously not understood. Science is still debating the research, what this means and how our philosophical worldview needs to change as a result.

ARISTOTLE'S HIERARCHY OF NATURE

Aristotle, another ancient Greek philosopher, was a student of Plato who was devoted to natural science. His views shaped not only medieval scholarship but continued to impact the Western world until the time of the Enlightenment.

One of his biggest contributions was his classification of living beings, whereby he created a hierarchy, or *scala naturae*, that consisted of eleven levels, from zoophytes to man. Living organisms were classified based on the complexity of their structure and their body function. The higher up the scale you went, the greater the vitality and capacity for movement.

Like Plato, Aristotle also believed in the notion that all living beings had souls, though this was different to our modern day understanding of what a soul is. Aristotle's definition of a soul was similar to what we could call the life-force of a living being.

Aristotle believed that there was also a hierarchy of souls, with the living beings at the lower end of the hierarchy possessing fewer functions of the soul than those higher up the hierarchy.

It's here that our anthropocentric Western worldview begins. Aristotle placed humans at the top of the hierarchy, both in terms of their external capabilities and soul functions.

He stated that there were three types of soul: *nutritive*, which belonged to plants based on their ability to self-nourish and reproduce; *sensitive*, which belonged to animals who could both self-nourish and reproduce, and move and perceive their environment; and *rational*, which belonged to man and man alone. Man possessed all the soul qualities of plants and animals along with something uniquely his: intelligence.

It was this work that medieval scholars developed to create the belief system called the "Great Chain of Being", a hierarchal structure of all matter and life that was believed to be the way in which God had intended the world to work.

At the top of the chain sat God, and immediately below him were his angels. This hierarchy descended through the stars and moons down to humans who were classified according to kings, princes, nobles and the common man. Below humans sat animals, themselves categorized depending on whether they were wild or domesticated. Then came trees and other plants, followed by precious stones and minerals before lastly coming to the Earth itself.

The Great Chain of Being explained that although the Earth existed, it was not alive, thus laying to rest Plato's notion of a world soul, along with any ancient religious and spiritual ideas of the Earth as a living organism.

This contradicted the ancient and universal tenet called the Circle of Life, which was a belief held by many indigenous cultures that the world existed in a cyclic nature with everything in life united, whole, and infinite. With the acceptance of the Great Chain of Being, the idea of the universe as a continuous circle was broken.

Nevertheless, Aristotle still made a major contribution to our understanding of how the world works through the development of empiricism. This is a belief that knowledge comes primarily from sensory experience and is gathered through the processes of experimentation and experience. How we organise, identify, and interpret this sensory information is the way in which we perceive and understand the environment around us. As we looked at the world, this viewpoint provided a disciplined framework and helped expand our knowledge of how nature really works.

NATURE OUTSIDE REFLECTS NATURE WITHIN

In the early twentieth century, the development of quantum mechanics by Albert Einstein and other scientists fundamentally changed the way we view the world. By bringing physical matter down to an atomic and subatomic level, we have been able to grasp the connection between energy and matter in a way we've never been able to understand it before.

Physical matter—the ordinary stuff we can see and touch—is made up of atoms. Atoms consist of particles known as protons, neutrons, and electrons. These particles are so small that atoms consist of mostly empty space. Despite the illusion of solidness with the human body, and everything else in the universe, the universe actually consists of more than 99.999% space. It's this space that connects us as humans to everything else in the universe. On a fundamental level, we are all connected. We are all one.

Furthermore, the atoms within our bodies are continually exchanged with others in the universe. Physically, despite the illusion otherwise, your body is not the same body that it was a couple of years ago. The atoms within your body have been exchanged with those from stars, rivers, mountains, oceans, trees, and the Earth itself.

Research also shows that once particles have been connected physically they stay connected even when they are separated by physical distance. When a change affects one particle it affects any other particle that was once connected to it.

The implications of this have not been fully integrated into our current Western worldview. We still view ourselves as separate from the natural world around us, but this is a deeply flawed belief.

As quantum mechanics reveals the fundamental truth that on an atomic level we're all connected and are all one, we have to realise that if we're at war with nature, we're at war with ourselves. The way that we try to control and dominate nature is the same way in which we try to control and dominate ourselves and others.

And if we care for nature, we care for ourselves.

On an individual level, we fight a continuous battle between what feels good for us and what our society and culture have told us is good for us. We see this played out as we stay in jobs that don't fulfil us for the sake of money. Believing that they're not achievable, we sacrifice our dreams, and are encouraged to believe that owning more things will make us happy. We stay in relationships that aren't healthy and struggle with the demands of all the different roles we have in life. We hide aspects of ourselves thinking that they're unlovable and that we're unworthy. Yet all the time we're secretly dreaming of more.

This plays out on a societal level as we experience racism, sexism, and homophobia within our society, and conflict and war around the world. Instead of acknowledging the parts of us that we feel uncomfortable with, we project them onto others. We judge them as different from us and see them as the root of all our problems. If only *they* weren't different, we wouldn't have the problems that we do in life.

Global warming, climate change, deforestation, land degradation, intensive animal and crop farming, ocean acidification and pollution, and their negative health effects upon us, are the Earth's way of warning us that we are fundamentally disconnected and out of balance, not just with the nature *around* us but also with the nature *within* us.

A New Way of Sensing the World

If we truly want to create global transformation and live in a world that benefits all living beings along with the Earth itself, we have to start with our own personal transformation.

This transformation starts with becoming aware that we are all one and we are acting from this place of unity. It's not just about understanding this on an intellectual level; it's about embodying this on a cellular level.

Unfortunately, many of us are disconnected from our own bodies because we've been taught to hate them. In particular, we see this reflected in the unhealthy and unrealistic attitudes towards our bodies in the media. Women, and increasingly men, are taught to judge their bodies by some unrealistic image of perfection that we're never going to live up to.

Furthermore, we've been taught that our bodies and their natural functions are dirty. Things like burping and farting are considered impolite and disgusting. Crying is seen as being too emotional and a sign of weakness. Never mind the conditioning that we've received that has told us that it's wrong to feel pleasure in our bodies!

Instead we've been trained to be overly dependent on our minds, which run riot with all the voices of the social and cultural conditioning that we've received ever since we were born.

When we stay in our minds, we don't have to feel the pain from all the unhealthy conditioning we receive. In some ways, it's easier. Going into our bodies and feeling the pain of our mental anguish on a physical level can be intense, especially when we try to face it ourselves.

That's where nature comes in. Nature's way of communicating is non-verbal. It communicates on a full sensory level, and the only way in which we can truly understand what nature is saying is by experiencing this communication through our bodies.

When we allow this communication in, we become fully supported by nature as we let go of the stress and anxiety that keeps us stuck in the same patterns and discover how creative and innovative we truly are.

We are able to give our stress and anxiety to the Earth and allow it to be recycled into something new. Yet many people dismiss this as nonsense or are afraid to do this. Our current environmental view is of the Earth as weak and fragile and as something that needs to be protected. The truth is dramatically different.

The Earth is far more powerful than we give it credit for. Think of the power of a tornado or of a volcano erupting. The Earth can create new landmass in a matter of days and destroy existing landmasses in a matter of minutes. It can wipe thousands of us out in a matter of moments.

In contrast, our stress and anxiety are nothing more than a tickle of discomfort for the Earth before the energy that we release into it is transformed anew into something that supports not only the Earth's growth but our own.

I'm aware that this might sound strange, especially if you've never considered that the Earth is a living organism before.

Yet the Earth welcomes our stress and anxiety because it's through this that the Earth experiences itself. It has the capability to take our stress and anxiety then transform it into ecstasy, which is then given back to us when we view a brilliant ball of red fire as it rises across the Earth's horizon or when we splash in fresh, cool water, feeling its wetness against our skin. In this way, we re-create the Circle of Life and allow ourselves to truly experience the nature within us and without in a way that sustains life rather than destroys it.

The Earth has been in existence for 4.6 billion years, and nature—the universe—has existed for 13.7 billion years, something which I'll refer to again. In contrast, we humans, in our modern form, have walked this planet for a scant two hundred thousand years. When we allow ourselves to experience a full-bodied connection to nature, we allow the ancient wisdom that is inherent within it into our lives, so that we create not only personal transformation but planetary transformation as we build a world that works for all life on Earth.

THE EMERGENCE OF ECOPSYCHOLOGY

Ecopsychology is a term coined by North American, Theodore Roszak in his 1992 book, *The Voice of the Earth*. It focuses on the relationship between humans and nature, not only from a psychological perspective but also an ecological one. What's interesting is even though Theodore Roszak coined the term he was not actually a psychologist. He was in fact a historian!

That the field of ecopsychology was – and is – developed by people who are not psychologists is a common occurrence. As a result, much of the early writing on ecopsychology was very philosophical, arguing that ecopsychology is not a sub-discipline of psychology but rather a framework that should define how we view psychology altogether. Today, there is much more empirical evidence to support the necessity of a human/nature relationship, some of which will be mentioned throughout this book.

Ecopsychology emerged from San Francisco and the field today is still dominated by a North American perspective, though as more people are starting to adopt and use ecopsychological practices in other parts of the world, this is slowly changing.

Even though the term ecopsychology only started being used in 1992, the idea of the human/nature relationship, along with using wilderness settings for therapy and education has been around since the nineteen-sixties. One of the pioneers of this early movement was North American, Dr Michael. J. Cohen. The Nature Process is based upon, and inspired by, the work he's developed over the last thirty-odd years in his Project NatureConnect program.

Furthermore, the Swiss psychiatrist and psychotherapist, Carl Jung, as far back as the 1950s, wrote extensively on the importance of nature and his concern over the loss of connection to nature that the modern world was creating.

Ecopsychology is still emerging as a field within psychology and there is intense debate about what ecopsychology actually is. Within its roots is a combination of deep ecology, experiential learning, wilderness experiences, environmental activism, and spiritual philosophy and practice. What is exciting about this is that you can define ecopsychology in a way that makes sense to you. This is what The Nature Process is all about; offering a practical way to engage directly with the natural world and discover what the human/nature relationship means to you on a deeper level than before.

Now, there are fundamental assumptions contained within ecopsychology, that The Nature Process supports. You'll discover more about these as you go through the book, though I want to clarify them here.

First, the Earth is a living system and human beings are fundamentally interconnected with the Earth.

Second, it is the current disconnect between humanity and nature, which is a key element of civilisation, which is the root of our personal, social and environmental challenges.

Third, there is an innate drive within humans to live in harmony with the natural world and its rhythms. The biologist, Edward O. Wilson coined the term *biophilia* in 1984 and refers to an urge to connect with other forms of life.

Fourth, we can learn about our relationship with nature not just from science but also from spiritual teachings, ancient knowledge and indigenous wisdom, as well as from our own experiences.

Lastly, when we connect to nature we remember the truth that we are nature and experience a new way of living with ourselves and with the natural world around us.

Why You Need to Get Outdoors

Aside from the fact that you probably already know that you feel good when you go outside, there are now over sixty-seven researched benefits to spending time in nature.

In 2015, there was a journal article published in the Ecosystem Services by Paul Sandifer, Ariana Sutton-Grier, and Bethney Ward. It offers the most comprehensive list of benefits from spending time outdoors that I've ever come across.

In contrast to my expanded definition of nature at the start of this chapter, they define nature as "plants and other living things, natural and semi-natural areas including coastlines and mountains, parks, forests, wildlife sanctuaries, views of seascapes and relatively undeveloped landscapes".

The following lists are a summary by category of all the benefits currently researched.

Mental processes and behaviours

- Psychological well-being
- Attention restoration/perceived restorativeness
- Decreased depression, dejection, anger, aggression, frustration, hostility, stress
- Increased self-esteem
- Positive/improved mood
- Reduced anxiety and tension
- Increased prosocial behaviour/improved behaviour
- Increased opportunities for reflection
- Increased vitality and vigour/decreased fatigue
- Increased creativity

- Increased happiness
- Increased calmness, comfort and refreshment
- Improved body image for women
- Reduced ADHD in children
- Improved emotion, social health of children; self-worth
- Improved quality of life

Cognitive function or ability

- Attentional restoration
- Reduced mental fatigue
- Reduced confusion
- Improved academic performance/education/learning opportunities
- Improved cognitive function
- Improved cognitive function in children
- Improved productivity/ability to perform tasks/positive workplace attitude

Physical function and/or physical health

- Better general health
- Perceived health/well-being
- Reduced illness/cough/mortality/sick leave
- Stress reduction/less stress-related illness/improved physiological functioning
- Reduced cortisol levels (indicative of lower stress)
- Reduced blood pressure
- Reduced mortality from circulatory and respiratory disease
- Reduced headaches/pain
- Reduced mortality due to income deprivation
- Reduced mortality from stroke

- Reduced COPD, upper respiratory tract infections, asthma, other inflammatory disorders and intestinal disease
- Reduced obesity
- Faster healing/recovery from surgery/illness/trauma
- Improved addiction recovery
- Reduced cardiovascular and respiratory disease
- Reduced pulse/heart rate
- Decreased sympathetic (fight or flight response) nerve activity
- Increased parasympathetic (relax and enjoy) nerve activity
- Increased levels of natural killer cells and anti-cancer proteins
- Decreased blood glucose levels in diabetes patients
- Decreased type 2 diabetes
- Increased physical activity
- Reduced exposure to pollution
- Increased longevity
- Better health of children
- Reduced preterm birth and low birth weight
- General health/convalescence/better health near coasts

Reduces the incidence of infectious disease

- Reduction in spread/amplification/of some infectious diseases including some zoonotic (can be passed from animals to humans) diseases

Individual, community or national level

- Increased/facilitated social interaction
- Enables social empowerment
- Reduced aggression, crime rates, violence, fear
- Enables interracial interaction
- Enhances social cohesion and social support

Cultural and spiritual well-being

* Aesthetic appreciation
* Increased inspiration
* Enhanced spiritual well-being
* Increased recreational satisfaction

Material goods and benefits

* Supply of food, raw materials, medicines, and other values
* Contribution to biomedical advances
* Increased value of property/housing; money
* Economic value of recreation

Personal and community ability to withstand impacts and remain healthy

* Sustainability/pro-environment awareness and behaviour
* Supply of ecosystem services critical for human health and well-being
* Supply of ecosystem services that support communities and enable community resilience

I don't know about you but I find that list very attractive. I want all of those benefits in my life!

QUICK REMINDER

What I've presented in this chapter is an oversimplified view of our history and our relationship with nature. It focuses particularly on a Western cultural and historical approach. To go into detail and present an in-depth multi-cultural and historical perspective of humanity's relationship with nature is beyond the scope of this book. I'm a woman who's grown up with a Western worldview and I'm making the assumption that you grew up with a Western worldview too.

The idea behind this chapter is not to dive deep into the themes I've presented. It's about giving you enough information to consider that there is a different way of thinking about nature and helping to prepare you to be open to experience The Nature Process. For those of you who wish to read more, I've included suggestions for further reading in a section at the end of the book.

Be aware that as you read what I've written, your mind may want to argue with it and find holes that challenge what I've said here. This is a mind-based trick that prevents you from engaging with the material presented. This book is not an intellectual exercise. It's an experiential one. Don't fall into the trap of intellectualizing this book. Stay open to the material that's presented, engage with the process and experience it first.

Before we dive fully into The Nature Process, I want to share a bit more about my background and relationship with nature so that you get a better picture of the author behind the book.

MY JOURNEY BACK TO NATURE

I've always been a bit of a nature geek. It comes from spending most of my childhood growing up in small Scottish villages. If I wasn't inside reading a book, you'd find me outside – when I wasn't ill. It was an era when you'd take your bike and see how far you could cycle. Your only commitment was to be home for tea. It was a time of adventure and excitement, and it saddens me that this isn't a typical upbringing for everyone, especially nowadays.

We've always had cats and dogs in my family. I like dogs but I adore cats. They're just way cooler. The cats' favourite place to sleep was on my bed. The doctor told me that it wasn't a good idea, as it would make my asthma worse. I ignored him. There was something compelling about a small, warm body curled up against mine. It brought me peace and I couldn't sleep properly without a cat on my bed. Turns out that was a great decision on my part. Research now shows that being exposed to nature helps boost your immune system, and that the best activity for a child who experiences asthma and eczema is getting down and dirty in nature.

Growing up, the world didn't make sense to me. I couldn't understand why people were starving and the environment was being destroyed, yet nobody seemed bothered by it. Every year I took part in World Vision's twenty-four-hour famine fundraiser, because even as a child I couldn't watch what was happening in the world and do nothing.

By the time I was seven, I had read the entire children's section – both fiction and non-fiction - in the library going through three or four books a night. The librarian phoned my mum and said she needed to speak to me as I kept on taking books out and returning them without reading them. My mum assured her I was.

The next time I went to the library, the librarian opened a book, read a section of it and asked me about it. After I enthusiastically told her about the story I became the only child in the village with an adult's library ticket and permission to borrow up to ten books at a time!

Reading exposed me to culture, history, geography, mythology, philosophy, psychology, the occult, romance and sex in a glorious mash up. I dreamed of adventure and making a difference in the world.

Yet, my teenage years were painful. After growing up in an environment of domestic abuse with much emotional abuse directed towards me, I had no confidence and extremely low self-esteem. I felt awkward around my peers as if I was somehow different to them. I so desperately wanted to fit in. I stopped talking about nature to others after my best friend at the time asked me how many friends I actually had. When I told her that the cats were my best friends, she scornfully replied that they weren't 'real' friends.

At the same time, I was researching into environmental activist groups such as the Animal Liberation Front and the Sea Shepherd Conservation Society. While their direct-action approach was appealing, there was something about the use of violence in defence of the Earth that didn't resonate with me.

Whilst walking out in the woods I received the insight from nature that if I truly wanted to change the system, I had to be part of it. This left me feeling confused and unsure about how I could make a difference in the world.

So when I discovered drugs and alcohol, they initially seemed a way of fitting in. Instead they became a way of numbing myself to the pain I felt inside. They also numbed my connection to nature, and I gradually forgot about it along with my dreams of adventure and making a difference.

I left home when I was seventeen. My behaviour was challenging for my mum and I blamed where we lived for all my problems. I thought that moving to the city would mean that I would escape my problems too.

That's not exactly what happened. I still experienced similar problems, but with drugs and alcohol I was able to numb my way through life and keep surviving.

That's where I was when my brother Peter died. I was high on drugs and just floating along, struggling to keep my head above water, though I don't think anyone would have realised. I was studying psychology at university, had a part-time job and my own flat. I seemed to be doing well.

After Peter's death, I returned home to stay with my family for the summer. It wasn't just a return home. It was a return to nature and the start of reconnecting with my inner being.

I rediscovered everything I'd forgotten about as I'd escaped the pain of my past by moving away. In blaming the place I grew up in as the source of my suffering, I'd disconnected myself from the strength and solace I'd received from the land around me.

Just like before I'd left, I went to the woods to deal with the pain I was experiencing, and spent hours walking around. Then I'd spend hours just sitting outside staring at the stars in the sky. As I did, something within me re-awakened.

I started to sense that nature was communicating with me. I had no idea what it was saying – or even if it was real. Jumbled images, sensations, and thoughts crowded my mind. Yet even in my confusion I felt peace and comfort.

Combined with the experience of sensing my brother's spirit still around me, I felt as if I were losing my mind. I couldn't explain what was happening to me and other people around me didn't understand.

The next few months were an internal battle that I'm happy to say I've never experienced again. Grief and peace raged within me. I had no idea how to reconcile the two. After months of self-harming and failed suicide attempts, I shaved my long red hair off to become completely bald before spending three days in a psychiatric hospital. This was my rock bottom. The only way from here was up.

My brother gave me strength. I loved him so much that I decided to dedicate my life to his memory. To make it the best I could and live enough for both of us. And to show the world what's possible when you truly love someone. I went from being a patient in the psychiatric hospital to working in it.

At the same time my mum and I realised that I always became depressed during the dark months of winter. We invested in a light box to see if that made a difference. It did.

This reaffirmed that I had a connection to nature that I didn't fully understand. The only thing that was certain for me was that if I felt peace in nature, then I had to spend more time there.

In the city of Edinburgh, where I lived, I started looking for nature. Thankfully it wasn't hard to find. There were pockets of woodland hidden throughout the city, with a canal that ran through it. Close-by were the Pentland Hills and Arthur's seat, a mountain peak of an ancient volcano which sat in the centre of the city.

By the time I returned to university after taking two years out after my brother's death, I was spending regular time in the nearby wooded areas close to my home and at university. I'd amuse myself by thinking that I could hear the trees talking to me but I wasn't really convinced it was anything more than my imagination.

At the same time, I'd started taking psychic development classes and meditating regularly. I could still sense my brother around and I wanted to reassure myself that I wasn't actually crazy. If I wasn't talking to trees in the woods I was talking to my brother. I still wasn't sure if I believed it but it brought me comfort. As my interest in spirituality grew I found myself more and more drawn to be outside and started reading about nature-based spirituality.

I eventually gave up taking the bus to my work at the psychiatric hospital, instead preferring to spend an hour on foot (or thirty minutes on the bike) traveling along the canal to arrive there. This gave me two hours a day to be outside in nature in a mindful and meditative state.

Even in winter. *Especially* in winter.

There are so many stories about staying away from deserted places in the city. Perhaps ironically, I felt safer walking along the desolate canal than I would have been in the city streets themselves. No one else was ever there. I had the place to myself.

Despite spending hours of my day outside in nature, I still felt something was missing in my life. Following my brother's death, I'd founded a charity in Edinburgh to help young adults affected by bereavement. I received national recognition for my work with it through award nominations and media coverage but I wasn't fulfilled. I felt numb inside and started drinking and taking drugs again.

I felt trapped by the charity I'd created.

I'd bought a flat and felt trapped by the limitations of staying in one area.

The thought of my potential future, of actually going ahead to do a PhD in clinical psychology and working within a mental health system that, for me, didn't always support the needs of the patients, made me feel trapped even more.

I was working crazy hours. I gave all my time to the charity for free. It was an act of love for my brother, or so I told myself. I worked full time at the local psychiatric hospital and ended up doing nightshift for a while. I was tired and burnt out.

I'd created what I'd thought was the perfect life only to find I hated it. Something had to change. The thought of going on like this was unbearable. I needed something more but I had no idea what that was.

One day I saw an advert on the internet for a holiday in Spain. All I had to do was pay for my flights and speak English to Spanish students, and in return I'd get five days in a five-star hotel for free.

I nearly didn't go. I mean, a foreign country by myself where they don't speak the language? Was I off my head? Travelling to London by myself when I was eighteen had been a big thing for me and they spoke the same language there!

Yet the more I thought about it, I realised that it would be a challenge.

Something new.

Something exciting.

Something that I'd never done before.

The fact that my brother's nickname was Pedro, which is Spanish for Peter, convinced me to go. It was like he was telling me I needed to do this.

It was a way of honouring my childhood dreams of adventures in other countries.

As cliché as it sounds, those five days changed my life!

I stayed in a small rural village with a wide river running through it. Everywhere was green and alive. The hotel garden was filled with butterflies, darting from flower to flower. The warmth of the sun was unbelievable. The land spoke to me in an even deeper way than the land had in Scotland.

Before I knew it, I had applied for a job teaching English and nine months later I moved to Spain to start a new life.

After two months teaching English I was promoted to co-ordinator, though I still had to teach. I ended up in a beautiful part of Spain called Galicia. Known as the land of a thousand rivers, it's shrouded in mist and magic. It also has Celtic roots, so I felt very much at home.

Teaching English full time was demanding and left little time for me. I worked from nine in the morning until six in the evening. All this time I was teaching. The method the company used was intensive, focused, and demanding. Any additional paperwork had to be done in our own time. The time I spent in nature gradually decreased until I was lucky if I had two hours outside a week.

After two years, I found myself in the same condition I'd been in before: tired, stressed, and burnt out. The curse of a high-performing perfectionist with low self-esteem! I took a month off work and spent as much of it as possible out in nature. Immediately I began to feel better. Yet it was more than that. I could sense that there was something even more powerful and magical about nature than I'd ever experienced before. This is when I had my experience with the old oak tree that I mentioned in the introduction.

Over the next few months I saved and planned as I created my exit strategy from teaching English. I got myself a coach, started coach training myself, and found another job in a nearby town with fewer hours so that I could devote more time to doing what really inspired me.

I also started spending more time out in nature again until I was back up to more than two hours daily outside. The insights I received led me to start my Masters in Applied Ecopsychology so that I could figure out how to share what nature was teaching me.

The grief I'd felt over the death of my brother might have been transformed into acceptance and peace, but there were other challenges ahead. My eczema flared up until it covered eighty-five percent of my body. My relationship with my Spanish partner was breaking down. I loved Spain but I knew I needed to return home to Scotland.

The next year and a half was a period of deep healing for me as I built up a coaching practice focused on helping people transform their grief while I healed my relationship with the land in Scotland. This was a time of rebalancing my whole being with nature's support. As this happened I realised that I was no longer attracted to working in the field of grief despite just having published my first book about it and spending the last couple of years rebuilding my credibility in the field.

I stopped taking on new clients and got another job teaching English, this time in Barcelona. It was a testament to how far I'd come. Not only did I manage to teach English full time but I also managed to maintain my connection to nature despite living in one of the most densely populated cities in Europe.

My situation gave me the time and space to allow my business to evolve into the work I do now. When I knew my time in Barcelona was coming to an end, I started thinking about where I needed to go next.

Through a series of synchronistic events I was led to the island of Ibiza. Having made the decision to move there before I'd even been there, I thought I'd better go and visit.

I only had one day. I quickly found my accommodations before spending nine hours driving around the island visiting many different natural spots. The energy of the nature there was so alive that by the time I'd left I'd spent most of my visit in an altered state of consciousness.

The six months I spent there—from January to July, 2014—were the most incredible of my life. What I learned from nature there became rocket fuel for my life and business. I started working for myself full time and have never looked back.

It's not always been easy. Yet, whenever I feel blocked I go to nature. The process you're about to learn in this book is the same process that I use daily in my life. In fact, I wrote this next section as I sat at the top of a mountain in Andorra, the landlocked microstate in southwestern Europe, located in the eastern Pyrenean mountains and bordered by Spain and France. Years later, my memory of this experience is hazy. Yet I still remember how it made me feel.

August 2014:

The sky is bright blue with soft, fluffy clouds. While it's warm there's a gentle breeze that causes the long grass surrounding me to dance in joy. Everywhere I look there are mountains, many of them covered in trees. A cricket chirps and a bird calls.

It brings chills to the very core of my being. My shoulders ache slightly from the sunburn I got yesterday and my legs feel the rough pressure of the stone I'm sitting on.

Just before I started writing this, I was attracted to a rock that I saw in the distance on the mountain. I could feel its presence calling me. As I walked towards the rock I felt that I had received permission to climb it. The rock had to be at least six feet in height.

I found myself drawn towards one of its corners. There in the rock face was a small ledge. As I attempted to climb it for the first time I felt fear rise up within me, and my foot slipped off the ledge.

Undaunted I tried again. As I felt for a handhold in the rock, part of it came away in my hand. Scary. Yet underneath the fear was trust. I used all my senses to find the right way to climb up the rock and the next thing I knew, I was standing on top of it.

As I looked around, it seemed as if the rock communicated with me that I was to jump off it and land on a certain point in the soft grass. I immediately thought, eh no. That looks far too high. I felt a sense of powerlessness and hopelessness rise up in me. Here I was stuck on top of a rock like an idiot with no way down.

I sat down on the rock and started speaking angrily to it. Thankfully no one was around to witness what undoubtedly would have looked like a crazy girl arguing with a rock!

As I ranted and raved at the rock I realised that my journey up the rock was a metaphor for how I was feeling about a new program I was launching within my business. Everything that was happening in that moment was a reflection of how I felt about the challenges I faced with this program.

With this insight, my fear dissipated. I already knew how to get down. The rock had told me. Excitement rose up within me as I went to the edge of the rock and jumped. I landed safely on the grass just as the rock had said.

Clearly I heard the rock say, "Again!" This time I had no hesitation. I quickly climbed up onto the rock again and this time enjoyed standing for a moment on it. As I looked down to where I was to jump off I still felt some discomfort rise within me. Yet I jumped again and landed safely.

Emboldened, I needed no encouragement to do it again. I climbed immediately up the rock, moved straight over to the edge, and jumped without hesitation. This was one of the most powerful lessons I had ever received from nature, and when you think about it, all I really did was climb a rock and jump off.

That moment is perfectly preserved through the words I wrote at that time so that you can read them now, years later. Since then I've had many more magical moments like that.

This is what I want for you too. The Nature Process is not just about reducing your stress and anxiety. It's about reminding you of that joyous state you experienced as a child, where the world was filled with wonder and hope. It's about helping you to access your imagination and see the teachings learned while in nature helping you to live a more creative and fulfilling life.

Come into my world. Discover what a connection to nature can do for you.

Start your journey by reading the chapter summary in "Key Points to Remember" and then reflecting on the questions that follow.

KEY POINTS TO REMEMBER

- Nature is not only the natural world and the universe around us, it's also our inner nature and what we create from that. Everything is nature.
- When you go beyond the label of "Mother Earth" you go beyond the stories into a direct sensory experience of nature.
- Many other beliefs and cultures different from the Western worldview believe that consciousness exists in all of life – and research is starting to show that animals and plants are far more conscious than we've previously thought.
- Aristotle's hierarchy of nature helped create a classification system that places humans above all elements of the natural world. This is something that's been embedded into the core of Western Culture and civilisation for over two thousand years.
- We are created from the same atoms and particles as the natural world around us. On a quantum level, we are all one. How we treat nature is how we treat ourselves and vice versa.
- It's through the recognition that we are all interconnected that we can create global transformation. As we start to transform ourselves, we transform the world. Through connecting to nature, we tap into 13.7 billion years of natural intelligence.
- Ecopsychology is an emerging field that focuses on the human/nature relationship and studies how we can use the human/nature relationship to promote personal, societal, and environmental well-being.
- There are currently sixty-seven researched benefits to spending time outside in the natural world.
- We all have our own story of our relationship and connection to nature. A new chapter in your story is about to begin as you start to learn and practise The Nature Process.

QUESTIONS FOR REFLECTION

- What does nature mean to you?
- What does Mother Earth mean to you?
- What are some of the cultural stories about nature that you've grown up with?
- What do you believe about animal and plant consciousness?
- Do you believe that we are all interconnected? Why? Why not?
- How do you view your current connection to and relationship with nature?
- What's your own nature story?

CHAPTER 2

The Nature Process

☙ ☙ ☙

*A new type of thinking is essential if mankind is to
survive and move toward higher levels.*

- ALBERT EINSTEIN

SINCE THE DEVELOPMENT OF THE Nature Process many people have commented that this is what they experience when out in nature but they never knew it was a "process". This is because The Nature Process isn't really something that I've created. It's what happens naturally when we are open enough to mindfully connect with nature and be guided by it. All I've done is observe on a detailed level what happens within myself and my clients when in nature and clarify it into a simple process that can be taught to others, using the foundations of Dr Michael J. Cohen's work on applied ecopsychology. This is the culmination for me of fifteen years of study into how humans and nature interact.

Ancient humans would have embodied this process without conscious thought. However, the challenge today is that most people now aren't able to experience this naturally. Through no fault of our own, we've become psychologically disconnected from nature. Our modern civilisation has created a fundamental disconnect in the way we think that separates us from nature.

Nevertheless, we are still biologically connected to nature and it's this biological connection that can help support our psychological reconnection as you'll discover when we go into The Nature Process in depth.

Nature has existed for 13.7 billion years. The Earth as we know it has existed for 4.6 billion years. In that time both nature and the Earth have managed to keep themselves in a constant state of growth and evolution with a 100% success rate. We can learn from that.

When we realign ourselves with nature's wisdom we're re-aligning ourselves with the natural intelligence that will not only help us survive both individually and collectively, but also to thrive and create a sustainable world for all.

This chapter outlines the five-step process of The Nature Process so that you can deepen your connection to nature and harness the natural intelligence within you. It's important to remember that while these five steps form the basic process, they are also independent principles that can be used in different ways once you've mastered the steps.

As you continue to explore The Nature Process I encourage you to use your own judgment and change the order or use only some of the processes instead of always using it in its basic format.

NATURAL PRESENCE

Starting The Nature Process means entering into a state of natural presence. This is the ability to let go of any thoughts of the past or future and come into the present to experience a deep awareness of the natural world around you. When in a state of natural presence, the chatter in your mind becomes silent as your full attention and focus move to observing the sensory information you receive about the natural world.

The key to entering a deep state of natural presence is to use your fifty-four senses to receive more information. An awareness of these additional senses, which I'll talk more about in the chapter on natural presence, allows you to experience the natural world in a completely different way.

Natural Presence is part of what some people might call mindfulness, which, despite its spiritual association, is nothing more than an awareness of what's happening in each and every present moment. It's a mental state that allows you to acknowledge and accept, without judgment, any feelings, thoughts, and sensations as they arise. It's also about clearly observing what's happening around you, free from any stories in your head about why it's happening.

However, natural presence goes beyond mindfulness. Its main focus is to explore the natural world that exists around you. When you experience nature without your sense of self psychologically blocking the connection, you are able to experience each and every moment without attaching any human stories to it as a way of explaining what's happening. In a state of natural presence you are able to break free from the past, forget about the future, and focus on the only place in which you have any power to make changes to your life: the present.

Your success with The Nature Process depends on your ability to master natural presence as fully as possible. The deeper your state of natural presence, the deeper your connection to the rest of the principles/steps of The Nature Process, the deeper your connection to nature and the more you can reduce your stress and anxiety.

If there's only one thing that you take away from this book, I want it to be the ability to master natural presence. Doing so allows you to enter this state at will and begin to come from this place of being more and more. This deepens your creativity and encourages you to create new ways of living your life that support growth in all areas of it.

Imagine that you are an alien recently landed on Earth in the middle of the wilderness. Nothing is familiar. You don't know the labels that humanity has given to the natural world that you're witnessing. You don't know how anything works. What would you do?

You'd explore the natural world through the senses you have. Your natural curiosity would allow you to experience the world as it is, without preconceptions.

In order for you to develop your natural presence you need to experience your awareness of the Earth as if it were the first time you'd ever encountered anything like it.

Natural Body

From a place of natural presence you are able to turn your focus inwards from the outer nature around you to the inner nature of your natural body. This is about being fully present in the body and experiencing it without interference from stories or judgments. It's about feeling the body, sensing into how it's working and what wisdom it has to share.

It's through our bodies that we are connected to the Earth and the environment around us. There is a non-verbal wisdom present within the body that receives information from the environment and sends this information to our brain to be processed.

When we are caught up in stories and judgments, this information is filtered through these and we end up with a distorted view of reality and the world around us. These stories disconnect us from the body's wisdom and can lead to injury and disease, as you'll discover later on in the chapter on natural body.

However, our bodies only exist in the present, which means they respond only to what is happening around us. Being fully in the natural body allows us to experience the moment and let our bodies help bring us into a state of balance and health.

Right now, as you're reading this, there are a multitude of processes that you are not aware of occurring within your body to keep it functioning.

A lot of these processes involve other organisms. Ninety percent of your cells are made up from microbes and not human cells. Your body is actually a mini-Earth capable of sustaining life for more than 90 trillion inhabitants.

Tuning into your natural body is the key to making The Nature Process work for you. I've had clients in the past who have told me that they have difficulty using The Nature Process because they can't sense what is happening within the body. The more you take time to develop your awareness of your natural body the more you'll be able to sense when you are in a state of stress and anxiety or when a thought or a story is impacting your health.

It's through working with the body that you will be able to let go of stress and anxiety and bring yourself back into a state of balance and harmony that supports your well-being and that of the planet. You make different decisions when you're not stressed and anxious. The reason behind this will be fully explained later on as you learn how your body works and understand how to listen to your body's wisdom.

NATURAL ATTRACTIONS

Natural Attractions is a way of thinking like Nature and thinking as part of Nature. Since the dawn of our universe there has been a dynamic interplay of invisible forces at work that has allowed our universe to develop and expand. This invisible force has allowed the Earth to form and life to develop on it.

We still don't fully understand what this invisible force is. Over the years, some people have called it God, while other people have called it evolution. NASA science calls it dark energy and notes that more is unknown about this invisible force than known. Once you are connected to both your natural presence and your natural body you are then able to start to focus on your natural attractions and experience this invisible force at work.

Since birth we've grown up with a multitude of stories and beliefs about the way life is. These stories and beliefs shape the way in which we see ourselves. Too often we find ourselves taking action that goes against our natural attractions such as working in jobs we hate or not taking time off to rest when we need to because we're worried about money. As a result, we end up stressed, tired and struggling with life's challenges

Our thoughts and actions in life are shaped by these beliefs and stories. Yet in Nature there are no beliefs and stories. There is only constant growth and evolution. This growth and evolution in Nature exists in an interconnected web with everything in existence related to everything else. Nature knows how to keep itself in balance. When we use our own natural attractions, we are able to tap into Nature's wisdom and learn how to keep ourselves in balance too.

We can fully experience life in a state of trust and openness knowing that the actions and behaviour we have is part of this interconnected web of life rather than stories and beliefs that create separation and stress.

As part of The Nature Process, natural attractions guide us to connect with a part of nature that can give us the support we need to let go of stress and anxiety and enhance our productivity and creativity. This is how we ensure that each and every time we consciously create a connection to nature we are brought back to a state of balance and harmony.

When we become fully present to the Nature around us and the Nature within us through natural presence and natural body we also become fully present to natural attractions and are able to harness their power and make it our own. We rely on sensory information to guide our behaviour instead of past stories and old beliefs.

Natural attractions help you to establish a connection between the thoughts, feelings, and sensations you experience in the moment and whatever part of nature you are drawn to in that same moment.

That part of Nature has a message about the truth of who you are, and reflects back to you the highest part of yourself that your fear and doubts often hide. By ensuring that you focus on a part of Nature that makes you feel good, you guarantee that you're also accessing the full potential of who you are too.

NATURAL COMMUNICATION

After establishing which part of nature you feel a connection with by following your natural attractions, the next step is to move into a state of natural communication. Natural communication is the ability to not only experience the way in which nature communicates with us, but to also understand that communication.

Nature is non-verbal. It has language, but the language is sensory in origin and can only be understood through engaging with the fifty-four senses.

This is why we first need to be in a state of natural presence and connected to our natural body.

We are born able to experience the natural communication of nature. Children are masters at natural communication because they haven't yet been taught differently. Most cultures and societies today unintentionally weaken this ability as we grow up.

As adults we have to redevelop this innate skill. To do this we need to re-learn how to translate the communication that we receive from nature around us and reconnect to nature within.

Western society, in general, has learned to go against our natural attractions and not enter into natural communication. Much of our unconscious behaviour towards nature dominates and oppresses both nature and ourselves. We've come to view the Earth and its non-human inhabitants as natural resources available for us to use and abuse.

By entering into a place of natural communication, we shift this perspective into one of consent and co-operation with nature, even radically asking permission to interact with the natural world around us. As a result, we experience more of nature's abilities to heal and transform us.

As part of The Nature Process, natural communication allows us to experience a conscious connection to nature that enables us to sense that we are part of the complex dance amongst all life on Earth.

NATURAL RELEASE

After connecting with Nature from a place of natural communication, you then move into natural release. This is when you are able to sense a connection between yourself and the rest of Nature, to feel yourself as part of a greater whole. From this place of connection, you are able to let go of stress and anxiety and tap into your natural productivity and creativity.

Natural release works on a sensory level and allows you to bypass the neural pathways in your brain that have been created from worries and doubt. The brain literally works differently when you are connected to Nature. This allows you to create new neural patterns that support you to return to a state of balance.

You are able to experience sensations within the body as it releases stress and tension without engaging in the stories of what this means. When you understand that you are a part of Nature, it allows you to experience the natural intelligence within it. There is a dynamic interplay of chemical reactions as your body responds to the natural environment around you. You don't even need to do anything except allow this to happen.

For many, this is the most challenging part of the process. There is a sense that you need to do something, which can come from the cultural stories we've absorbed that we need to *do* something to achieve a result. There are guided exercises available later on in the chapter devoted to natural release to help with this. However, results come with The Nature Process by merely *allowing* Nature to do what it does best.

Some of my clients, as I guide them through The Nature Process, have said to me, "But I don't know how to shift this." The thing is that you don't need to know what to do. The intelligence inherent within Nature knows what to do. All you have to do is relax, let it happen, and allow the body to do what it needs to do to rebalance itself.

Natural release is a safe and gentle way of letting go of stress and anxiety. It allows you to feel supported and nourished by Nature as you bring yourself back into balance with the Earth.

THE NATURE PROCESS IN ACTION

When all five principles/steps of The Nature Process are practised together, they become a seamless experience that you can complete in as little as thirty minutes. This makes it easy to implement it into your daily life. It's something that can be practised on your lunch break from work, while you walk the dog, relaxing in your back yard or on the beach. Once you're skilled enough you can even practise The Nature Process walking around a city!

The reason that I teach you to actively experience each part of the process separately and then build it upon the other parts is that your understanding of how it works becomes far more complete. As a result, you have deeper and deeper experiences when you do. Some of my clients have been practising The Nature Process daily for years now and they are amazed at how much more intimate and powerful their own connection to nature continues to become.

Furthermore, the idea behind The Nature Process is that you successfully learn how to do this yourself so that you don't have to rely on another person to facilitate the process for you. I know the work is done when clients no longer need the support of The Nature Process facilitator or coach to practise The Nature Process. This is something that I teach everyone who trains to become a facilitator or coach. The ultimate goal is for anybody they work with to master The Nature Process themselves.

One of the reasons that I do recommend people to work with The Nature Process facilitator or coach is that they are able to help you go deeper into the process far quicker than if you were initially doing it yourself. It's a way of accelerating the power of the process and seeing clear benefits of it for yourself. This helps you continue to engage and practise the process so that it becomes a part of your daily life.

Example of The Nature Process in Action

When you have examples of The Nature Process in action, it's easier for you to get an idea of how it works and what you should be doing when you're out in nature by yourself using The Nature Process. One of my clients, Sara Sanderson wrote a blog post about her experience of The Nature Process with me and gave me permission to share it here with you:

> *The day of the session I felt called to go to a local cemetery where I'd been for the first time in years just the day before with a friend. It turned out to be an ideal place for what unfolded.*
>
> *With Tabitha asking the questions, I first became present in nature by describing my surroundings and then noticed what I was naturally attracted to. I sat barefoot on the grass, an area of the cemetery I was guided to by a squirrel, who then ran up a tree and sat there the whole time. It*

was like he was watching over me during the session. Every now and then I could hear him moving around high up in the branches.

I sat feeling safe and comfortable as I held on to a short stem of a plant explaining to Tabitha what I wanted to explore during the session. However, when I asked for permission to connect with it to support me during the session, the answer was no; and it was an adjoining leaf, soft and smooth to the touch, where I found permission to continue.

The texture of the leaf was gorgeous to touch, delicate yet strongly rooted to the ground and firmly connected to the Earth. With the support of nature, I explored what was at the core of my perceived block to receiving my birthright of abundance in monetary terms. Delving into my unconscious mind, I sensed there was an invisible force-field that protected me, and although I had room to move around within this bubble with its transparent force-field wall, I felt it was preventing certain things from getting in (such as my fullness to health, money and intimacy).

I used the support of the leaf rooted in the Earth to start altering the force-field. In my mind's eye, I visualized the force-field pulsing, and then it started to vibrate rapidly. As the intensity grew so did fear rise up inside me, so I stopped before any damage to the force-field occurred. It just didn't feel safe to break it.

The reasons why included "I would die if it came down" and "I wouldn't be strong enough without it." Clearly these are not logical responses but our unconscious mind, and how it affects the nervous system, is real to the body and has an impact on our external circumstances and situations.

Tabitha asked whether there was another part of nature I was attracted to that might help support me further. As I looked around, a butterfly flew past and my eyes followed it and then my body moved too. I relocated to another patch of grass where I felt drawn to what I described to Tabitha as a warrior leaf.

Tabitha was quick to explain that the warrior was, of course, me (the whole nature process is a reflection of self). As I held on to the warrior leaf I could easily embody my inner warrior, and together we shook and vibrated the force-field until it shattered into a billion pieces.

I no longer felt fear, in fact I felt expansive and powerful wanting to scream out loud "Freedom!" I was reminded by the lines sung by Caliban in Shakespeare's The Tempest, and for me it was a clear reminder to my mind that it's not the master of who I am:

"Ban, 'ban, Ca-caliban Sara

Has a new master. So get a new servant.

Freedom, what a wonderful day, wonderful day, freedom, freedom, wonderful day, freedom!"

Tabitha supported me to anchor this feeling of freedom, and being in and supported by nature so I could draw upon it whenever I choose.

I noticed a single ant on my hand and a single worm circling around the base of the warrior leaf. It didn't occur to me at the time how unusual it was to have seen only one squirrel, a single butterfly, a single ant, and a single worm. As I call upon symbolic meaning in the coaching I do (the unconscious uses symbols and metaphors to communicate), I decided to look up what each creature meant, and was delighted by what I read as each one supported my nature process experience perfectly.

I feel a shift certainly happened and transformation is taking place regarding abundance flowing and being received. There may well be more work to do in keeping down the perceived need for a force-field around me. I will continue to explore with the support of nature as I progress my business and continue to create and manifest my heart's desires.

Experience The Nature Process

Now, if you haven't already downloaded the complimentary guided The Nature Process meditation by Master Coach Sami Aaron from our website, do so now. This thirty-minute meditation will give you an experience of what The Nature Process is all about and give you a taste of what Sara experienced, before you dive deep into mastering each principle/step of The Nature

Process. Go to www.thenatureprocess.co and enter your name and email address to get access to it.

KEY POINTS TO REMEMBER

- Natural Presence: Step into a deeper experience of the natural world as you become aware of your 54 senses.
- Natural Body: Connect to the wisdom of the body.
- Natural Attraction: Let go of stories and beliefs you have about life and learn to think like Nature and as a part of Nature.
- Natural Communication: Experience and understand the non-verbal language of Nature.
- Natural Release: Feel yourself as a part of a greater whole, Nature, and use your sensory connections to return to a state of balance and well-being.
- Practised together, these five principles form the basis of The Nature Process which can be done daily in as little as thirty minutes.

CHAPTER 3

Natural Presence

※ ※ ※

*The basic laws of the universe are simple, but because
our senses are limited, we can't grasp them.*

-ALBERT EINSTEIN

WHILE NATURAL PRESENCE MIGHT SEEM the simplest part of The Nature
Process, it's actually the one that people struggle with the most. If you don't
get a proper experiential understanding of natural presence and realise just
how deeply aware of nature you can become, then the rest of The Nature
Process is not going to be as powerful as it could be.

This is the root of the process. The stronger and deeper your roots, the
greater you'll be able to reach for the stars. Just like a tree.

Mastering natural presence takes time and effort. You'll know you've
achieved mastery when it becomes a part of your daily life. You won't need to
make an effort to maintain a state of natural presence. In fact, you'll notice
immediately when you start to become disconnected and be able to take action to move yourself back into this state.

Being outside in a natural environment and practising the following techniques in this chapter will help you to experience more of the benefits of
interacting with nature that I mentioned back in chapter one.

What's great about learning to master a state of natural presence is that
you can practise it anytime in as little as five minutes a day. You can practise

natural presence looking at a photo of a natural landscape, staring out of a window to a natural environment, walking from your house to the car and stepping outside your workplace for a short break.

Many clients ask me if they're able to practise The Nature Process when they don't live in the countryside. This is the beauty of this process. You don't need to be in a national park or the wilderness to practise The Nature Process. You can do it anywhere there is nature. To give you more ideas about how do this, I've included a section later on in the chapter that addresses this specifically.

As I mentioned in the previous chapter, natural presence is the ability to enter into a deep awareness of the natural world around you as your mind becomes silent and you engage in a sensory exploration of your surroundings with your fifty-four senses. In a way, it's very similar to a meditative state.

THE CONNECTION BETWEEN MEDITATION AND NATURE

Meditation has become mainstream. It's no longer weird or woo-woo to talk about it. Researchers have begun to investigate its benefits, and are showing that meditation can help to reduce stress and anxiety. It helps us cope with pain and challenging emotions. It can boost our immune system and helps us get to know ourselves better.

All of this is wonderful, yet there's a mental block within many people when it comes to meditation. Despite there being many different ways to practise meditation, the traditional image that comes to mind is someone sitting cross-legged and trying to empty their mind to find inner peace. This stereotype stops many people from experiencing the benefits of meditation.

For some, the drawback of meditation is that it invites people to go *within* as a way of receiving these benefits rather than simply focusing on what's already around us. What is incredible is that you can get the same benefits as meditation simply by going out into nature. In fact, you don't even have to go outside. Having a view of nature from your window can trigger some of the same effects.

One of my favourite ground-breaking studies was done by a researcher named Roger Ulrich in the nineteen-eighties. He was looking at patients who had been in hospital for the same operation. During the recovery after the operation, half of them were given a nature view. The other half saw only buildings. What was fascinating is that those who had the nature view experienced less pain, recovered quicker, and had fewer complications than those who just had the building view.

Now, before you get excited and pull up an image of nature on your computer, this idea of a nature view was taken further and tested to actually see if technological views, as in computer images of nature, have the same effect. The research shows there is something about the actual natural view and the way that it is created that supports us. You can't just look at nature online, like so many people do with TV documentaries. You have to be looking at the real thing to get these benefits.

However, in extreme cases there are benefits to watching nature imagery – especially when you are deprived from accessing nature any other way. Ground-breaking research is being carried out at Snake River Correctional Institute in Oregon, U.S. Prisoners in the maximum-security section spend twenty-three hours a day locked in a small cell. During the hour that they are released for exercise they were given the option to watch a nature film. Researchers found that those prisoners who watched the nature films experienced less aggression and distress than those who didn't. As a result, prison guards are now taking a pro-active approach and using the nature videos as a way to prevent violent prisoner outbursts.

If you are someone who can't get outside, looking at nature images on technology is better than nothing. However, when we do go outside, the benefits increase even more. Nature starts interacting with us on a physical level. Plants and trees produce chemical compounds called phytoncides, and when we're outside and surrounded by plants we breathe them in. These chemicals help boost our immune system and help reduce stress. There's even bacteria in soil that triggers the production of serotonin in the brain!

These additional physical benefits make meditation in nature far more powerful than if you were to stay indoors and meditate. Furthermore, you can be active and moving around outdoors which helps bring the body into your meditative state. Also, further research published in 2015 highlights that people who have mystical experiences through being in nature are encouraged to take better care of the environment. Meditating/being in nature seems to be the catalyst for wanting to take better care of the world around us.

The Earth's Connection to Our Brain

Our connection to nature goes beyond the physical aspects. There's also a brain based response that happens when we go outside in nature. Research in 2015 discovered that going for a walk outside in a natural area reduced activity in the subgenual prefrontal cortex – the part of our brain responsible for repetitive negative thoughts.

The pre-frontal cortex is also active in planning complex behaviour, the expression of our personality, making decisions and helping us determine how to act in social situations. This is the area of our executive functioning. What this suggests is that our brains work better when we are outside in a natural environment.

Research into the Japanese art of forest-bathing, *Shinrin-Yoku* also supports this. Researchers found that spending a minimum of half a day in a forest environment can boost mental cognition for up to a month.

The most interesting discovery though, was back in the 1950s when a physicist named Winfried Otto Schumann scientifically measured and confirmed that within the earth's electromagnetic field there are a set of electrical discharges that occur naturally between the earth and the ionosphere.

Schumann measured these discharges and discovered that they exist at a frequency of 7.83Hz. They became known as the Schumann Response even though these frequencies were originally discovered by Nikola Tesla, the man who invented much of the twentieth century technology that we have now come to rely on.

Within our brains we have electrical discharges too. In fact, this is what enables our brains to transmit information through our neural pathways. The type of information we receive is varied by our brainwave frequency.

Science has discovered that we have four different brainwave states measured by their frequencies; the Beta, Alpha, Theta, and Delta states. There's also a fifth brainwave frequency known as Gamma, but we'll not be exploring this state in the book.

The state that we spend most of our time in is the Beta brainwave state, which functions at a rate of 14-40Hz. This is the fastest brainwave state when we are most alert and our minds are most active. This is the state that we're in when we experience stress and anxiety, when we're working on trying to reach a deadline or dealing with the challenges of modern life. It's the state we're in when our inner voice is the loudest.

Then we move down into the Alpha brainwave state, which functions at a rate of 8-14Hz. This is where we start to experience relaxation, start to daydream, fantasize and experience visualizations. Our mind becomes quieter and we enter a meditative state. Yet we're still alert and focused.

When our brains enter the Theta state this is where magic happens. This brainwave state functions between 4-8Hz. In this state our mind becomes still and we experience silence. Total silence. Our conscious mind is, in effect, switched off and we're able to access the depths of our subconscious. This is the realm of deep knowing, intuition, creativity, and of our connection to ourselves and to the world. It's the place of spiritual insight and high-functioning brain states. This is where our natural presence lives.

It's no coincidence that the magnetic frequency of the earth is the same. While there is currently no scientific research that clearly demonstrates this, I suspect it will only be a matter of time. From my personal experience, and that of my clients, I've discovered that when we go outside, become aware of our brainwave state and focus on the natural environment around us we're able to connect with the frequency of the earth and bring our brains into sync with that energy. It becomes far easier to enter a Theta brainwave state.

This is where you need to arrive in order to enter a state of natural presence. Fully connected to our subconscious, we can unravel the patterns that keep us stuck in a state of stress and anxiety where we're lacking creativity and innovation.

Furthermore, research into the different brainwave states shows that when we're trying to change our behaviour or create new thought patterns, it takes thousands and thousands of repetitions in the Beta brainwave state.

If we change our behaviour or create new thought patterns while in the Theta brainwave state, we only need one or two repetitions to create successful change. It becomes far easier to remove any obstructions that are stopping us from improving our well-being and enhancing our life.

Incidentally, children up until the approximate age of seven spend most of their time in the Theta brainwave state. This is why unconscious childhood crap is so difficult to leave behind. We're trying to remove deeply ingrained behaviour learned while in the Theta brainwave state through working on it while in a Beta brainwave state as adults. Duh! No wonder enhancing our lives seems difficult at times.

Delta brainwaves are the home of psychic capacities and high levels of empathy. It's where gut decisions come from. Delta brainwaves function at a rate of 0.5-4Hz and is where we experience a state of deep dreamless sleep and total relaxation.

With The Nature Process, we are actively working on enhancing our Theta brainwave state. Working with delta brainwave states in The Nature Process is something I do with only my most advanced clients who have successfully mastered entering the Theta brainwave state.

This is only a brief introduction to brainwave states so that you understand the changes that will happen as you start to spend more time outside.

CONNECTING TO DIFFERENT ASPECTS OF NATURE

So far I've been talking about developing your natural presence within nature in general. Yet within nature itself there are many different parts that make up the whole. Not only are there living plants and trees to connect to, but there are also seemingly inert things like rocks and rivers.

Plants and trees are more accessible than rocks and rivers. What I've found over the years as I've worked with clients is that it's easier for most people to connect with plants and trees rather than rocks and rivers because generally, in the Western word, we can accept that plants and trees are alive but struggle to think the same about rocks and rivers. That's why I always recommend people to initially focus on connecting to nature through plants and trees. It's easier for us to do so.

Not only are trees and plants obviously alive, but they also have an ability to help us connect to them. Whilst science is yet to fully explain how this works, one example of this is that when we actually go and put our hands on trees, the flow of their sap regulates to the same rhythm of our blood flow. There's also further evidence that suggests the possibility that plants and trees may in fact be conscious, which I'll talk more about in the chapter on natural communication. But, for now, we're going to look at what's possible when you utilise your senses to their full capacity.

DANIEL KISH: HUMAN ECHOLOCATION EXPERT

After having both eyes removed when he was thirteen months old due to an aggressive form of cancer in his retinas, Daniel Kish has been totally blind. He's the president of World Access for the Blind, a non-profit organization, whose mission is to help people with all forms of blindness to create self-directed achievements and increase public awareness about what blind people are capable of doing. To date this organization has helped over 7,000 people in thirty different countries.

Despite being blind, Daniel still has the ability to "see." As a child, Daniel taught himself how to use echolocation by clicking his tongue. This in itself is not remarkable. There have been other cases of blind people teaching themselves echolocation. What's unique about Daniel is that he's amazingly good at it, and he's the first person to have figured out how to teach this to others.

He teaches this technique to blind people through the work of his organization, and has also successfully taught it to people who are sighted. In 2009, a group of researchers from the University of Alcalá in Madrid conducted a study into whether it was possible to train sighted people to echolocate with Daniel's support. Despite some people believing the idea was ridiculous, the study showed that after just a few days of training, the participants had all gained basic echolocation skills.

Traditionally we've thought of echolocation in terms of how dolphins and bats communicate, but we've never thought of it as a human capability. Yet Daniel has been able to tap into his own sensory nature, connect this to the natural world around him, and develop a skill that is naturally ours by birthright.

Daniel models what he teaches to other people. He lives alone. He does not follow the norms that are commonly associated with people who are blind, who are taught to keep their environment the same and adapt to that, rather than let the environment adapt to them.

Daniel doesn't stick to familiar routines, nor does he use a white cane as his main method of "seeing." He's out there in the wild going camping by himself, climbing trees, and even mountain biking, and he's teaching others like him to do the same.

Just like any revolutionary approach that challenges mainstream thought, there's been a lot of criticism around what Daniel's doing. It requires time and commitment to achieve a high level of expertise in human echolocation. People don't experience immediate results, which leads those who are impatient to question the validity of this approach.

Why doesn't every blind person do this? In fact, blind children intuitively click their fingers, clap their hands and stamp their feet to make noise that will help them develop the skill of echolocation. But sadly, too often blind children are actively discouraged from doing this by their well-meaning parents, because this is not considered acceptable behaviour in society. Think about it from your own perspective—how many times have you been told off for making noise that wasn't appropriate for where you were?

We are born knowing how to use our senses so that we can connect to the world. Unwittingly, not just in blind children but in all children, we shut down these capabilities by training them to respond to social rules and behaviours that are not in their best interests.

Daniel and his work remind us that we as humans have sensory capabilities far more powerful than we realise that allow us to connect to nature on a level that we have previously not thought possible.

THE REALITY OF OUR SENSORY NATURE

For the last couple of thousand years we've been told that we only have five senses; sight, hearing, taste, smell and touch. This belief is so pervasive that we tend to accept it as fact, even as science recognises that humans have far more senses than the traditional five.

A quick google search on senses will bring up thermoception (sense of temperature), nociception (sense of pain), equilibrioception (sense of balance), mechanoreception (sense of vibration) and proprioception (sense of movement).

You may also be familiar with what some people call a sixth sense. This enables us to connect to a world that we can't see. It's the sense that leads people to say they can see ghosts, among other things, as popularized by the film of the same name starring Bruce Willis.

There is growing evidence of the fact that humans have more than five senses. In 1978, the science and philosophy writer Guy Murchie identified thirty-two different senses that humans share with all other creatures and provided biological and anecdotal evidence to support this. However, as Murchie himself pointed out, the classification of these senses is controversial, with many of them appearing ambiguous and vague. Furthermore, many of them could be considered instincts or capacities instead of senses.

This didn't stop Dr Michael J. Cohen from basing his work on these thirty-two senses and expanding them into fifty-four, based on the experiential practises of himself and his students. It's this approach upon which The Nature Process and natural presence are built. I'll talk more about the fifty-four senses in the next section. First, I want to explain how our ability to sense information from our environment works.

There are a number of scientific theories that suggest the information we receive from our environment is held within a temporary mental store within the mind. This information is then filtered for meaning, with irrelevant information being ignored and discarded.

Indeed, recent developments in neuroscience have highlighted a physiological process within the brain which filters information to prevent our central nervous system from being overwhelmed by irrelevant sensory information. This process is called sensory gating.

Stephen Harrod Buhner, herbalist and senior researcher at the foundation for Gaian Studies argues that this sensory gating can be intentionally controlled via the senses, although he himself suggests there are only six senses. Buhner suggests there are three ways of intentionally controlling these neurophysiological processes:

1. By focusing attention on a task that allows greater sensory data to enter conscious awareness;
2. Experiencing the world as a child in the first few years of life would;
3. Alternating gating channels themselves through altered states of consciousness induced by such things as meditation and psychedelics.

As you go through The Nature Process you'll find that it uses all three of these concepts (but doesn't advocate the use of psychedelics) within the process to help you expand and explore your fifty-four senses as you deepen your ability to enter into a state of natural presence.

THE FIFTY-FOUR SENSES

As mentioned, the fifty-four senses were developed by Dr Michael. J. Cohen from Project NatureConnect. Dr Cohen has spent the last fifty years devoting his life to a sensory exploration of how a connection to nature affects our personal, social and environmental well-being. His work is radical, and quite frankly, highly unscientific at times.

However, where Dr Cohen is a genius, and why I studied for a MSc. in Applied Ecopsychology with him, is because he has an incredible ability to guide people in how to have an experiential (rather than just intellectual) understanding of a relationship with nature.

Dr Mike categorised the fifty-four senses into four categories, which are based on Guy Murchie's original categorisation; radiation, feeling, chemical, and mental. Since working with the fifty-four senses in The Nature Process, Sami Aaron, The Nature Process Master Coach and myself have expanded these categories into six; radiation, feeling, chemical, mental, communal, and spiritual. We found that doing so helped people to relate more to the senses and understand them better. We've also renamed some of the senses to help people recognise them more easily. Our objective in doing so was not about being scientifically accurate but rather in helping people experience their fifty-four senses to allow a deeper state of natural presence.

As humans, we are subjective beings. Our reality is based upon what we experience. Our extended senses – whether six, thirty-two or fifty-four, are those sensations, feelings and thoughts that allow us to experience the world in a far deeper, more intimate manner than just the ordinary five. They are a non-verbal way for us to experience the world in which we live. Our senses existed before we developed the capabilities of language. As Derrick Jensen, a North American writer and radical activist states, they are a language older than words. Our senses allow us to fully connect with the natural world around us and experience it through all facets of our body. This is what we want to facilitate.

In the following sections I offer a short description of each of the fifty-four senses so you can explore them for yourself. To offer you a detailed explanation of how each sense works along with the scientific research that already exists on it, is beyond the goal of this book. The main purpose of this exploration is to help you recognise and experience how you receive information about your environment beyond the traditional five senses. I recommend that as you read each of the fifty-four senses you stop and reflect on your own experience and understanding of this sense. It's also important to note that many senses work together rather than separately.

There's a risk that as you read this book you'll start to intellectualize the information in it. Your mind will read the information about the senses but you'll not actually take the time to experience them. It's only when you take new information and experience it fully that you truly understand what is being taught. That's why, after exploring the fifty-four senses, I offer an additional way in which you can continue to experience them with a guided meditation that I've used with The Nature Process clients.

Even if you already think you have a deep connection to nature, it's possible to go even deeper through experiencing the fifty-four senses. As one participant of The Nature Process highlights:

I've spent a lot of time in this forest and a lot of time in the sea. Yet it was like I saw everything for the first time with the colours and the light. It was such a rich experience, doing something that I always do but seeing it as if for the first time.

I think that was an awakening. Seeing the world with such vivid colours, shapes, forms and connectedness. I saw a lot of magic. I'd look into a flower and see a whole world. A lot of synchronicities would happen afterwards that would make me think, "that's related to the flower I was really observing and taking in".

The fifty-four senses opened me to more and more of nature. I realised that I mainly use my eyes. Now I'm aware of things like the weight of my body, the warmth of the sun, and the sensation of the breeze. It was a real strong opening for me on how to look at nature and how to perceive it in ways that I would never have previously connected to being in nature.

RADIATION SENSES

These senses relate to our ability to perceive invisible waves such as sound, light, electricity, and magnetic pull.

Sense of light and sight (#1)

Light is a type of electromagnetic radiation that our eyes have the ability to perceive and process so that we can make sense of our surrounding environment. However, out of all the electromagnetic frequencies known to man, only a small section of them are visible to the eye. Our sense of sight and light tends to be one of the most dominant senses we have and is used to help us perceive many other of our fifty-four senses.

Sense of seeing without eyes (i.e. heliotropism) (#2)

This is the movement of plants, such as sunflowers, that adjust their position to follow the direction of the sun. It also exists in animals who have a tendency to move towards light and has an impact on muscle tone. A latent positive heliotropism exists within humans that is noticeable in new born infants or in brain-damaged individuals.

Sense of colour (#3)

Colour is created through changes in the visible electromagnetic frequencies that our eyes can process. When this visible light hits an object, only some of the electromagnetic frequencies are reflected back into our eyes, giving us the particular colour of an object.

Sensitivity to radiation other than visible light (i.e. radio waves and X-rays) (#4)

Some radiation, known as ionized, is powerful enough to change the basic structural components of a physical object, which is why radiographers are required to protect themselves from repeated exposure to x-rays. Other forms of radiation are known as non-ionizing, which means that they're not powerful enough to cause changes within the body or impact human health.

Sense of hearing (includes resonance, vibrations, sonar, and ultrasonic frequencies) (#5)

Soundwaves are non-electromagnetic forms of radiation that are caused by movement. These sound waves enter the ear and cause movement of hairs within the ear that the brain translates into sounds. Sonar soundwaves are what dolphins and whales use to communicate. Ultrasonic soundwaves are not audible to the human ear.

Electromagnetic sense and polarity within the body, ability to generate
current as in the nervous system and brain waves (#6)
The human body could be considered an electrical machine. Information
we receive from the environment around us is translated into electrical
currents that transmit information in the brain and throughout the body.
These electromagnetic fields are subtle, yet with practise, it's possible to
sense them.

Sense of electromagnetic fields outside the body (#7)
Electromagnetic fields are both naturally occurring and man-made.
Thunderstorms can produce these fields while the Earth's electromagnetic
field points towards magnetic north and allows birds and animals to use it as
a tool for navigation. It depends on the strength of the electromagnetic field
as to whether it can be sensed or even impact the body.

Awareness of temperature (#8)
Thermoception is the scientific name given to an organism's ability to perceive temperature. In humans, our temperature 'sensor' is located in our spinal column and information received is transmitted through the skin to the
brain. It would seem that the expression 'shivers down your spine' has its roots
in a real physiological basis!

Awareness of weather (#9)
Before we had weather forecasts, people were able to tell what the weather was
going to do from observing minute changes in the surrounding climate. This
sense is still active in many people who live in rural areas and is a combination
of other senses at play. For example, when it's going to rain, there's a change
in the appearance of the sky along with changes in temperature and pressure
as humidity in the air increases.

FEELING SENSES

These senses relate to physical sensations including touch, weight, balance, space, pressure, pleasure, and pain.

Sense of touch (especially on the skin) (#10)

Our sense of touch is created by what's known as the somatosensory system, a complex system of nerve cells that respond to internal or external changes in the body. There are sensors on our skin, body tissue, muscles, bones, joints and body organs. All these sensors are connected to a special chain of cells in the spinal cord that collate and send the information to the brain where it's processed into sensations.

Sense of seasonal changes (#11)

Our sense of seasonal changes is processed through many of our other senses such as sense of light and sight, temperature, colour, meaning attached to colour, pressure and movement. These seasonal changes have a physiological impact upon the body, which can lead to the development of seasonal affective disorder (SAD) in some people during the winter.

Awareness of pressure, particularly underground, underwater, and to wind and air (#12)

Our sense of pressure is also part of the somatosensory system. The cells that sense pressure are known as mechanoreceptors that exist all over the body. There are four different kinds, based on their speed of adaption and size.

Sensitivity to gravity (#13)

Gravity is the force that attracts physical objects towards the centre of the earth. It affects us every single moment of our lives. Without gravity, our bodies wouldn't work properly and we tend to only become aware of gravity when this sense isn't working properly.

Without gravity, we would experience bone and muscle loss, puffy faces from fluid not moving fully through our body, de-conditioning of and decrease in heart functioning, lengthening of the spine and back pain, problems with our inner ear and balance and, challenges with our sleep and performance. These are all things that astronauts who stay in outer space have to deal with!

Sense of appetite or hunger for food, water and air (#14)

This sense involves internal sensors within the brain. Some of these sensors monitor our need for food as a way of maintaining energy flow in and out of the body. Other sensors monitor the level of carbon dioxide in the lungs. There are also sensors in our circulatory system that monitor the levels of salt and trigger our need for water if our salt levels get too high.

Sense of excretion (includes releasing toxins, waste elimination, protection from enemies, and marking territory) (#15)

This is another sense that is connected to internal sensors within the brain. It's also related to some of the communal senses such as sense of territory and sense of self. However, there are also sensors in the bladder and rectum that create sensations of fullness and the need to excrete our bodily waste.

Sense of weight and balance (#16)

Our sense of balance is also known as equilibrioception. It involves our sense of sight and space along with the physical functioning of the ears where the same hairs used in our sense of hearing are activated. Visual sensory information is transmitted to the brain and translated into information that the muscles and joints then receive to stop us from falling over.

Space or proximity sense (#17)

For this sense to function effectively we must first have a well-developed sense of self that allows us to map where we are in relation to other objects. Our sense of space comes from a series of cognitive processes that are interpreting information received from other senses such as sight, movement, distance, position, and speed. If this sense is undeveloped we end up bumping into other objects.

Sense of motion; body movement sensations and sense of mobility (#18)

Our sense of movement is also known as our kinaesthetic sense or proprioception. In our muscles and tendons there are sensory receptors called muscle spindles. These connect to our central nervous system and send the information to our brain which gives us our experience of movement.

Coriolis sense or awareness of effects of the rotation of the Earth (#19)

The Coriolis sense is where anything that moves on or above the Earth's surface doesn't move directly in a straight line but instead drifts off course due to the rotation of the Earth. Not only does it impact airplanes but it also impacts ocean current and hurricanes too. It also impacts how we perceive the movement of the moon at night. While it seems as if the moon is arcing across the sky, in reality the moon is staying in the same place while the Earth rotates.

Sense of pain (#20)

Our sense of pain is called nociception and is caused when the sensory nerve cells, called nociceptors, receive chemical, physical or thermal stimulation. The information received travels along the nerves of the spinal column up to the brain where it is then processed into our subjective experience of pain.

Sense of emotions (includes happiness, distress, joy, contentment, pain, and grief) (#21)

Our sense of emotions is created by the limbic system within the brain. This part of the brain is also connected to our sense of memory and smell. We process information from our environment, information from the body and prior information about objects and situations simultaneously which creates an emotional response. Science is still in the process of understanding fully how this works.

Sense of fear, dread of injury, death, or attack (#22)

Our sense of fear is created through a process of learning from information gathered from our other senses. It's a combination of biological and psychological responses that have a dynamic interplay between them. The part of the brain that is most commonly associated with our sense of fear is the amygdala. We'll be exploring more about the stress-responses triggered within the body as a result of our sense of fear in the following chapter on natural body.

 Note: Our senses of pain (#20), emotions (#21), and fear (#22) are three special senses in that when they are over-activated they represent a warning flag that lets us know we are out of balance and that we need to take action to re-balance ourselves. They let us know that we are disconnecting from both our inner nature and the natural world around us. Once we reconnect to nature, we reconnect to ourselves and these senses subside.

Sense of pupation (includes dormancy, cocoon-building, and metamorphosis) (#23)

In humans, this is not a biological sense but rather a psychological one. It is a sense processed by the brain that relies on meaning and interpretation of certain events.

Urge to hunt and gather food (#24)

This is related to our sense of appetite for food and water. While small internal sensors let the body know it needs food, there's a whole psychological aspect to food that includes the meanings we give to different types of food and also how we feel about hunting and gathering specific food types. This is connected to our sense of self, smell, taste, humility and ethics.

CHEMICAL SENSES

These senses relate to our awareness and recognition of the meaning and uses of hormones, scents, and tastes.

Sense of smell (#25)

We possess little sensors called chemoreceptors in the nose that pick up chemicals and translate these chemicals into electrical impulses which are then processed by the brain. Our sense of smell is also connected to parts of the brain that process emotions and memory. We have more capabilities of smell that we realise. Research has shown that blindfolded people have been able to follow specific smells across a busy university campus.

Sense of taste (#26)

We possess chemoreceptors in the taste buds on our tongue that process chemicals in the same way as our sense of smell. Our brain combines information from our senses of smell, touch, temperature and pain to help us create a complete picture of the flavour of different foods.

Sense of humidity and moisture (#27)

Hygrosensation, or the ability to sense humidity, is still not fully understood. Unlike certain insects, humans and other animals don't have humidity sensors. Instead, we rely on a combination of the senses of touch, pressure and temperature upon our skin and airways that are then processed by the brain.

Hormonal sense (as to pheromones and other chemical stimuli) (#28)

Hormones are chemicals that are produced in various parts of the body by the endocrine glands and help control functions of the body such as hunger, reproduction, growth, emotions and moods. These hormones are secreted directly in the blood and transported around the body to specific tissues and organs. We can sense the impact of hormones through how our body functions.

Horticultural sense (the desire and ability to nurture gardens and cultivate crops) (#29)

When we garden, we experience a chemical response within the body that can help reduce fatigue, anger, stress, depression, anxiety and pain while improving concentration, memory and mood. Research shows that there is an interconnected relationship between chemicals in the natural world and the human body. For example, there is bacteria in soil that triggers the production of serotonin within the brain, which creates a happy, positive mood.

Mental Senses

These senses relate to perception and expression of intellectual and emotional thoughts and reactions using the mind and reasoning.

Sense of mind and consciousness (#30)

There is great debate about what our sense of mind and consciousness actually is and whether it's a by-product of the functioning of the brain or if it's a key non-physical component to our existence. In simple terms this sense allows us to be aware of what's going on around us and within us. It's a key sense that enables the processing of many other senses into what is our subjective experience of reality.

Sense of language and articulation, used to express feelings and convey information (#31)

The scientific study of this sense is called linguistics and focuses on the form, meaning and context of words used. In humans, language is processed within many different parts of the brain and is heavily influenced by our communal senses.

Sense of reason, memory, and the capacity for logic and science (#32)

The part of our brain responsible for processing our sense of reason and memory is also the same part of the brain responsible for our sense of emotions. It's directly related to the rise of philosophy, science, language, and math.

Sense of form, design, and function (#33)

Our sense of form refers to our capacity to understand the elements of an object and how those elements combine together along with the purpose of the elements individually and together.

Sense of play, sport, humour, pleasure, and laughter (#34)

Our sense of play, etc. uses many of the same skills (and brain functioning) involved in solving complex problems. Connected to many of our other senses, this one helps us make sense of the world and connect to others.

Sense of physical place, navigation senses, awareness of land and seascapes, and of the positions of the sun, moon, and stars (#35)

Through our sense of place, we are able to build up a mental picture of the world around us that allows us to move through it without getting lost.

Sense of time and rhythm (#36)

Chronoception is the psychological name of our sense of time. While we have no specific sensors in the body that allows us to perceive time and rhythm, research has shown that there is a specific system comprised of various parts of the brain that allows us to perceive time.

Sense of biological and astral time (i.e. movement of the stars), awareness of past, present, and future events (#37)

This sense uses a combination of other senses processed in the brain to enable an experience of past, present and future.

Sense of meanings, moods and emotions attached to colours, textures, and sounds (#38)

Colour psychology studies the impact of human behaviour related to colour while psychoacoustics studies, amongst other things, our psychological response to music and sound. Our gender, age, experience and culture can also affect the meanings, moods, and emotions we attach to colours, textures, and sounds.

Sense of excessive stress and surrender (#39)

Our sense of excessive stress will be explored in more detail in the following chapter when we look at how the body responds to stress and what we can do to reduce this. When we give in to excessive stress we stop resisting the body's physiological stress response. As our body starts to rebalance we experience a sense of surrender due to the physiological changes of the body moving out of the stress response.

COMMUNAL SENSES

These senses relate to our innate desire to be part of a community for physical as well as emotional support and survival.

Sense of emotional place, of community, belonging, support, trust, and thankfulness (#40)

A sense of place develops from the interaction of childhood experiences, family connections, societal meaning and community events that are connected to a specific location. As a result, special meanings are associated to specific locations and can impact a person's sense of self and identity. Activation of this sense shows that people are more likely to take care of a natural area because they feel connected to and have a relationship with it.

Urge to procreate (includes sex awareness, courting, love, mating, and raising young) (#41)

Our awareness of and interest in sex deepens as we reach puberty due to the sex hormones that are released. Courting, love, mating and raising young are also impacted by the chemicals that are released as we experience these events. These chemical responses are intertwined with the societal and cultural stories we receive, many of which can contradict the natural urges within the body.

Territorial sense (includes possession and ownership; sense of home) (#42)

Our territorial sense consists of our relationship to a specific location associated with our family, society or culture. This sense is intertwined with some of our mental senses such as memory, language and physical place and is also impacted by our sense of emotional place and sense of self.

Sense of awareness of one's own visibility or invisibility and the ability to camouflage (#43)

This sense relies on our mental capacity to see ourselves from other's perspectives and understand what needs to be done to attract or detract another being's attention to or from ourselves. This can relate to actions we need to take as individuals or objects we can use to help us. It's a sense that develops as we mature. Think of young children who hide their face and assume they are invisible because they can't see you, even though only their face is hidden. Pee-ka-boo!

Awareness of the capacity to persuade, mesmerize, or hypnotize other creatures (#44)

This sense is closely connected to our capacity for leadership and is connected to the mirror neurons that fire within our brain. Mirror neurons allow us to imitate other people's behaviour. Someone who has this sense well-developed is able, through speech and behaviour, to trigger a specific response within another individuals' mirror neurons that can influence their behaviour and thoughts.

Sense of self (includes power, control, dominance, and submission) (#45)

Our sense of self is better known in psychological terms as the 'ego'. Our ego is how we define ourselves as separate from others and create a sense of an autonomous individual who is capable of exerting influence on ourselves and the world around us.

Urge to travel, migrate, emigrate, and colonize (including compassion and receptive awareness of all the earth's living beings) (#46)

Throughout the history of humanity, we've been a species that has moved from one part of the world to another, whether that's been for adventure, exploration, necessity, food, etc. This sense is also about the awareness and recognition that to meet our needs we have to have an awareness of our relationship to other living beings in the same location. This is not a physical sense. Like many others of our communal senses it's psychological, though there may be a biological basis underpinning it.

Sense of survival through joining a more established organism (#47)

This sense reflects the awareness that if we are separated from a bigger organism, whether that be biological (as in the Earth) or socially constructed (as in tribes, family, society, religion, corporations), we have less chance of survival.

SPIRITUAL SENSES

These senses relate to advanced thoughts including aesthetics, humility, ethics, as well as conscience, joy, sorrow, spirituality, and unity.

Aesthetic sense (includes creativity and appreciation of beauty, music, literature, form, design, and drama) (#48)

Our aesthetic sense allows us to have an emotional response to beauty, music, literature, form, design, and drama. Through focusing our sense of awareness upon an object that we perceive as attractive aesthetically, we are able to explore deeply the symbolic meaning of the object and experience a deep emotional connection to it.

Sense of humility, ethics, morality, and fairness (#49)

This sense helps us gain a perspective of our relationship to the world and decide what we consider to be fair, just and right in how we want to treat others.

Intuition or subconscious deduction sense (a.k.a. sixth sense) (#50)

This sense is also referred to as a 'hunch' or 'gut feeling' and refers to the ability to receive knowledge without conscious reasoning, proof or evidence. Some theories suggest that the subconscious mind is able to process and filter information faster than the conscious mind, thus arriving at knowledge without our understanding why.

Sense of relaxation and sleep (includes dreaming, meditation, and brain wave awareness) (#51)

This sense is perceived through the multiple processing of many other senses, especially those within the feeling category. Combined with our sense of self and mind, it enables us to create physiological changes within the body that support its well-being and growth.

Psychic sense (includes foreknowledge, clairvoyance, clairaudience, psychokinesis, telepathy, astral projection, and certain animal instincts and plant sensitivities) (#52)

Our psychic sense, or extra-sensory perception (ESP), allows us to access very subtle information that is beyond the traditionally accepted realms of knowing. There is huge controversy about the existence of this sense, with some scientists and psychologists dismissing it as pseudoscience. Other branches of psychology seek to understand and explore this sense due to the increasing numbers of individuals who report psychic experiences.

Spiritual sense (includes conscience, capacity for divine/universal love, ecstasy, deep joy, profound sorrow, sacrifice, and compassion) (#53)

Our spiritual sense is how we express ourselves on the deepest level possible. It's through this sense that we explore the values and meanings of the world around us and consider our place within the world.

Sense of interconnectedness/oneness/unity (#54)

A sense of interconnectedness is a felt sense of connection between all life on earth. In a traditional religious or spiritual sense this can be considered an altered state of consciousness that connects you with God/Divine/Allah/ Nature, etc. In a more secular context this is a felt sense of the relationships that exist economically, socially, and politically and the recognition that fundamentally these relationships must work for the benefit of all, not merely a select few.

EXPERIENCE YOUR FIFTY-FOUR SENSES

You don't need to be outside to start exploring your fifty-four senses. In fact, you've probably started experiencing the senses as you read through them all. Great! The simple act of reflecting on each sense as you read it is a fantastic starting point.

Remember though, as individuals, our senses differ depending on the experiences we've had. Some of us will have senses that are more developed than others. I probably have some senses that are stronger than yours and vice versa. Think of Daniel Kish; his sense of "seeing" without the eyes is incredibly strong. I doubt anyone reading this book could experience right now that sense the way he does.

The problem we face with our senses is that modern society has created an environment that deadens some of our senses and imbalances others. When we recognise this and start exploring our weaker senses, we are able to strengthen them.

Think about your sense of hunger and thirst. There's a lot of information out there about how people mistake their sense of thirst for hunger because they're unable to recognise the difference between the two. Maybe you're actually one of them. I know I used to be. When you focus on exploring the difference between aspects of the same sense or different senses, you're able to discern the difference and enhance your sensory capability.

There is no right or wrong way to experience and explore your senses. There is only your way. We are all different. That means you need to explore what works for you.

One way of exploring the fifty-four senses is to close your eyes and see what senses you can identify with your eyes shut. We take in a lot of information through our eyes. In evolutionary terms we've been trained to rely on our eyes, as they've been useful tools in helping us to sense potential danger. When we close our eyes, the senses that are more dominant are deactivated, so we have to start experiencing our other senses.

Once you've noticed the awareness of your senses with your eyes closed, open your eyes. Explore what senses you can identify now and observe any difference. Keep the book close by so that you can refer to it as you sample different senses.

Personally, when I'm outdoors I find it easier to keep my eyes open and to notice all the different senses I'm experiencing in that moment. I then focus on my ears and explore what senses I'm aware of through them. I very rarely close my eyes outside in nature, and when I do it's not for long. Other people who have participated in The Nature Process Group Program have commented that they have to close their eyes before they can open up their other senses. Play with this and find out what's right for you.

As you explore your different senses take a moment to label them. This helps keep the mind engaged so that it's easier to slip into the Theta brainwave state. Start an internal dialogue in which you consciously focus on saying, "Look at those leaves on the tree. I'm sensing the greenness of them and the round shape of them. I'm sensing movement as they're dancing in the wind. In contrast to the green leaves, the branches are brown, which again is my sense of colour."

The more that you have this internal conversation with yourself (and it can be very powerful to actually verbalize it if no one else is around), the more you'll become aware of nature. The more you become aware of nature, the easier it is to drop into the Theta brainwave state.

It probably will be challenging for you at first, which is why it's so important to consciously engage your mind along with your sensory experiences. We're most used to spending time in the Beta brainwave state. Most people don't even believe that it's possible to experience silence of the mind. Even in meditation, teachers say that it's not about silencing the mind *per se,* but allowing thoughts to arise without becoming attached to them. Play with your senses and discover the truth. Silence of the mind is possible.

If you have children, get them involved in this adventure. How much nature can you sense and how many senses are activated whilst you're doing so? The act of involving children can also help to activate the communal senses of urge to procreate (raising young), and sense of emotional place, of community, belonging, support, trust, and thankfulness.

Don't underestimate the power of doing this on a regular basis. Developing your natural presence is not complicated, yet many people choose to make it so, especially by focusing only on a few of their senses at the expense of others.

Make developing your natural presence part of your daily routine. When you leave your house, stop and take a moment to observe the nature around you. Every time you look out of a window, stop and take a moment to observe the nature around you. Slowly but surely you will increase your natural presence.

When you have free time, make it a priority to get outside, even if it is just for five minutes. The more time you spend outside, the easier it will be for you to experience the Theta brainwave state whenever you sense nature. A short time is better than no time!

If you're attracted to exploring your fifty-four senses in depth, you'll find the 'Reactivate Your Fifty-Four Senses Exercise' on page 209.

EXPLORE YOUR SENSES IN DIFFERENT BRAINWAVE STATES

Different senses can be experienced in different brainwave states. If you look at the last spiritual sense, which is a sense of interconnectedness/oneness/unity, this is not a sense which can be experienced in a Beta brainwave state where most people experience themselves as completely separate beings from others. In order for us to experience this sense we need to lower our brainwave frequency. Explore the senses through brainwave states. What senses do you notice as most active in a Beta brainwave state? How about if you calm yourself into an Alpha brainwave state? What ones are most noticeable when you move into a Theta brainwave state? If you struggle to identify which brainwave state you are in remember that the Beta brainwave state is lots of thoughts, the Alpha is relaxed and calm while the Theta is complete silence.

EXPLORE YOUR SENSES IN THE CITY AND THE COUNTRY

Traditionally, a lot of connecting to nature is focused on taking people out of modern day society over a period of a few days into the last remaining pockets of wilderness. The challenge with this is that not all of us have the time and resources to do this. It's also not necessary.

If we truly wish to maintain our natural presence, it's imperative that we're able to do this whether we are out in the countryside or within the city limits. We have to learn to live within the world as it exists now and develop a connection to nature no matter where we are in the world.

Some people have to commute hours to work. You need to be able to be present and aware of nature while you're travelling in your car. When you walk down a really busy and crowded city street, you need to be able to tap into and connect with the nature that already exists there.

Developing your natural presence in the countryside is really easy. Once you're there, there are no distractions. You simply throw your senses open and experience everything that nature has to offer. Dropping into the Theta brainwave state is relatively easy.

This is why most people who live there do not have a conscious awareness of their senses. They don't need to know about them. They can just experience them. It is also important to note that many people in the countryside are experiencing an eroding of their senses without even being aware of it. They believe that because they live in the countryside, they are fully connected to nature. There's a little bit more to connecting to nature than merely living in it – especially if you live most of your life in a Beta brainwave state. I'll talk more about this in the next chapter.

Developing your natural presence in the city is a whole different story. Not only is it far more challenging, but you also have to approach it differently. If you just throw open your senses and experience everything in the city, you become overwhelmed with negative sensory input that is damaging to your well-being.

In the year before I ran The Nature Process, nature challenged me to live in Barcelona for a year. Barcelona happens to be one of the most densely populated cities in Europe and one of the six biggest.

As you know I'm not a city person. I grew up in a village of six hundred people. I've been a country girl my whole life. Even when I lived in Edinburgh, which is known as "the big village" because it's so small, I lived on the outskirts and hardly ever went into the centre.

Living in the centre of Barcelona gave me an opportunity to truly understand how to develop and maintain a connection to nature when everything around you is busy, bustling, and chaotic. If you live in the city, the chances are good that you don't have the opportunity to go for a two-hour walk through the forest every week. It's more likely that this is a special treat for you.

In order for you to develop your natural presence in the city, you need to experiment with the following techniques. These techniques also work for those who are living in the countryside as well and are a great way to deepen and expand your connection to nature.

First of all, you need to get house plants. You will learn a lot from having plants in the city. It's a wonderful way to bring nature into your living space. You can also bring them into your workplace. Research shows that productivity and creativity are boosted just by the presence of plants.

Secondly, you can't just throw open all your senses in the city. If you do, it's likely that all the noise and pollution will overwhelm your senses and actually make you ill. What you need to do is to focus on one particular aspect of nature. You pay attention to it and create a specific connection to this aspect of nature. This requires a little bit more focus than when you are out in the countryside, due to the fact that there are so many other distractions.

In a city, one of the easiest aspects of nature to focus on is the sky. Observe this aspect of nature and explore what different senses you can engage to experience it. Challenge yourself to see how aware you can be of the sky throughout a certain time period. A reason why the sky is so powerful is that no matter where you are it's easy to sense the shifts from day to night. This shift triggers many different senses. If you look at the sky for long enough, and relax your eyes, you'll start to see a shimmering, translucent field over the sky. That's its energy field. Looking where trees meet the sky can help you see this. You'll also notice this on pristine white snow

You can also focus on the wind in the city. That's nature too, and easy to sense whether you are inside a building or outside on the street.

In some cities, there are a lot of birds. When you focus on them, what senses are you aware of?

Look at the sidewalk and see if you can sense any plants/weeds growing in the cracks and gaps.

Nature is everywhere. All you need to do is expand your senses to become aware of it.

Whether you live in the countryside or in the city, make this an adventure. Explore your fifty-four senses out in nature. This is how you incorporate your natural presence into your daily life. As you do this you will naturally reduce your stress levels and start experiencing life through a different lens.

Even if you go no further, mastering just this one part of The Nature Process will create fundamental changes in your well-being and your life. That's how valuable this is.

EXERCISES TO PRACTISE IN NATURE

* Take this book outside with you, find a quiet spot to sit down and explore how many of the senses you can activate and recognise as you go through the list of the fifty-four senses.
* Focus on one specific sense and spend at least fifteen minutes discovering what you can learn about it as you explore a natural area.
* Go to an area where there are lots of plants and trees. Study them to discover how many senses you can observe at play within them and their relationship to the environment.
* Choose a category of senses and focus on exploring them in more detail.
* Experience a sense in nature, such as sense of touch, through stroking the bark of a tree, then close your eyes and imagine the sensory experience without the stimulation.

KEY POINTS TO REMEMBER

✓ Spending time in nature is just as powerful as meditation.

• ✓ Nature changes the way our brains work and impacts the frequency of brainwave state.

• ✓ The lower the frequency of your brain, the easier it is to feel connected to the world around you.

• ✓ Trees and plants are easier aspects of nature to connect to than rocks and rivers.

• ✓ You connect to the world around you through your senses.

• Our senses are more powerful than we think.

• We have more than five senses; we have fifty-four and they are grouped in six categories.

• Radiation senses deal with our capacity to perceive different types of invisible waves.

• Feeling senses relate to physical sensations.

• Chemical senses focus on our awareness of hormones, scents and tastes.

• ✓ Mental senses relate to perception and expression of intellectual and emotional thoughts and reactions using the mind and reasoning.

• Communal senses relate to our innate desire to be part of a community for physical as well as emotional support and survival.

• Spiritual senses relate to advanced thoughts including aesthetics, humility, ethics, as well as conscience, joy, sorrow, spirituality, and unity.

• You can explore your fifty-four senses indoors or outdoors; in the city or country.

• It takes time and repeated practise with your fifty-four senses to develop them fully.

• Commit to making natural presence and the development of your fifty-four senses part of your daily routine until you are able to maintain a state of constant natural presence.

QUESTIONS FOR REFLECTION

* What's your favourite memory of a time or place in nature and why?
* What sensations do you particularly remember about that experience?
* How do you feel after you've spent time in nature?
* How often do you feel present and engaged outdoors and in?
* What do you think about the fifty-four senses and why?
* How often do you engage in conscious sensory exploration of the world?
* What can you do to activate more of your senses in your daily life?

CHAPTER 4

Natural Body

❦ ❦ ❦

Body and soul are not two different things, but only two
different ways of perceiving the same thing.

- ALBERT EINSTEIN

HAVING FOCUSED ON THE NATURE of the external natural world around you, it's now time to understand more about the nature that exists within you before connecting the two together. This chapter is designed to give you a basic understanding of the how the natural body works so that you can apply it to yourself. The more you engage experientially with the information in this chapter, the deeper you will understand how your own body works.

We are all individuals, which means that there will be certain things your body does that are unique to you. I can't tell you what they are. You need to discover them for yourself. This chapter will help you do that.

While your natural body can be experienced by itself, independent of your natural presence, it's far more powerful to link the two of them together. If you wish to practise The Nature Process in its entirety, this is a necessary part.

The stronger and deeper your ability to experience your natural presence and your natural body together, the deeper your capacity for understanding your own capacity for reducing stress and anxiety and becoming a fully productive and creative person able to function at your full potential.

You'll know you've mastered the two parts of this process together when both nature and your body become such a part of your daily life that you don't need to make an effort to get outside and move your body in nature.

To refresh your memory, the natural body is a state of being fully present to the inner nature of the body so that you can tap into its wisdom without interference from stories or judgment. Your natural body is how you connect to the environment around you and process the information you receive.

As part of The Nature Process, your natural body is the means by which you translate the information you receive through the fifty-four senses. It's also the means by which you are able to reduce stress and anxiety while encouraging productivity and creativity in your life.

If you are disconnected from the body, then it's highly likely that you'll be unable to fully complete The Nature Process. Should that be the case then I recommend finding a movement practice that helps you engage with the body on a deeper level. Running, yoga, strength training, dance, martial arts, weight lifting and tai chi are all great activities provided they are practised in a mindful way that connects you to the body and its movements.

In this chapter, I'll share more about the impact of the mind upon the body and how you can prevent the mind from disengaging from the body. If you are someone who is already active with the body, this chapter will help you work on an even more embodied level than before. As a result, any physical activity you undertake will have a far more powerful impact upon the body.

THE BODY AND STRESS

Stress is a combination of a psychological threat with a physiological process. When a person perceives an event as a threat, whether that be getting stuck in a traffic jam, doing a presentation in front of hundreds of people, moving to a different house, financial difficulties or family problems, there is a hormonal response within the body.

As a result of the chemicals released, blood is pumped into our arms and legs. Our heart and lung capacity increases. We begin to breathe more rapidly and our ability to mentally process conscious thoughts is reduced. Our digestion slows down or stops completely. We may also experience shaking and flushing while our hearing and vision can be affected.

This is commonly known as the "fight, flight, or freeze response." These changes occur to give us increased body strength and speed in anticipation of what's to come. Once the threat is gone, the hormones reduce and the body returns to normal.

However, in today's modern world, this stress response can be activated on a regular basis which means the body can struggle in discharging the stress experienced and instead holds on to it so that the effects of the stress become cumulative.

As a result, our hormonal levels become ineffective in returning to their normal levels. In the 1970s, researchers at St. Vincent's Hospital, London, were the first to show that severe and continuous stress reduces the ability of our immune system to function effectively, thus making us more susceptible to illness.

Furthermore, if stress hormone levels remain high, they can block our ability to produce serotonin, which is the happy drug that regulates our mood. As a result, we can become depressed.

This leads not only to certain food cravings as the body attempts to rebalance the serotonin, but it can also cause stomach aches, shallow breathing, nausea, dizziness, sweaty palms, cold hands, lack of concentration, sleeplessness, anger and a sense of being overwhelmed.

When it comes to the natural body, understanding the stress response is key. The sooner you recognise that your body is experiencing the symptoms of stress, the quicker you can take action to rebalance yourself and deal with the situations that are causing the stress. This prevents a build-up of stress hormones repressing the immune system and causing illness and disease.

THE BODY-MIND CONNECTION

Despite Descartes' prevailing idea within the medical approach to health and illness that the body and mind are two separate entities, research shows that the body and mind are, in fact, the same thing. Without the body, there is no mind. Guy Claxton, one of the UK's foremost thinkers on creativity, education and the mind, and author of *Intelligence in the Flesh,* highlights that much of the intelligent activity we attribute to the brain actually comes from the body instead. This is a wisdom and intelligence inherent within the body that we've become disconnected from.

The way our body communicates with us is through our emotions. The physician, Gabor Maté, author of *When the Body Says No,* highlights that ill health and disease comes from the stress created by repressing our emotions. What's more, the body can only exist in the present moment and deal with whatever is happening in that moment. The best way for the body to cope and deal with stress and the challenges of life is to recognise them as they arise.

However, our sense of mind has the capability of existing in the past, present and future. When the sense of mind and sense of past, present and future combine together through repressed emotions, you can end up with a feedback loop that causes the body to experience whatever thoughts and feelings you are holding onto - whether these belong in the past, present, or future.

Our modern lives are already filled with low-grade stressors such as work deadlines, traffic jams, bills, family and relationships. Our body is already experiencing stress. When we add thoughts about the past or future into this, we exacerbate this stress. When you think about challenging experiences from your past, especially if it's traumatic, or a future event that you're not looking forward to, the body responds as if the event were happening in that moment.

In the case of a past event where you still have repressed emotions, conscious of them or not, what happens every time you *think about* that event is that the stress response you initially *experienced* during that event is replayed out within your body's hormonal system. This is caused by the sense of helplessness felt in that moment.

Our body-mind connection isn't helped by our societal and cultural stories that teach us to repress our emotions instead of learning to regulate them. The challenge we face is that if we are not able to feel and recognise our emotions, then we are not aware of when we are feeling stress. This leaves us responding irrationally to events in the present because they contain a reminder of something emotionally unresolved from the past. If we are unable to create distinctions about the past and present we start to perceive more danger where none exists and therefore create more stress.

How often do you get caught up in thoughts about what you could have done differently, or how some event in your past has affected your life? The brain in its Beta state can obsess over past events, taking you back over the event again and again and making you relive your experiences.

Your body relives them too.

This response is what can block you from entering a deep state of natural presence. It's also why many people can be out in nature and still be disconnected from it. If your thoughts while in nature are overly concerned with the past or future, instead of the natural landscape around you, then you're potentially keeping yourself in a state of stress and anxiety and negating the health benefits of spending time out in nature.

TENETS OF EMBODIMENT

We can learn a lot from being aware of our body's language. Embodiment expert Mark Walsh (www.embodiedfacilitator.com) has summarised his key teachings into the following tenets, or principles, based on his experience. Mark has not only worked with large and small organisations teaching people how to become an embodied leader but has extensive experience in leadership, stress management and conflict resolution in countries around the world. Mark has also developed Embodied Yoga Principles (www.embodiedyogaprinciples.com) and trains yoga teachers to bring psychological self-awareness into yoga and apply yoga skills to daily life.

T0. Layers tenet

Our situation, relationship, culture, disposition and environment are all embodied. We contain layers of each of these within the body that are adapted to respond to our history.

T1. Tenet of comfort

The body reveals what's familiar. What we have practised feels easy.

T2. Tenet of joy
Delight reveals what's needed or longed for.

T3. Holographic tenet
The body reveals our way of being in all things.

T4. Tenet of deviation
An inability to follow a form reveals habitual pattern. Habits assert themselves and are exposed by form.

T5. Guidance tenet
The body can guide our life. When listened to, the body gives wisdom.

T6. Practice tenet
We become what we practice. We can learn to embody new ways of being

T7. Tenet of contrast
The body reveals and learns by exaggeration, contrast and differentiation

T8. Social tenet
We learn in relationship, and naming is powerful. By being witnessed and naming something we deepen insight and declare new futures

T9. Integration tenet
We can transfer embodied learning into daily life by creating micro indicators that tell us what's happening within our body, through working on yoga postures, and by designing a practice routine.

SUPPLEMENTAL TENETS:

T.10 Tenet of process
The body is a process and it benefits us to listen and follow.

T.11 Tenet of self-regulation
The fight-flight-freeze and craving responses can be managed

T.12 Trigger tenet
Our shadow is revealed by triggering and infatuation

These tenets reveal the power of working with the body. It expresses what we've learned from the environment we've grown up in. It shows us what's comfortable and lets us know what we really want. Our body communicates how we are in life, offers us wisdom and shows us what we need to work on. The more we are in the body, the more guidance we receive. The more we consciously play with the body, the more we learn about ourselves and how to be different in the world. Our body learns best when it's interacting with others and we can choose what to learn simply by listening to the body so that we can help change what it's communicating. This is something that we once knew and many animals still retain.

HORSES: MASTERS OF BODY AWARENESS
In his book *Waking the Tiger*, which explores how the body stores trauma, Peter Levine poses an interesting question: "How on earth can a zebra be out in the plains, get attacked by a lion, get mauled by a lion, yet the next day be out grazing and not affected by the traumatic experience?"

This question stuck with me because zebras are cousins of horses. They share similar processes in how they deal with danger.

Both zebras and horses are prey animals. This means they have to be fully aware of predators, because if they're not present to the environment and present to themselves by being in their body, they can end up getting eaten. It's a serious matter of life and death.

Horses are sensory animals with highly developed specific senses. It's what they rely on. Because horses are prey animals rather than predators, their senses have evolved to ensure they stay alive. They can hear noises miles away that we human are incapable of hearing. They can run fast, over long distances. They are able to pick up information through the ground via their hooves.

When something happens that they perceive as a threat, which means their stress response is triggered, they instantly go into flight mode. This is their first natural response.

It's really interesting when you observe horses because they're able to read body language of people and other animals extremely well. That's what helps keep them alive. That's why horses are being used in therapy. They have sensory capabilities beyond what humans are capable of, because humanity has developed by relying on its mental senses at the expense of the other senses.

I knew nothing about this until I had my first experience with Equine Assisted Learning. As part of my Masters in Applied Ecopsychology, I spent a month at the Healing Hooves, Healing Humans, Horse Sanctuary in Sunnyside, Washington State a few years ago learning about Equine Assisted Learning from its founder, Betty Hames (who is trained in and works with The Nature Process).

Equine Assisted Learning is a client-centred approach that allows people to work directly with horses. This approach helps people better understand how their behaviour and actions affect others. It impacts their lives through receiving direct feedback from the horses which is then translated with the help of a trained facilitator. Great for team building and understanding how others perceive your behaviour!

I was really nervous as I didn't have a lot of experience with horses and I am allergic to their dander. The first time I went out to meet the horses they reacted to my fear. They started getting frantic, moving dramatically, running around, neighing and snorting in a way that made my fear even worse. It took me a few days to become fully comfortable around the horses.

Every day I would go out to the corral and watch the horses. What fascinated me the most was watching what the horses did after they'd experienced a stressful event and once they realised that the perceived threat had disappeared. I observed this happening again and again during the month that I spent at the horse sanctuary.

Whenever their stress/fear response was triggered, they wouldn't immediately return to a state of normal relaxation. There was a gradual process that they would go through. I watched as they would stop running and return to standing in one place.

Yet they weren't still. As they stood, their muscles would ripple and their bodies would shake. They'd stamp their feet, blow heavily through their nostrils, or breathe with deep sighs.

This really got me thinking about what Peter Levine said in his book about the zebras. It made me reflect deeply on how we process our own stress responses.

It also relates to what I said in the last chapter about blind children intuitively clapping their hands and making noise to try to teach themselves to see through echolocation, but parents and society stopping them from doing this.

The same thing happens to us with the ways in which we process our own stress responses. Just like the horses, we have our own physical ways that help us shift the energy of the stress hormones from our bodies. Yet we're often prevented from fully rebalancing these hormones. We're told to sit up straight and don't fidget. It's not polite to burp in public, so we're trained not to do that. Our behaviour patterns have been separated from our natural body by what we consider appropriate social behaviour. Unlike horses, many of us are not able to rebalance the hormones of the stress response within our body. Instead we keep them elevated, weaken our immune system and end up in a state of disease, which is an extreme imbalance within our body.

We can learn a lot from horses about how to process our body's stress response. This is what developing your natural body is all about; being able to tap into the intuitive process that removes the effects of stress upon the body and brings it back into a state of harmony.

The challenge for us is that we have to unlearn all the ways in which our civilised behaviour has stopped the wisdom of the body from naturally expressing itself and become comfortable with the natural functioning of our body.

How the Body Naturally Releases Energy

Crying is one of the ways that we release energy generated within our bodies. Recent research shows that a variety of chemicals are present in our tears depending on the reason that we're crying. This is huge. When crying is triggered by a stress response, our tears contain enkephalin, which is a natural painkiller that helps us process harmful experiences.

Yet look at the cultural messages we have around crying. Apparently, it's only girls that cry (because we're awesome enough to not be afraid of our emotions!). If you're a man, the cultural message is that 'strong men don't cry'. In the United Kingdom, we even have the idiom, *Keep a stiff upper lip*. This traditionally encouraged us not to show our emotions, because emotions and tears were considered a sign of weakness.

Like horses, we also process the energy of our stress response through movement. Think back to the very nature of the stress response. It's preparing us to fight or flee. That's why the horses tremble, move, and stomp their feet. We need to do the same. Yet again, movement like this has not been considered socially appropriate.

In the past in the United Kingdom, we had a belief that children should be seen and not heard. To some extent it still exists. That means that we were trained from birth to not respond naturally to the body's stress responses.

No wonder we have such a reputation for high alcohol consumption. It's traditionally been one of the few socially acceptable ways to process our stress responses. And then we get to blame the alcohol for our behaviour, instead of our emotions!

The hormones from our stress responses also affect our digestion. This means that it's normal to experience energy releasing from the stomach. An example of this is burping, which is something I do a lot when I release the energy of a stress response. Taken to the extreme, this is why some people actually vomit when experiencing severe stress and anxiety.

Sweating is another way of shifting energy within the body. It's why we sweat when we have a fever. The body is working to bring itself back into balance. If you have strong body odour, this is a sign that your body is releasing toxins, which are imbalances within the body, through your sweat.

Going to the toilet is a way of shifting energy within the body.

Making primal sounds is a way of releasing energy within the body.

Trembling and shaking is a way of releasing energy within the body.

Yawning is a way of releasing energy within the body.

The key to success in mastering your natural body is to become comfortable with what your body naturally does. Every involuntary function within your body is designed to bring your body back into a state of balance. When we stifle these functions, in accordance with societal beliefs about how we should act, we stifle our body's ability to stay in a state of balance and health.

Think about how the earth works. Whenever there is a build-up of pressure and tension, it causes the earth to shift its tectonic plates causing an earthquake. Or a volcano erupts. Or there's a tornado, or some other natural phenomenon. That's the earth bringing itself back into balance.

Your body functions in the same way. However, we have a host of cultural stories and beliefs that we've been exposed to since childhood that get in the way of our natural body expressing itself in the way it needs to. I'll talk more about the impact of these cultural stories in the following chapter on natural attractions.

The challenge in developing your natural body is moving beyond any fear you may have about bodily functions. Rather than treating the functioning of your body as something to be embarrassed about, you need to learn to see the wonderful mechanisms at play within the body that are designed to help it stay in balance.

Think about when you need to go to the toilet. You're desperate to relieve yourself. Your senses of pain and distress are activated. Your stomach feels full and uncomfortable.

Then you sit down and release. You've got to admit, it feels good. The elimination of waste brings your body back into balance.

Have you ever noticed that after a night of too much self-indulgence with alcohol, when you have a bowel movement the next day you actually feel better?

Society tells us that we shouldn't really talk about stuff like this in polite society. Yet it's *not* talking about stuff like this that has contributed to people's ill health. If we don't talk about it then we don't know what's normal. If we don't normalize the way our bodies release energy, we experience shame and guilt towards ourselves. That is the biggest disconnect of all – and it's one that, quite literally, can make us ill.

THE BODY'S RESPONSE TO EMOTIONS

As I've already mentioned, there's a growing body of research that suggests that specific body parts or ailments are actually connected to specific issues or emotions. A study published in 2014 by a group of Finnish researchers highlighted how emotions impact specific areas of the body. They conducted five different experiments with groups having a range from thirty-six to three hundred and two participants in each. The participants were given a picture of a body coloured in blue and were asked to draw where they felt physical sensations associated with an emotion, such as sadness, anger, depression, love, happiness, etc.

The study demonstrated a significant correlation with body sensations experienced by the participants. Sadness created a sense of coldness in the arms and legs with a neutral sense in the rest of the body, apart from some mild sensations around the heart and head. Anger was found to create a sense of activation in the head, shoulders, upper body, arms and feet. Depression was found to shut down the body completely with a numb core and very little energy in the head, arms and legs. On the contrary, love created a sense of heightened activity and warmth in the centre core of the body that spread up into the head, while happiness lit up the whole body with a warm glow.

This study shows a direct correlation between the body and our emotional responses. The thoughts and stories that we tell ourselves about things that have happened impact the way we feel. The way we feel impacts the health of the body.

Conduct your own experiment and notice where in the body you experience sensations when you feel angry. Then, notice how you feel when you are happy. Play with other emotions. Become familiar with your body's response to emotions.

Sometimes, in order to be able to work with the body's response to emotions, it's necessary to explore the thoughts behind the emotions – especially if you're struggling to come into a state of natural presence.

What can be helpful is to explore what author and speaker, Byron Katie calls "The Work". This is a method of exploring yourself to find a way of changing the thoughts that are creating the emotions you're experiencing.

It's based upon four questions:

1. Is it true? (If no, go straight to question three)
2. Can you absolutely know that it's true?
3. How do you react, what happens, when you believe that thought?
4. Who would you be without the thought?

For example, say your boss at work has really annoyed you. You feel angry. You want to punch or kick something and no matter how much you walk outside you are so aware of the energy in your body that you can't ground into a state of natural presence. All that's going through your mind is the thought, 'he shouldn't expect me to do that!'

First of all, if you are able to sense into the emotions that's a great thing. You are more in your natural body that you think. However, how you respond is the challenge. Using Byron Katie's approach, you ask yourself if it's true that your boss shouldn't expect you to do that. Be honest with yourself. I don't think I've ever found a time that I can say that I absolutely know that my thought is true.

The third question offers you a chance to reflect on your reaction and observe what happens both within the body and as a result of your anger towards your boss. Do you end up having an argument with a loved one? Maybe you drive the car slightly more erratically? Or maybe you go and buy a big bag of sweets and eat them all? There's no right or wrong answer to this question. It's simply a way of gaining a new perspective on your emotional response.

The last question offers an opportunity to go deep into the body and sense how it would feel without the thought that your boss shouldn't expect you to do that. The idea behind this is to create a physiological change within the body that creates a sense of peace. Use an exploration of the physical sensations associated with your emotions to help facilitate this, based upon the previous study mentioned. Once you know what peace feels like in your body, it becomes easier to consciously move your thoughts and emotions into that state.

This can be a very helpful exercise to do outside while walking in a natural area surrounded by lots of greenery. The walking and greenery will help support you as you engage with your emotional response and explore it with Bryon Katie's questions.

Another way to explore your body's response to emotions is through the work of Louise Hay. Louise is the founder of the publishing company Hay House, which is the biggest mind-body-spirit publishing house in the world.

In the 1980s she wrote a book called *You Can Heal Your Life,* in which she explained how physical illness can have its roots in the way we think. This book has sold over thirty-five million copies worldwide, making her one of the largest selling women authors after J.K. Rowling, Danielle Steel, and Barbara Cartland, who all wrote fiction. That's a pretty impressive claim to fame!

The companion guide, *Heal Your Body,* offers an extensive list of ailments and their root mental causes, along with affirmations to change the way you think. I'm not particularly a fan of affirmations myself and tend not to use them with my clients. Nevertheless, referring to the list of ailments within this book is a great starting point to see if there's any connection between your ill health and emotions that you're not fully recognising.

BODY AWARENESS EXERCISE

The following exercise is designed to help you reconnect to your natural body and strengthen your awareness of it. Take a moment and familiarize yourself with the exercise. Make sure you are in a place that's safe, comfortable and warm – whether inside or out. The exercise assumes that you are sitting in a seat but you can also do it standing up or lying down.

Get comfortable wherever you are sitting. Make sure your buttocks fill the seat and put your feet flat on the ground, feeling the sense of pressure as you do.

Ensure you're relaxed and comfortable for this exercise. If you need to, move your shoulders and stretch so that you can become fully comfortable. Make any other adjustments you feel are necessary to your body.

Come into a place of stillness, no movement. Close your eyes, knowing that some of your natural senses will be activated as you do so.

Take a deep breath in. And a deep breath out. Take another deep breath in. And another deep breath out.

Activate your sense of memory and remember the nature experiences that you've had in the past. Think about being outside in your local area experiencing a sense of spaciousness; a sense of desire to connect; a sense of peace, tranquillity, and silence.

Remember the different colours, shapes and textures of the natural world around you.

What was the temperature like?

What was the weather like?

What noises did you hear?

Remember the emotions these sensory experiences created within you.

Acknowledge that in your mind you are there. Your body doesn't know the difference. Bring this awareness of nature fully into your mind and body with every breath you inhale and exhale.

Anchor yourself within these moments, to these experiences. Harness the sensory experience of nature. Know that you are safe and you are supported by nature, that nature is helping you to sense the nature within you.

Now start sensing your body. Start at the feet. Become aware of the pressure, that sense of pressure underneath your feet, the sense of contact and the sense of temperature.

Are your feet hot?

Are they cold?

As you move up into your legs, sense your legs and notice if there's any twitching. Sense your body and understand the way that your body wants to work. If you need to move, move.

Trust your body. Trust that your body knows exactly what you need.

Allow your senses to keep exploring up your thighs. If you're attracted to using your hands to help you sense your thighs, then do so. There's no right or wrong way to do this. There's only your way.

Keep on sensing that energy. Sense what is going on within your body for you, paying attention to any thoughts, feelings or sensations that arise.

Bring your awareness up through the groin area, up to the hips and the back. Pay attention.

Do you have a feeling of balance or is there a feeling of stress?

Is there tension?

Is there something that needs to be moved?

If you do, move. Trust your body to do exactly what you need in the moment.

Bring your awareness further up into the stomach, into the heart. If it helps you, imagine the heart beating and pumping all that blood through your body.

Stay focused on your sensory experience of your body. Are you able to stay present, without the mind becoming distracted?

Can you feel your body?

As you keep on breathing, are you able to feel your lungs expanding and contracting?

Is there movement within the stomach that supports this?

Observe all the different sensations that you're experiencing, with the awareness that the information you're receiving is coming in through fifty-four sensory gateways within the body.

As you allow these fifty-four senses to send you more information, be aware of any new and different experiences you're having with the body.

Keep hold of your awareness and bring it up into the shoulders. Again, if you need to move, do it.

Feel your arms. Notice your sensory awareness. Move your arms right down to your fingers and if you want to, move your fingers. Feel the air surrounding your fingers as you do so.

Can you feel this movement in you?

The muscle moving underneath the skin?

Make a little movement with your fingers. Again, just keep all of the awareness of your fingers, your arms, your shoulders and neck. Remember that if you need to move, move. Your body knows exactly what it needs.

Ignore the sense of mind. Focus on the other senses. Bring your awareness up into the head.

Feel your whole body as you are just now from a state of loving. Respect the wisdom of your body. Your body is a wise beacon of knowledge on this physical plane. It deserves order and respect for its ability to be here as part of the earth, sensing itself.

How does it feel to acknowledge this?

Take a few moments to sit with whatever sensations are arising. If you get the urge to cough or make noises, let them out. Nobody else matters. There's only you present.

Give yourself a moment. Offer thanks to your body for the wisdom that it contains, for the natural wisdom, full of power and strength. Your body knows intuitively how to bring you back into balance.

How does it feel to be reminded of the body's power?

Offer thanks, especially if you are suffering from any illnesses. Offer thanks to your body. Your body is not weak because it is ill; your body is the strongest it has ever been.

If you're suffering from an illness, your body is working twice as hard to bring you back as much as it possibly can to a state of balance and wholeness. That is incredible. That is power. Feel this and give thanks.

Take a deep breath in. And then out. Feel the aliveness and energy within the body. Then, when you're ready, open your eyes and re-engage with the world around you.

If you need to take a moment to reflect on your experience, do so. If you'd like to journal about your experience, get a paper and pen and start writing. It's worthwhile to do this exercise again and again so you can get to learn more about your body and how it works.

Connect to Your Natural Body

Use your fifty-fours senses to focus fully on your natural body. Instead of sensing nature outside of you, you're now sensing nature within. You don't have to be outside to sense your natural body, though I will talk about connecting your natural body to your natural presence at the end of this chapter.

You are with your body one hundred percent of your time. Without your body, you wouldn't exist. Not only does your body express who you are but it's also your way of being in the world. Yet so many of us are caught up in the Beta brainwave state that we disconnect from our bodies and the sensations within it. As you read this book, how aware are you of your body?

Take a moment and bring your awareness to your body right now. Is it comfortable or are there aches and pains present? If so, what are would feel good for you to do?

As I wrote the first edition of this book, I noticed that as I typed these words I was conscious of tension in the shoulders. Earlier that morning I'd gone for a jog, which had helped release the tension in my shoulders from the day before. Yet the tension had come back. It was a sign that I was spending too long at the computer and that my posture was not supportive of what I was doing. Even with regular breaks to stretch and move my body, the tension still remained.

At the moment, my body was requesting that I take a break and move the body more. Yet the sense of mind was fully engaged with what I was writing and didn't want to stop. The compelling urge to continue writing, even as my body asked me to stop, was a clear sign that I was in full Beta brainwave flow.

Writing the second edition of this book, the right side of my neck feels tight and I have an ache in the lower back from slouching in bed to type rather than sitting up properly. This awareness has me sitting up straight, adjusting the pillows and the laptop so I can continue to write in a more body-friendly way.

This is part of developing an awareness of your natural body – by tuning into it at regular intervals and discovering what it needs. In a world where many of us have sedentary lives and jobs it can be challenging to develop awareness of your natural body. That's why I included the previous exercise. It can be done while you are sitting at a desk, on the sofa, or even if you're stuck in traffic. You can do a quick scan of your body in as little as a few minutes.

Every time you check in with your natural body, ask it what it needs and then give that to the body. Find a way to develop the awareness of your natural body in line with your pre-existing modern day life commitments.

As I've already said, The Nature Process is about finding a way to connect to nature, both within and without, in the midst of your daily life. This is where the true power of this process lies.

Check in with your body when you wake up in the morning and before you get out of bed. Check in with your body at night before you go to sleep.

Another great time to focus on your natural body is when you eat. Pay attention to the sensations you experience as you eat your food. Notice the different sensations that arise in your body depending on what you eat. Are there foods that make you feel more energized? Happier? Or is what you're eating triggering your senses of pain, distress, and fear?

If you're a woman, learn the rhythm of your menstrual cycle and discover the changes that occur in your body from month to month.

Notice how your body feels before, during, and after exercise.

How does the body feel as you walk? How does the body feel while you're sitting?

The more you check in with your body, the more you create a habit that helps you learn to understand what your body wants and needs at all times.

How to Adapt Your Natural Body to Physical Disability

During one of The Nature Process Live online programs, one of the participants asked a question about how to adapt the exploration of the natural body, especially with regards to the Body Awareness Exercise, as she was a paraplegic and couldn't experience some of the things I mentioned in the exercise. The following is a guideline for anyone who has some form of physical disability.

You need to start with where you are and what you can already sense. Don't focus on what you *can't* sense; that's counterproductive to developing your natural body and will only lead to frustration. Remember from the last chapter that pain, distress, and fear are sensory signs that you need to engage other senses for your own well-being.

When you focus on what you can sense, follow that sensation as far as it goes. Then push your awareness further and see what other sensations you can notice.

Repeat and play with this process. Is it possible to expand your awareness of your natural body beyond what you currently sense?

To help you explore your natural body more deeply, get a massage. This is a great way to tune into sensations and feelings in the body without having to make an effort. It also has the added benefits of stimulating circulation, helping the nervous system to function more effectively, and relieving pain and muscle tension.

See if it's possible to get a massage out in nature. This will help you shift into the Theta brainwave state so that not only are you connected to nature but you'll also be able to tap into your body's wisdom. It will tell you how best to move and expand your natural body.

If you have a physical disability, it's even more important to connect with your natural body and learn to trust it. It will give you the best wisdom possible about what you're capable of sensing, experiencing, and doing.

CONNECT YOUR NATURAL BODY TO NATURAL PRESENCE

Once you've become aware of your natural body it's time to go outside and connect the natural body into a state of natural presence. If you feel attracted to doing the previous exercise outdoors you can, but it's not necessary. At the end of this chapter I offer many more exercises to explore your natural body outdoors in nature.

Mastery of the natural body is about having continual awareness of the dynamic interplay of the external nature around you and how it's impacting the inner nature within the body. In essence, this is how often you are aware of how your environment is impacting your physiological and psychological health so that you can take action to ensure an optimal state of well-being.

It's also about being aware what the body needs and wants, especially when it comes to movement. One of the challenges when people are moving, whether it's with exercise or in daily life, is they're not really connected to their natural presence nor their natural body. This is when accidents and injuries occur.

Start from where you are in the moment. Maybe all you're attracted to doing is sitting outside. That's ok. If you want to walk, great, but don't force yourself. Let nature within and without guide you through this. Trust the wisdom of the body.

As you tap into your natural presence you're silencing your mind and becoming aware of nature. When you turn your focus and attention inwards, you connect nature outside of your body with the nature that is part of you.

Nature will start reducing stress and boosting your immune system on a physiological level. All you need to do is to pay attention to the sensations and feelings in your body as they arrive and move your body in a way that feels good.

Natural presence and natural body are only the first two parts of The Nature Process, and already you should be starting to challenge how you respond to stress through deepening your connection to nature – provided you are practising what you are reading!

It's important to note that you might not be attracted to going outside. That's ok. Remember that a nature view from a window has powerful healing effects. If you don't have access to a natural view, this is where you use the Body Awareness Exercise from earlier in the chapter. You use your sense of memory to activate a previous nature experience that allows your body to sense that it is present in nature.

This is something that comes up again and again for many of my clients. They aren't attracted to going outside to practise The Nature Process and then feel guilty that they aren't taking action. You start where you are. If your body wants to rest more than it wants to be outdoors that's ok. If the thought of going outside and going for a walk seems stressful, don't do it.

If your sense of concentration is weakened and you can't focus enough to do this, enlist the help of someone else. Share your nature memory with them and ask them to share their own nature memories with you.

Just like with your natural presence, the more you practise connecting your natural body and your natural presence, the easier it becomes. You're also training yourself to use this part of the process as your default response to stress and anxiety. By doing so you spend less time sensing pain, distress, and fear, which turns into stress, and more time connected to nature within you and around you.

If you're attracted to you can take your awareness of the natural body further with the 'Expand Your Awareness of the Natural Body Exercise' on page 215.

Exercises to Practise in Nature

* Find a quiet spot where you won't be disturbed. Bring yourself into a state of natural presence and allow your body to move in whatever way it's attracted to. Focus on movements that feel good.

* Go to an outdoor exercise class and bring yourself into a state of natural presence and natural body as you perform the exercises. Observe the thoughts, feelings, and sensations that arise as you do.

* Go for a long walk. Pay attention to your breathing, ensuring that you are able to take deep breaths in and out. Focus on the sensation of your feet moving across the ground. Notice how much pressure you put on the ground as you take steps. Pay attention to how the body feels as you continue to walk.

* Go outside with a child. If you don't have one, find one to borrow. Allow them to set the pace and direct the journey. Pay attention to

how they move and copy them. Notice the thoughts, feelings, and sensations that arise within the body as you do.

* Spend time in a garden, park or other natural setting. Notice the thoughts, feelings, and sensations that arise in the body as you do. Observe the differences within the body upon arrival and as you leave.

KEY POINTS TO REMEMBER

* When the body is exposed to stress it produces hormones which can negatively impact the body's health if these hormones build up within the body.
* Our body and mind are actually the same thing. Repressed emotions from the past, or worries about the future can trigger a stress response in the present moment that adds to any stress we are currently experiencing, potentially weakening our body's capability to stay healthy.
* We can learn a lot from listening to the wisdom of our body.
* Horses have the capacity to let go of their stress response fully by ensuring that the hormonal stress response leaves their system through shaking and stamping their feet.
* As humans, we let go of our stress response by crying, yawning, trembling, shaking, burping, and making primal sounds. We have been conditioned out of these natural responses and need to reconnect with them as they are part of the body's intelligence that keeps us in a state of balance and harmony with ourselves – and the world at large.
* Our emotions create physical sensations within the body. Our emotions in turn are generated by the thoughts we think. When we are able to change our thoughts, we are able to change our emotions and subsequently the stress response within our body.
* The more you develop your awareness of your natural body, the more you will recognise when you are feeling stressed and anxious and then be able to tap into the body's intelligence to help yourself rebalance.

- Use your fifty-four senses to tune into your body on a daily basis and discover what it's trying to tell you about your day.
- If you have a disability, focus on the senses you can tap into and what you can sense rather than what you can't.
- Being outside in the natural world and entering a state of natural presence before connecting to the natural body provides support for the body's immune system and helps you connect to your natural body. It is also okay to use a natural view if you are not attracted to going outside, as research shows this also has a positive impact upon the body's health.

QUESTIONS FOR REFLECTION

- How much do you understand about how your body works and what could you do to learn more?
- In what ways are your mind and body connected?
- How do you normally deal with stress in your life?
- What others ways could you deal with stress in your life?
- What kind of thoughts do you observe within you during the course of your day? Do they give you energy or do they drain you?
- How often do you listen to what your body needs?
- What can you do to listen to your body more?

CHAPTER 5

Natural Attractions

❧　❧　❧

*Try and penetrate with our limited means the secrets of nature
and you will find that, behind all the discernible concatenations,
there remains something subtle, intangible and inexplicable.*

- ALBERT EINSTEIN

*Dude, engage your fifty-four senses through your natural presence
and natural body and connect them to natural attractions.
Then you'll understand the secrets of nature much better!*

- TABI JAYNE

IF YOU'RE USING THIS BOOK like an instruction manual and practising the exercises as you go through the book, by now you should be engaging more and more with the fifty-four senses and using them to experience both a state of natural presence and your natural body. As you start to go deeper into connecting with nature using The Nature Process it can be easy to get lost in an exploration of nature and forget that the purpose of using this process in its entirety is to reduce stress and anxiety so that you can experience greater levels of well-being that enhance all aspects of your life.

Through The Nature Process, you are learning how to experience a deeper relationship with the natural world than you've ever had before. It's exciting and never-ending. There is no finish point where you will reach the stage where you realise that you've discovered everything you need to know about being deeply connected to nature.

Natural attractions are a pivotal point of the process. It has the potential to both challenge and excite you. It's also the part that will cause you to question yourself and nature the most. Some people I've worked with have found that this is as far as they're able to go when they initially start working with The Nature Process. That's ok. It's important to honour yourself and your journey as you take your time to fully experience and integrate each principle/step of the process.

Don't rush. Lao Tzu, a philosopher and poet of ancient China, said it best: "Nature does not hurry, yet everything is accomplished." It takes time to develop a deep state of natural presence and, depending how much experience you've already had practicing body awareness, it takes time to be able to feel its natural wisdom and desire.

Mastering natural attractions means that you're able to live every second of your life in a state of flow and harmony with your inner nature. However, this is far more challenging than it sounds. I've already shared with you how civilisation controls the body and its responses. In this chapter, we're going to go deeper into this concept and discover just how much civilisation controls the way we think.

Recently, I was working with one of The Nature Process coaches doing some training. Despite having practised The Nature Process for nearly two years, this coach's ability to fully embody The Nature Process was still being challenged by the stories and beliefs that she held. We had to do some deep exploration to uncover these stories before the trainee could go deeper into her own natural attractions. It takes time and commitment to be able to master your natural attractions.

To refresh your memory, natural attractions is a way of thinking like Nature and thinking as part of Nature. This part of the process helps you to discover the relationship between the thoughts, feelings, and sensations you experience in the moment as you focus upon and interact with a specific aspect of nature.

That part of Nature, your natural attraction, has a message about the truth of who you are, and reflects back to you the highest part of yourself that your fears and doubts tend to hide. By ensuring that you focus on a part of Nature that makes you feel good, you guarantee that you're also accessing the full potential of who you are too.

WHY YOU NEED TO FOLLOW YOUR NATURAL ATTRACTIONS

When you listen to and follow your natural attractions, you're following the wisdom that has existed within nature for 13.7 billion years—the dawn of our universe. Following our natural attractions allows us to exist in a beautiful dance with life, one that allows our stress and anxiety to be subsumed into nature so that we remain in a state of balance and harmony with ourselves and with the world.

This is the quickest and simplest way to bring balance back into your body and your life. Nature is fully balanced at all times. As soon as there is imbalance, action naturally occurs to restore equilibrium.

We see this truth reflected back to us in global warming and climate change. For every action taken by humanity that brings the planet out of balance, there is a corresponding response to restore equilibrium. For example, we humans create lots of carbon dioxide that is released into the atmosphere and takes the amount of carbon dioxide to levels not seen in hundreds of thousands of years. In response, the average temperature of the Earth's climate has risen which has resulted in the polar ice caps melting, the temperatures in the ocean rising, and extreme weather events.

Until we understand that as individuals we must first explore our inner nature to help us with the natural environment around us, the symptoms of global warming and climate change will continue to increase. It's nature's way to get our attention and communicate this message to us.

Our fifty-four senses are fundamental to both hearing this message and applying it to ourselves. Right now, within most of humanity our collective senses of pain, distress, and fear are fully activated – with good reason - but we don't know what to do with them. We need to activate the rest of our senses and allow natural attractions to bring us back into a state of total balance so we can improve our well-being and then take action to enhance our own life and the lives of others.

The Essence of Natural Attractions

1. Stop doing things that make you feel bad.
2. Focus on what makes you feel good and do more of that.
3. Harm neither yourself nor others.

These are the cardinal rules of natural attractions. When you do more of what makes you feel good, you are re-aligning yourself with the power of nature. In the book, *Darwin's Unfinished Business: The Self-Organizing Intelligence of Nature,* Simon Powell expands upon Darwin's theory of evolution by highlighting that evolution is not just about the survival of the fittest (which really means the best fit for the environment) but rather the survival of clever and sensible behaviour. Evolution in nature is not down to random chance but rather, it's down to a system of self-organizing intelligence. When you follow your natural attractions, you are tapping into this self-organizing system, which science is still in the process of exploring and fully understanding.

Neil deGrasse Tyson, a North American astrophysicist, cosmologist and author argues that it's possible to understand the fundamental truths of how nature operates. What we need to do, however, to achieve this, is to understand the complex dance of evolution that includes the Earth's origin within our solar system, the origin of structure in the universe as well as the origin and evolution of the universe itself.

To discover clues, evolutionary biologist, Elisabet Sahtouris, has drawn parallels between the evolution of cells and the evolution of human society as she compares and contrasts the healthy self-organisation of cells with the unhealthy organisation of our current human society.

How is it that nature can organise itself into balance and harmony, while we humans struggle to do so? Put simply, nature knows how to follow its natural attractions. Humans, on the other hand, especially in the Western World with our culture and beliefs, have created a system that fundamentally goes against our natural attractions. This is reflected in the growing numbers affected by stress, depression and anxiety along with various other 'first-world' physical health issues such as obesity. Focusing on money and power, as we are discovering, does not lead to happiness.

Yet we seem stuck. We have a collective belief that change and growth is difficult. It's only difficult when we stay in our senses of pain, distress, and fear and try to change and grow from there. Pain, distress, and fear are signs of stress and anxiety. As you learned in the last chapter, your body under stress acts differently as it is preparing itself for a state of survival.

When we activate the rest of our fifty-four senses and use them, change and growth become joyful, fun, and easy. Your body is able to move into a state of relaxation and the energy it was planning to use for survival can then be used for growth.

This is why the fifty-four senses are fundamental within Natural Attractions. The more aware you are of your senses, the more aware you are of what feels good for you in each and every moment – whether you are outside in nature or not. The more you are aware of what feels good for you in each and every moment, the easier it becomes for you to rebalance and follow your own natural attractions.

The Challenge of Following Your Natural Attractions

What stops us from following our natural attractions is thousands of years of family, social, and cultural conditioning that is embedded deep within our psyche. Doing things that make us feel good can create a sense of guilt and shame, especially when they contradict things we've been taught to believe.

For example, how often have you stopped yourself from doing something that makes you feel good through a sense of obligation, guilt, or fear of upsetting a loved one? Your sense of mind offers all these wonderful justifications of why you shouldn't and as a result you don't do whatever it is that you want to do.

It's important to note here that following our natural attractions is *not* about indulging in hedonism. Too often when people follow their hedonistic tendencies they end up hurting themselves and others. This clearly contravenes the third tenet of the principles of natural attractions; to harm neither yourself or others. There is a difference between pursuing pleasure at all costs (which usually doesn't make people *really* feel good) and doing what intuitively makes you feel good. For example, if you feel ill, do you take time off work and allow yourself to rest, because that's what feels good, or do you force yourself to continue on as you consume a high dosage of medication to alleviate some of the pain you're experiencing just so that you don't lose out on earning money?

This is the part of The Nature Process that is going to challenge you the most. Our identity is so closely entwined with our beliefs that there is a fear of not knowing who we are without them. Our beliefs offer us a false sense of security, even as they keep us trapped in our senses of pain, distress, and fear. This can be so strong that we will argue to the contrary even when presented with alternative evidence.

If at any point, you find yourself becoming angry or defensive or feel a desire to let people know you're right and justify it with your personal experience, then it's time to stop and celebrate. Natural attractions are showing you that there is something out of balance with who you truly are. There is a family, cultural or societal story at play that you believe in and it's impacting your ability to follow your natural attractions.

The more you remember this, the more you will be able to follow natural attractions by activating your other senses. You will then spend less and less time in stress and anxiety than you currently think is possible.

The problem with these family, cultural and societal stories is that the more we believe them, the harder it is to experience our natural attractions in flow. We follow rules and regulations rather than our own natural attractions.

However, collectively we're becoming aware that the stories our world has are life-destroying instead of life-enhancing. As we gather more and more evidence, thanks to how technology has made the world a lot smaller by allowing us to share information freely, we are seeing systemic racism, discrimination, sexism, violence and corruption for what they truly are and creating new systems and stories to counteract them.

THE INSANITY OF CIVILISATION

The fact is that our modern world has created a way of living that is damaging our personal, social, and environmental well-being. This is because a key tenet of our human civilisation is that it perceives itself to be separate from and have domination over the natural environment.

In his book, *Endgame, Vol 1*, Derrick Jensen presents an analysis of the insanity of civilisation. He makes the observation that the real reason both the Egyptian and Roman civilisations ended was because they consumed too many of the available natural resources in their respective regions and were unable to maintain their growth and expansion.

There's a lesson in this for us with the current state of our own modern civilisation, which derives many of our beliefs and attitudes from these extinct civilisations. Einstein allegedly defined insanity as doing the same thing over and over again but expecting different results. This quote has never been more relevant than it is when it comes to our civilised behaviour. Our current Western way of living is unsustainable. It doesn't make us feel good and it doesn't make the Earth feel good either.

If we don't change both our individual and collective behaviour, then it's highly likely that we'll be going the way of the dodo. And just like it was human behaviour that was directly responsible for the dodo's extinction, we'll have no one to blame for it but ourselves.

Now, I'm not asking you to destroy modern civilisation and go back to living a life in nature devoid of all the wonderful comforts we've developed that make our life easier. This is in contradiction to what nature teaches us as the essence of life: evolution.

What you need to do instead is to question which comforts are necessary for your life and make clear decisions about which parts of civilisation you want to support.

Personally, I love technology. I'm naturally attracted to using it to improve my well-being and enhance my life. If it weren't for the development of asthma inhalers and nebulisers I would probably have been dead a long time ago.

The internet allows me to work with clients around the world. Apps such as Skype allow me to stay in contact with both friends and clients in many different countries and speak to my nieces when I'm away.

Even though airplanes are highly damaging to the environment, I still love the fact I can travel from one part of the world to another in a day. I'm not attracted to staying at home and not travelling because of this. I'm attracted to finding an alternative fuel source that doesn't cause as much harm.

However, do I want a huge wardrobe filled with the latest fashions that have been made by cheap, exploited labour and negatively impacts the planet's well-being? No thanks. I'm happy buying nearly all my clothes in second-hand shops – especially when I see what other people throw away!

Or do I want to get caught in the trap that I'll only be beautiful if I spend a large amount of money on beauty products that may or may not be environmentally friendly, filled with questionable chemicals and are potentially (still!) tested on animals? I'd rather buy fewer products and go for the natural look.

We are so conditioned to being consumers and having more things in our life. It's important to stop and question, not only if they really make sense for you to use them, but also whether they really make you feel good or not.

Exercise and Natural Attractions

Think about cats. Unless you overfeed them, they naturally maintain a sleek and healthy body. You don't see the cat setting an alarm to get up and go exercise at five o'clock in the morning before it goes to work. You don't see it counting how many times it's jumped up to try to get the fly that's buzzing around. A cat doesn't even make an effort to exercise. When a cat feels attracted to moving its body, it does (just like small children do, much to their parent's annoyance!).

Cats in general are able to stay fit and healthy without excess fat with no effort at all. In contrast, we humans struggle to stay fit and healthy, and obesity is a rising epidemic. The fitness industry in the United Kingdom alone was worth £3.92 billion in 2013. That's a lot of people going to the gym instead of just getting outside, having fun in nature, and playing when they're inspired to do so.

What's of even more interest is that going outside for a run burns more calories than running on a treadmill. Green Exercise, which is exercising outdoors, has a whole host of health benefits that go beyond just basic fitness. For example, research by the University of Essex discovered that a thirty-minute walk outside in nature each day is potentially just as effective as anti-depressants for mild to moderate depression.

Yet when you think about it how often do you move your body in a way that feels good – either indoors or outside?

Work and Natural Attractions

Now, think about your job. You probably spend up to forty hours a week working just to bring in the money you need to satisfy your basic human needs. Meanwhile, you feel frustrated that you're not spending enough time with your loved ones or being able to do what you really want with your life. There is no other animal on this planet that does this. Every other animal lives from their natural attractions.

I went outside and tried to think of an example that would contradict this but I couldn't find one. As I watched the ants scurry about industriously over the ground, on whatever mission they were on, I realised this wasn't work for them. It was merely what they were attracted to doing.

Furthermore, the ants don't have to drag their asses out of bed and into work just for the sake of earning some money to survive. They just get on with creating what is necessary, not just for themselves to thrive individually but for their whole ant colony, which could be comprised of millions of ants.

Ants are complex social insects that are able to organise themselves, modify their habitat, tap into natural resources, and defend themselves in such a way that it puts us humans to shame. They're so successful at what they do that it's been estimated that they comprise of up to twenty percent of the biomass of land animals.

The most interesting part of the organization of an ant colony is that not all the females reproduce. This is left up to the queen ants of the colony. Now we might think of them as the leaders of the colony, which is not strictly true. The authority and decision-making processes lie with each and every individual ant that is part of the colony. Could you imagine what our human lives would look like if each of us was endowed from birth with the authority and decision-making to make our world as healthy and productive as possible for all living beings?

Queen ants are the only ants to have wings. They need them to reproduce and start a successful colony. In this way, they are leaders. After reproduction, the queen ants either detach their own wings or let the worker ants in their colony chew them off.

Think about this in comparison to the leaders we currently have at work and in government. How many of them would sacrifice themselves to put the good of their people first?

DEATH IN NATURE

One of our greatest challenges as a civilisation is death. We create elaborate stories about what happens after death and have numerous expectations about who should die and when. We believe that children should outlive their parents, people should only die when they're old and we should fight against death when it arrives.

Yet, what we label "death" nature calls "transformation". If you don't believe me I challenge you to go out into nature and find an example of death. You won't be able to.

When a tree "dies," it transforms into a source of new life. Fungi grows on it. Insects and animals make their home in it.

When an animal "dies," its body decays and becomes a food source for other animals. Unless, of course, you're a human animal, because ever since the rise of civilisation we've just pumped your body full of toxic chemicals to preserve you, stuck you in a box, and kept you fundamentally disconnected from nature even in death.

You might remember from the introduction that when we scattered my brother's ashes in the forest, small red flowers sprung up everywhere they'd touched the earth. Witnessing that was the start of my perspective shift into realizing that not only do I connect to myself out in nature, but I also connect to my brother.

This understanding of growth has fundamentally shifted my perspective on death and grief so much so that I can't relate to how most people experience death and grief anymore. It was one of the reasons that I knew I had to walk away from a coaching practise that worked solely with grief. Most people in the early stages of grief aren't able to consider a different perspective. Some people are never able to consider a different perspective and stay stuck in grief their whole life.

This is compounded by the language that we use around this topic. We tell people that we've lost a loved one. We don't lose our loved ones after death. If you choose to let them, they remain just as much a part of our lives as they did when they were alive. The bond continues on.

Relationships don't end just because people die. They continue on in our hearts and minds. It's just that the relationship has transformed and grown into a different one.

We talk about missing our loved one. I don't miss my brother. That would mean that I notice the absence of his presence in my life. Over the last fourteen years, I've worked hard on the relationship with my brother to ensure that he is present in everything I do. He's still here. He's just in a different form than before.

Discover Your Natural Attractions

This part of The Nature Process helps you uncover all the hidden stories and beliefs you may have that are creating stress and anxiety in your life. The last three topics I chose to talk about in this chapter were deliberately chosen as all of us have to deal with exercise, work and death. Did you pay attention to your thoughts, feelings and sensations as you read the sections? What came up for you as you read them?

It's important to pay attention to your thoughts not just about those topics but also with regards to many others aspects of civilised life. When you do, you'll start to become aware of the stories you tell yourself about your life and how you think it should be. If your identity isn't defined by these stories, then you'll be able to let go of them without much effort, along with the stress and anxiety they cause.

The stories that cause the strongest emotional response, which don't feel good for you, are the stories that you have unconsciously invested in and use to define how you see yourself. These are the stories that negatively impact your well-being and your life the most.

Stop a moment and think. What areas of your life are causing you the most stress and anxiety right now? What are the stories you're telling yourself that are contributing to the stress and anxiety?

All you need to do at this stage is make a note of them either mentally or physically. You don't need to go into them and spend time trying to figure out where the belief has come from. The more you engage with stories, especially the ones that repeat in your mind, the stronger you're reinforcing the neural pathways that are connected to that story in the brain.

When you put all five principles/steps of The Nature Process together, you are able to work on changing these stories to ones that support your well-being and your life. You do this by allowing nature to switch off the part of your brain that worries and stresses so that you can create a new empowering story and reinforce it through a sensory experience by being in the body. Once you reach the chapter on natural release, you'll find out exactly how to do this.

Changing their stories is where many people get stuck. They believe that they need to share their story, telling it again and again. While there are cases where sharing your story can be powerfully healing, most people tend to go over and over their story, reinforcing the stress and anxiety that is behind the story without doing anything to change it.

Think about a time that something happened that upset you. How many times did you share the story of what had occurred? How did it feel to share the story? Are you at peace with what's happened or do you still have a response in the body when you think about it?

THE POWER OF EXPLORING YOUR NATURAL ATTRACTIONS IN NATURE

Thus far, this chapter has focused heavily on explaining the challenges of following your natural attractions and how this can negatively impact your life. What you now need to learn is how to use nature to strengthen your natural attractions so that you can do more of what makes you feel good.

Ethan Kross, a researcher at the University of Michigan, studies self-talk and he discovered that when you speak about yourself in the third person it becomes easier for you to deal with stressful situations. His research explored how people practise self-talk in preparation for giving a speech with little time to prepare. Those people who used 'I' thoughts tended to be far more negative on themselves, filled with worry and doubt, both before and after giving the speech. However, those people who used a second or third person perspective tended to give themselves more positive messages.

This principle is part of what underlies the exercise I'm about to share with you to help you develop your natural attractions in nature. It can be easier to the truth of who we are when we're able to distance ourselves from it, especially if we're not used to being kind to ourselves.

We're going to use nature both as a mirror and as an extension of self. Doing so will allow us to see ourselves in a different way and help us address that inner voice that runs a dialogue of all of the ways in which we're not good enough.

That inner voice has been created from all the family, societal and cultural stories we've heard since we've been born. Here is where we use nature to combat this. There are no stories in nature. Stories belong firmly in the realm of humanity. It's one of the many things that make us unique. While stories have the potential to transform us, they also have the potential to keep us stuck.

Because there are no stories inherent within nature, it is a safe place for us to explore our human stories without judgment from others. You can share your deepest, darkest fears and doubts and nature will not react.

It will stay the same. And, as long as you focus on your natural attractions in nature, it will always reflect back to you the part of yourself that your fears and doubts prevent you from seeing.

THE NATURAL ATTRACTIONS IN NATURE EXERCISE

This exercise was originally developed by Dr Michael J. Cohen as one of over 100 exercises he created to help people reconnect to nature. Out of all of the exercises he's shared, this one is the most powerful, as it helps you see yourself reflected in nature.

The exercise itself is very simple.

When you are outside, pay attention to the part of nature that catches your eye or draws you to it. It might not even be something that you notice through your eyes. If you're attracted to the sound of a bird's song or the sound of running water, that's ok too. Maybe it's even the feel of the earth under your feet or the tree bark as you touch it with your hand. Trust in whatever natural attraction you feel pulled towards and experience it through all of your senses.

Once you've identified the part of nature that attracts you the most, complete the following sentence:

I like [this part of nature] because…

Trust whatever comes to mind. Once you have identified why you like this part of nature you then turn the sentence around so that what you like about this part of nature becomes what you like about yourself.

I like myself because…

Say the sentence out loud or to yourself a few times. What thoughts, feelings and sensations arise as you do?

That's it. The power of this exercise comes from turning the sentence back to you and then seeing how it relates to your life.

One of my clients, who has integrated The Nature Process into her daily life, shared this experience she had recently from using this 'Natural Attraction in Nature Exercise:'

I was having a difficult day. My thoughts were filled with doubt and confusion about how I experience myself in relationships. I'd realised from recent experiences that there was still a part of me that didn't believe people liked me. I couldn't focus on work so I decided to go for a walk.

As I left the house the cool crisp autumn air hit my face and swarmed around my body. Despite this, the sky was bright blue with only small wispy clouds. The sun shone brightly and I could hear birds singing in the trees.

With every breath, I could feel the crisp air filling my lungs as my feet crunched over the golden-brown leaves that had fallen from the trees. Reaching the old wooden bridge, I stopped and watched the sunlight sparkle on the calm surface of the river.

Suddenly a gust of wind freed more leaves from a branch and gently swirled them to the ground. I found myself staring at the tree, so strong and peaceful. It was content to be who it was and let go of anything it no longer needed. It reminded me that I too am strong and peaceful, content to be who I am and let go of anything I no longer needed.

This experience with the 'Natural Attraction in Nature Exercise' is simple to understand and the message clear. This person was attracted to the very part of nature that reflected back to her the key message she needed to help her make peace with how she was feeling.

However, sometimes the sentence you end up with is a bit more challenging and confusing to understand how it relates to you and what you're currently experiencing in that moment.

INTERPRETING YOUR RESPONSE

Sometimes you need to look at your sentence symbolically, especially if it doesn't immediately make sense.

For example, I'm really attracted to the golden fields of wheat that I see scattered across the Scottish countryside just now. It's late August and the harvest is just about upon us. Whenever I go out for a walk I see these golden fields, the grasses dancing and swaying in the wind. I see them as I drive across the country. As I sit on a train, writing this, I see more golden fields out the window. For days now, I've hardly been able to take my eyes off them.

But what is it that attracts me to them?

I like the golden fields of wheat because they are ripe and ready for harvest and they contrast spectacularly with the greenery of the trees that usually surround the fields.

That seems simple enough, until I turn it around and relate it to myself.

I like myself because I am ripe and ready for harvest and contrast spectacularly with the greenery of the surrounding trees.

What does it mean that I am ripe and ready for harvest? And how do I contrast spectacularly with the greenery of the surrounding trees. It doesn't seem to make any sense.

When you interpret the symbolic meaning of a sentence like this it is completely subjective. What you are looking for is a sentence that feels good to you. You may also need to spend some time reflecting upon the statement to arrive at a deeper understanding of it.

I am ripe and ready for harvest. Harvest is the time of year when you gather the crops you have planted earlier in the year and receive a reward for them. On a symbolic level, where in my own life have I planted something earlier in the year that is ready to harvest? What immediately comes to mind is all the work I've done developing the facilitator training program for The Nature Process. It's ripe and ready to go. When people start the training, it is going to bring in a reward for me. There are also many other things I've been working on both with Earth Self and The Nature Process.

In this case, the fact that I am ripe and ready for harvest highlights that I have been working hard and am now about to reap the rewards for doing so. Even this book you're reading is part of that harvest!

I contrast spectacularly with the greenery of the surrounding trees. It's the contrast of the golden colour against the green. During the summer, everything is green. It blends together in harmony. Yet now, the field has changed. It stands out. It's different. Again, this year has been about working on both Earth Self and The Nature Process so that as companies they stand out and are different from other companies.

For me, that I am contrasting so spectacularly means that I finally know what makes these companies different (from their business models to their ethics and values) and confirms to me that the effort I've put in on business development this year will be noticed.

The most interesting bit of this is that there has been a part of me recently that's felt stressed and anxious about the work I'm doing. At times, it feels very challenging. This example here is enough to help me relax and feel more confident with what I'm doing. Even though I wasn't consciously thinking about this stress and anxiety, it's clearly been there and playing on my mind.

When you use the 'Natural Attractions in Nature Exercise' you'll find there's a connection between the part of nature you're attracted to and the current story that active in your life. When I've worked with clients they have always been able to identify and relate with the answer they have received from doing this exercise. There's never been a client yet who hasn't!

The purpose of using this exercise is to help you create a new story that is stress-free, one that helps you feel happier and more positive about your life. It is a tool for reflection and insight into your own inner nature, free from the self-doubt and worry that you may experience only too often.

We all have stories that impact our lives. Fundamentally, they usually have one core root: that we're not enough. That who we are is flawed. That there's something wrong with us. The truth is that we're all perfect exactly the way we are. Through tapping into the beauty, power and strength of the natural world you are able to connect to that part of you which is already whole.

As you build up your experiential understanding of natural attractions, you'll want to go play with this part of the process again and again. It's my personal favourite part of The Nature Process and something I use by itself when I only have a few minutes to appreciate a natural environment.

When you use this exercise do it only with those parts of nature you are positively attracted to. Don't do it for negative attractions. When you do, you end up identifying things about yourself that you're not happy with. You already have enough of that in your life as it is. Focus on what's good. Focus on how you are already enough. Let the natural world around you reflect back the essence of who you are so that you can see the truth of your own power and potential. If you want to go deeper with your natural attractions, you can use the 'Re-Activate and Re-Energise Your Natural Attractions in Nature Exercise' on page 219.

EXERCISES TO PRACTISE IN NATURE

* Every time you go outside, find a part of nature that attracts you and do the 'Natural Attractions in Nature Exercise.'
* Practise the 'Natural Attractions in Nature Exercise' by using your family and friends as a part of nature.
* When outside, say only the word "attraction" whenever you come across a part of nature you're attracted to, paying attention to the rhythm and tone of the words as you do and how it makes you feel to recognise your natural attractions in this way.
* When you're faced with a challenge/opportunity for growth, go for a walk and contemplate the question "What am I attracted to doing in this situation?"
* When walking, use your natural attractions as a way of deciding which path/direction you're going to take.

KEY POINTS TO REMEMBER

- The essence of natural attractions is to do things that make you feel good and that reflect the core of who you are without harming either yourself or others.
- Learning to follow your natural attractions can challenge your beliefs and stories about who you are.
- We struggle to stay fit and healthy and have to create places to force us to exercise rather than doing it naturally outside.
- The only animals on Earth that work forty hours a week, doing a job they don't like for money, are humans.
- We find death difficult as we see death differently from how nature views death.
- Our civilised way of life is damaging our health and well-being along with that of the planet through its beliefs and stories.
- The events in your life that cause you the most stress and anxiety are the ones that you have the strongest beliefs about that don't support the event.
- You can use nature to change these stories into more positive and empowering ones that reduce your stress and anxiety.
- You do this by using nature as a mirror to reflect back to you the best aspects of yourself
- When you use the 'Natural Attractions in Nature Exercise' to help strengthen your natural attractions you:
  a. Find a part of nature you're attracted to
  b. Discover why you like it (I like this part of nature because…)
  c. Turn the sentence around so that what you like about this part of nature becomes what you like about yourself (I like myself because…)
- Think about the symbolic meaning of the words you've used to help you arrive at a better understanding of how an aspect of nature is reflecting back yourself to you

QUESTIONS FOR REFLECTION

- What examples of natural attractions at play in the natural world have you observed?
- In what ways do you follow/don't follow your natural attractions at work?
- How does your culture and society impact your natural attractions?
- What thoughts do you have that create stress and anxiety in your life and how do these thoughts impact your natural attractions?
- How often do you allow your natural attractions to guide you in life?

CHAPTER 6

Natural Communication

❧ ❧ ❧

I speak to everyone in the same way, whether he is the
garbage man or the president of the university.

- ALBERT EINSTEIN

THIS IS THE PART OF The Nature Process that can challenge people, in that communicating with nature is not something we consider normal in Western culture. We've been taught that we need to appreciate and respect all humans regardless of ethnicity, gender, sexuality and social background. Yet, when it comes to nature, there's a huge block. After all, how often have you spoken to nature in the same way in which you speak with another human being? This chapter focuses specifically on how you can communicate with nature both as part of The Nature Process and by itself.

What I also will do in this chapter is demystify communicating with nature. Think of all the negative stories we've been told about those people who do communicate with nature. Historically, we called those people, usually women, who spent time in nature, "witches". They spoke with their familiar – usually a cat or other animal – and had the ability to communicate with spirits. They could allegedly control the weather and damage the harvest. Over time, the term 'witch' has evolved into 'tree-huggers' and 'hippies', as labels to associate with those who believe in a relationship with and who take care of the earth.

Nevertheless, many animal lovers are already engaging in natural communication, whether they're aware of it or not, as are many outdoor enthusiasts. The reality of communicating with nature is somewhat different to the stereotype. If you're reading this book, there's a good chance you engage in natural communication, whether it be watching the communication of a honeybee's dance or listening to birdsong and being aware of the interaction between the birds while out in your garden.

Natural communication can also be the most fun part of The Nature Process. By suspending your disbelief over what's possible and allowing yourself to tap into the imagination of your childhood, you're able to develop new relationships with other-than-human beings.

This is the start of integrating your mind with nature's wisdom so that you too can think and act from a place of balance and wholeness. It's where you start to explore how we live as humans from a totally different perspective – one of co-operation and harmony with nature. It's also the start of expanding your creative and innovative capacities.

As part of The Nature Process practised in its entirety, natural communication amplifies the natural healing capacity of nature by helping you to continue to feel safe and supported by the natural world. Natural communication helps you befriend the natural world and learn to respect it.

In this chapter, we're going to explore how the earth is one living super organism and how simple it is to experience natural communication in a way that's not weird or "woo-woo". I'll then introduce you to a simple concept that allows you to encounter and explore nature as a living organism.

You'll know that you've mastered this part of the process when you find it easy and effortless to receive communication from nature, even when you're not consciously applying the process. As part of this, you'll have developed your own unique way of blending all your senses together, allowing you to translate nature's non-verbal communication into words so that you can share your experiences with others.

It's important to remember that nature is non-verbal and the way in which it communicates is sensory in origin. Using your fifty-four senses is key to understanding what nature is saying. Due to the subtlety of the sensory form of communication, it's essential to be in a state of natural presence and natural body, otherwise you're incapable of processing the information you receive.

Through entering into a place of natural communication with nature you are able to shift into a place of co-operation and harmony with it, treating it as you would an extension of yourself. Natural Communication is how you recognise and feel that you are part of the complex interconnectedness among all life on earth.

The Gaia Hypothesis

The idea that the earth is actually one big living organism was developed in the 1970s by an English independent scientist named James Lovelock, who was naturally attracted to this work through longs walks he took out in nature when he was a child.

He proposed that the earth, along with all the different parts of its atmosphere, is a self-regulating, complex system where the earth and its organisms intelligently interact with each other through a process called homeostasis to keep the earth in balance and capable of sustaining life.

Homeostasis is a dynamic interplay between many processes on the earth's surface that help regulate surface temperature, atmosphere, composition, and ocean salinity that's powered by changes in the heat and temperature of the earth. This process actively ensures that optimal conditions for life remain on earth even when threatened by terrestrial or external events.

When we look at the earth as a self-regulating organism, we learn that we do not live *on* the earth but *in* the earth, as its atmosphere extends out four hundred kilometres above where we live on the surface. This is a small distinction but it's an important one.

The preposition "on" signifies contact. The preposition "in" signifies that we are contained by the limits of the earth. We are not merely connected to the earth through contact with its surface. We are an integral part of the earth, being fully contained within it. If the earth is communicating with itself to bring itself back into balance, it must be communicating with us too because we are part of it.

Natural communication is our birthright. It's something that is natural and normal. We all possess this ability. The only reason we're not fully using it is because our social and cultural conditioning, as discussed in the last chapter and mentioned briefly again here, has trained us out of it.

This hypothesis demonstrates exactly how The Nature Process works, both for the earth and for us. It's changes in chemical compositions that help the planet to remain in balance. You'll remember from chapter four that stress and anxiety are on a physiological level, nothing more than hormonal imbalances in our body triggered by the fight, flight or freeze stress response. It's the dissolution of these hormones that bring us back into balance. It's the same process for the earth.

It's important to address the debates about how much sentience, awareness, and consciousness the earth actually has. Lovelock stated that the processes that keep the earth in balance are unconscious. In contrast, *we* human beings need to be fully conscious of this process in order for it to work. If not, the power of our sense of mind can stop us from functioning in harmony with nature. This is the first fundamental difference.

The second is that the earth doesn't experience human emotions. While it can experience pain, distress, and fear, it self-corrects so rapidly that it puts us to shame. It knows no shame, guilt, duty or obligation and doesn't spend hours deliberating over what action it should take and whether taking that action will hurt people it cares about.

Tilly Smith: Tsunami Heroine

Tilly Smith offers us a wonderful example of natural communication. She's not well known, yet her story demonstrates what happens when you're able to tap into your senses and recognise the communication of the earth for what it is.

The interpretation of her story, as I tell it, is told through the lenses of our fifty-four senses. Her story, as it was portrayed in the media, was an example of why education is so important. While this is true, it's also an example of the power of tapping into natural communication with the earth.

In 2004, Tilly and her family were on holiday in Thailand. At the time, Tilly was only ten years old. This is only a few years after children start shifting out of the Theta brainwave state, which means it's still easier for children of this age to drop into the Theta brainwave state than adults.

Two weeks before Tilly went on holiday, she had a lesson at school that had taught her all about tsunamis.

On the morning of the great Indian Ocean tsunami that killed over 230,000 people in fourteen countries, making it the biggest natural disaster in the recorded history of humanity, Tilly stood and looked out at the sea. Through her senses of sight, movement, proximity, colour and form, she noticed that the water had gone bubbly and frosty like beer as it started to recede. Her sense of memory was activated and through her sense of reason and logic she was able to correctly interpret what was about to happen.

Because she knew what was coming and the implication of it, this activated her senses of distress and fear. She told her mum, but at first her mum didn't listen to her as she was too busy reading a book. Yet Tilly didn't back down. Her sense of distress and fear was too strong and she was still too young for the societal and cultural conditioning that we experience, to override it. The more she was ignored, the more hysterical she became.

Finally, her dad listened to her and went to tell the hotel security. As a result, they evacuated the beach.

This beach was one of the few beaches along the stretch of the coastline that had no deaths. It's estimated that Tilly's actions saved the lives of over one hundred people.

What makes this story even more compelling is that there was also research done into animal behaviour at the time of the tsunami. One thing that was conspicuously absent as rescue workers were going through all the devastation left after the tsunami were the dead bodies of any animals.

As animals are more closely attuned to their connection to the earth than humans are, they were able to tune into the earth's communication that something terrible was about to happen. They started fleeing for higher ground to get out of harm's way. They probably didn't even know what they were fleeing. They just trusted their sensory nature that told them to run. In contrast, as the waves receded on many beaches and left fish flopping about on the sand, many humans went towards the water. They took photos of the fish and sea. If you go and look at some of the recorded footage from the tsunami on YouTube, you'll see humans just standing on the beach watching the tsunami race towards them, unaware of their impending death. You'll even hear the disbelief and horror of the people recording this as they watch them swept away.

Tilly's story is a powerful testament of what's possible when we trust our senses and pay attention to the Earth's communication. The death toll of the tsunami is a powerful testament of what happens when we don't.

HOW TO COMMUNICATE WITH NATURE

As you might have guessed from the way I told Tilly's story, we communicate with nature through our fifty-four senses. That's why they are so imperative, and why I offered an in-depth explanation of them in chapter three.

What happens when you're in the Theta brainwave state and you're using your fifty-four senses to connect and listen to nature's communication, it's like you switch on a universal translator. For those of you who aren't *Star Trek* fans and don't get the reference, a universal translator is a little piece of technology that can translate any language into the one you speak.

It can seem like nature is speaking to you verbally in your native language. However, what's really happening is that you're interpreting the sensory information you receive into a medium that's more comfortable for you. Your brain filters the information through your previous knowledge, experiences and beliefs to find a way in which you can accept the information you're receiving. This is why it's important to keep an open mind when experiencing natural communication.

What can help you integrate non-verbal sensory communication is deep listening to all the information your senses provide. It means listening with the whole body, and not just the ears, without trying to control or judge what you are experiencing. When you apply this to verbal communication with another human being, deep listening also means listening to what's not being said, along with the tone, tempo and intonation of what is being said.

The beauty of deep listening is that you don't need to start practising this in nature. You can practise it in any communication. The next time you're speaking with someone, make a conscious decision to listen more than you speak. If you're naturally introverted you'll find this very easy!

Another thing that can help with natural communication is trust. When you enter a Theta mind state you are, in essence, entering into an altered state of consciousness. You process things differently. Your experience of time is different. Even your sense of space is different.

As you leave the Theta mind state and re-enter the Beta mind state, it's easy to discount what you've experienced and put it down to your imagination. You can start to question what happened and doubt that it was real.

The problem here is that when you doubt what you experience, you weaken your trust in what's happened. This then makes it harder for you to go back and communicate with nature. Trust is like a muscle. The more you exercise it, the stronger it gets.

What you hear from nature is never wrong. It's just that sometimes you haven't activated your universal translator properly so that what you get is distorted by the stories in your mind. If you have never done this before, it's very likely that your universal translator is not going to be working at one hundred percent. Just keep trusting what you get anyway. As you do, you'll be able to fine tune the frequency. It just takes time and practise.

Sometimes you may receive the message, but it takes your universal translator a little while to understand the communication. For example, I wrote the first edition of this book while housesitting in France. I'd just got off Skype with a friend. As we were chatting I noticed a little insect on the ground. As I looked closer at it, it jumped up onto the coffee table in front of me. As I chased it away I noticed its beautiful golden colour and thought that it looked like a small cockroach.

I didn't think anything more of this until it jumped back up onto the table and started crawling over the television remote control. I interrupted my friend to tell her about this insect. As I did I felt an attraction to go onto Google and do a search for a golden cockroach.

Turns out my little friend is what's known as a tawny cockroach, and is actually not a pest but an important part of the ecosystem. Tawny cockroaches prefer to live outside in woodlands and don't like to co-habit with humans.

All of this might seem insignificant to you until you understand the deeper story behind this. When I arrived back in Scotland from Ibiza, another cockroach jumped out of my computer bag. My mum and grandmother wanted to kill it but I couldn't let them. Instead I saved him and created a small home for him in a terrarium.

Yet he was unhappy. From spending time in natural communication with the cockroach, I sensed that he'd rather be squished than live alone. As I did more research on cockroaches I found out that they were actually very social animals. I couldn't release him in Scotland as there's no known cockroaches in the area and I didn't want to create a potential ecological imbalance. Instead I promised him that I would take him to France and release him when I arrived, figuring that Spain and France must share cockroaches.

The day I arrived in France I did exactly this. However, a part of me was worried that Roachie, as I named him, would be ok. I didn't know if there were other cockroaches around. As I did all this research my universal translator finally kicked in. This other cockroach had come to let me know that Roachie was ok and had found friends. When I turned around to look again for him, he'd gone.

It might be easy for you in your Beta brainwave state right now to laugh at this and think I'm a bit insane. That's why you need to get out and experience your own natural communication. Then you'll know I'm not. And if I am, well, it's a great story!

MAKING NATURAL COMMUNICATION WORK FOR YOU

It's essential that you understand natural communication in a way that makes sense to you. If you're someone who believes that consciousness exists in everything (for example, Shamanism) then you'll be more than happy to dive in and engage with natural communication. However, if you're someone who thinks things like that are weird and unbelievable, you're naturally going to be a lot more sceptical of this part of The Nature Process.

Yet no matter what you believe, there is a way that natural communication works regardless of your beliefs about whether it's possible. Natural communication is a way of enabling you to communicate with yourself on a deeper level. That's it. What you define as 'you' is open to interpretation.

A good way to put this into practise is through the use of the following concept, which is integral to The Nature Process. This is the idea of asking permission from an aspect of nature before interacting with it.

If you are someone who believes that all living and non-living beings possess a spirit that you can interact with, then you can do this exercise by reaching out and asking permission of the spirit.

If you are someone who believes that we are all one, then you can do this exercise by recognizing the aspect of nature as yourself and asking permission of yourself to step deeper into understanding of yourself.

If those two options don't feel right to you, then the purpose of this exercise is to create a change in the way you understand your relationship to nature. By asking permission, you are programming your brain to become more conscious of the interconnected relationship you have with the rest of life on Earth. It is a way to discover yourself on an even deeper level.

Get Permission to Connect to Nature

Permission is a very simple concept, yet it's something that is misused and misunderstood again and again. One of the most common misconceptions is that once you get permission, you don't need to ask for it again.

Getting permission helps you to set a conscious boundary as a way of helping you to acknowledge the difference between merely being present in nature and being consciously connected. As you experiment with the permission exercise below, you'll be able to recognise the difference.

In asking for permission, you don't have to do it out loud – especially if you feel uncomfortable doing so. You can ask silently using a full question or just a word such as, 'permission' or 'connect'. It's worthwhile taking time to explore different ways of asking permission to find a way that works for you. My clients all have different ways of doing this.

Also, be aware that you might get consent from one part of nature but not another. For example, one time I was out and was attracted to climbing a tree. The tree was quite happy for me to do this but the bunches of nettles around the tree trunk weren't. I sensed them say that if I could climb the tree without stepping on them I could have permission. When I looked, I saw that this wasn't possible. Needless to say, I didn't climb the tree after all!

The Permission Exercise

The following instructions are adapted from Dr Cohen's book, *Reconnecting with Nature: Finding Wellness through Restoring Your Bond with the Earth.* They're the same instructions that I send to my private clients so that they have a guideline to remind them of how to get permission from nature.

Go to something in nature that you find attractive. Some suggestions are a park, a backyard, an aquarium, or even a potted plant.

When you get to it, notice how you feel. Are you able to offer thanks for any good feelings you may have?

Treat this area fairly as you would with a friend or equal. Ask permission for you to visit, enjoy and learn from this natural area.

Doing this increases your sensitivity to the area. Ask it if it will help you learn from it. Learning from it can't take place if there is a lack of safety and the potential for injury and destruction, either from it or you.

Wait for half a minute. Look for signs of danger such as thorns, bees, cliff faces, etc. If the area still feels attractive, or becomes more attractive, you have gained its consent.

If this portion of the natural area you visit no longer feels attractive, simply select another natural part that attracts you and repeat this process.

That's it. It's this simple. What's powerful about this exercise is that you can bring it into your daily life with every human encounter you have so that this becomes a natural and instinctive way to start any form of communication. Don't underestimate the power of this. It will revolutionize your relationships. Try it and see for yourself.

When you pay attention to consent in human communication, you'll find that a large amount of communication between us all is actually non-consensual. We automatically assume that people want (or need!) to listen to us and can get offended when they don't. Think about the number of times that you've got annoyed because someone isn't listening to you. Did you ask for their permission first?

How to Know You've Got Consent

It's easy to know if you get consent from another human being. All they need to do is to let you know with words. Nature has no words. Its consent is non-verbal.

As I developed The Nature Process I realised that understanding this consent can be difficult for people at first. Quite a few people were surprised to see what their experience of consent was when I personally guided them through The Nature Process. They were expecting something more. Sometimes consent can be nothing more than a subtle shift in your senses that is easy to override and doubt.

A client of mine shared that she was having difficulty in knowing whether she had gained consent or not, and believed that she wasn't capable of sensing it. I asked her to go out into nature, take herself through The Nature Process, and then share her experience with me.

It was a beautiful morning in the bush. I stopped at a large gum tree. It was from the same family as the one near my house. It was such a beautiful tree. At this time of year, the bark peels off the trunk in long strips. These strips catch on the branches below and reveal the smoothness of the white bark beneath. The rising sun was reflecting on the high branches. I could feel many sensations in my body especially a small feeling of warmth around the area of my heart. Not much was happening and I found my-self getting caught up in the thoughts within my head. This made me sad to think that my sense of mind had developed at the expense of my other senses.

I want to draw your attention to her comment about getting lost in her thoughts. If this is happening to you outside in nature, then this is a sign that you need to deepen your state of natural presence.

The warmth my client experienced in her heart was a sign of consent. It made her feel good and the tree stayed attractive to her. However, as she wasn't fully in a state of natural presence, that's all she could experience in terms of consent in that moment. It's important to remember that at times consent is given in subtle ways.

Here's another example of a client's experience with asking for permission:

I once deliberately set out to spend time in a garden I like, with an issue I was working with. There's a particular place I like to sit where there's a pool where the water cascades down to a lower level. I settled in, letting go of my "edges" and began looking and asking for permission. Nothing seemed to come to my attention. It was just being there but with no at-tractions. After a while I got up and was drawn to walk to the lower level pool where there was a lotus just coming into full bloom. It was magnificent and really drew me in close. The more I stared at it, the more attractive it became. Through the lotus, I found the answers I needed to help me. I described what I saw and related it back to the issue I was needing help with.

You can see in this example, that the attraction my client experienced came after she moved away, following her natural attractions to discover the lotus which became even more attractive to her. Again, consent is very subtle and you can miss it if you're not present.

Many of us unintentionally want to rush ahead, find the natural attraction, and connect with it so that we can let go of our emotional pain and limiting beliefs and get on with our life. We're impatient. This is a human trait that will interrupt your experience of The Nature Process.

It may take up to a minute before you sense signs that you have nature's consent. Take your phone out and set a minute on the timer. Close your eyes and wait. You'll find that this minute seems so long.

In today's busy, modern world we've come to expect instant responses through text messages and email. Nature doesn't work like this. You have to give it time to get your answer.

Remember the key lesson from natural attractions and apply it here. If you feel the goodness of nature in any way, you have consent. If you don't feel the goodness, you don't have consent.

Another client shared how she was in the woods. As she walked through she felt attracted to touching several trees and said to each one, "Hello, how are you doing?" As she did, she sensed a soft flow of energy coming back at her, but she didn't know what it meant. That again was consent, and the start of non-verbal communication, specifically here with trees.

Once you recognise what consent feels like, you can deepen your understanding of it. You can also experiment with this part of The Nature Process on its own. If your goal is merely to understand natural communication better, then you don't need to do the other parts of the process first. As I've mentioned before, the five parts of The Nature Process are both principles and steps, that once you've mastered, you can adapt and use in any combination you're attracted to.

If you're still struggling with the idea of asking nature for permission, look at it from the perspective of being in a sexual relationship with someone. Just because they've given their consent once to having sex with you doesn't automatically mean they give consent for you to have sex with them whenever you want.

Nature is in a constant state of change, just like us. Just because you got permission in the past from a part of nature or a place to connect, doesn't mean that you'll always have permission. Always take the time to check in and ask.

I learned this lesson myself when I returned to the Galician countryside. Behind my ex-partner's family house in the middle of nowhere is a beautiful forested mountain with old ruins at the top. I spent a lot of my time up the mountain experiencing my coursework for my Masters in Applied Ecopsychology. I have so many wonderful, joyous moments in my memory from there—following wild horses up to the windmills, standing on a rock and breathing in the essence of the trees, discovering a natural altar and creating my own ritual there, and standing naked in the mist as it slowly fell and turned everything around me to dense white. I returned there a year later after the end of my relationship. Excitedly I began walking up the mountain. As I did I threw open my senses and shouted internally, "Here I come!", which was my variation of not quite asking for permission but still connecting. I assumed I had consent so I didn't ask for it.

Immediately I felt as if a wall had been put up in front of me. Confused, I stopped and then I heard very clearly in my mind, "You're not welcome anymore." To tell you the truth, I was devastated. In fact, I thought that I'd heard wrong, but I hadn't.

As I sensed more and more into the mountain's communication I was told that if I went back up the mountain it would undervalue all the previous experiences I'd had up there. I could have ignored that and continued, but I didn't. Instead I turned around, headed in the opposite direction, found a grove of trees and sobbed my heart out.

This following experience, from one of the The Nature Process online program participants, Deborah Two Trees Birthing, highlights the power of asking for consent and also offers a glimpse into what can happen when you don't. It's also a beautiful story of the depth that's possible with natural communication and what Deborah refers to as being 'Humbled by a Madrone.'

"I journey with a vast Madrone tree over a three-day period, while supporting a Wisdom University vision quest in the Santa Cruz Mountains of California. In a dreamlike state, this powerful tree, with its peeling bark, speaks to me, revealing an angry voice that captivates my attention and prostrates my body upon the soil of its roots. The Madrone is firm in

its teaching. The depth of its voice, a knowing felt sense, vibrates the cells of my body and mind. Its passionate energy flows from the Earth, teaching me lessons in humility while speaking to the deforestation of the Earth.

During the opening circle of this gathering, in a newly prepared clearing of the forest, I perceive an energy coming from the trees encircling us. The next day, following a sweat lodge ceremony, I meet the Madrone as I lean against its large trunk to write in my journal. If I were to hug this tree, my arms would barely reach halfway around its huge body. I am amazed at its size and awed by its beauty. Its elongated limbs stretch out high above the labyrinth being constructed below. The red-orange bark of its leafy branches peels back, revealing its nakedness, and the smooth, yellow-green skin of its new birth.

Sitting upon the Earth in a layer of fresh sawdust mulch, back against the tree, I face the Inipi, a portable sweat lodge structure. It is something familiar in this new place. I write that my heart is filled with gratitude for its long journey from Central Texas, and the dedicated member of our Earthtribe Community, who trucked it to this mountain of majestic trees. With each ceremonial action we take, we are tapping into the sacredness of the land. Not unlike the peeling branches of the Madrone, we are exposing ourselves as we prepare for the birthing of visions. I intuit the eyes and ears of the trees watching, listening and questioning; I imagine them asking, who are they? What do they want?

Suddenly, something sharp and pointed is poking me in the middle of my back. The stabbing pain is piercing. I turn around to see what might be protruding from the trunk of this large Madrone. Nothing is visible. My hand feels the bark, finding no jagged edges. I am puzzled. My body aches from travelling the trails and roads of the 45 square miles of this retreat area. It is a logical place to rest my bones and write. Did I ask permission of the tree before sitting down?

I recall a cursory request, unconscious and distant, one spoken quickly without sufficient attention, without listening for a response. The message is clear. This tree does not want me to lean on it, or touch it for that matter. I sense an aversion toward me. Is it my humanness, I wonder? I send a heartfelt apology. The pain continues as though a pointed edge is embedded into my skin. As I reach back to examine the spot, I discover nothing, except the place where two moles were removed earlier this year, leaving a slight indentation, a small hole, where the skin is thin. I am surprised by the change in shape. What was concave is now raised. Later, I discover a spot of blood on my blouse.

Disturbed by this encounter, I am aware it carries the energy of a wake-up call. As the pain subsides, I sit upon the Earth in silence, facing the tree trunk for some time. Respecting its request, I do not touch it. Pondering the arrogant attitude of my actions, I begin to question my relationship with trees. I assumed I would be welcome, for I have touched and been touched by many trees this year.

At my Vision Quest the previous April, I was given the Nature name, Two Trees Birthing. I thought I carried the energy of these tree encounters within me. Now I pause to question what I bring to this relationship with trees. I have never met a tree with such adverse energy before. It seems angry, deeply irritated. I decide to sit with this to see what bubbles up, to see what this intimate encounter can teach me. I resolve to come back tomorrow to hear more of the story.

On Friday, I humbly approach the Madrone again. First, I spend some time shaking my egg rattle, in a healing manner, in a clockwise spiral, around the recently disturbed area and at the base of the Madrone. It is a soothing process. In doing so, I discover a hole in the tree, a small but deep opening. Immediately, I am drawn into the memory of a dream of being here in this forest, lying at the base of this tree. As in the dream, I prostrate myself upon the Earth, forehead down, arms raised with hands placed upon the trunk. Remembering to ask first, I am granted permission to touch its trunk.

Ceremonial practices from the night before, help me to open, empty, and become blank, seeking a place of resonance. Some time passes. I lose awareness of my surroundings. The voices I heard earlier, up near the sweat lodge, disappear. I receive a download of information from the tree. It is filled with a forceful, emotional intensity. Not only are the trees distressed by the disruption in the immediate area, they have a much bigger story to tell.

It is about the global rape of Earth, animals, trees and women. Trees hold the tension of the Earth in their roots. They are tuning devices seeking connection. It was a conversation of sorts, not easily explained, more emotions and images than words. The strength and deep sadness of the message enters my physical being. My entire body shakes, as I sob uncontrollably. The download of information holds an urgent message to speak on behalf of trees. The Madrone urges my alliance in a firm, compassionate voice.

This intimate encounter continues on Saturday morning. An energy worker of the Earth listens to my story, granting me permission to walk the not quite finished labyrinth, to see what more the trees have to share. First, I lay upon the Earth in the humble manner of yesterday. Each day I am welcomed a bit more. This morning, I am introduced to a nearby Sequoia with two trunks holding a bowl shape opening between. I understand it to be a supportive partner of the vast Madrone. We are all connected through our roots, they tell me. One of the returning Vision Questers asks to join me. Her energy is strong and welcome. We sing a song to honour the trees, before heading to the Naming Ceremony, where she receives the Nature name, Fearless Tree.

Walking the labyrinth comes later, just prior to departing this sacred mountain. It is quiet. Everyone is at lunch. Being here is all the nourishment I need. The Madrone and the Sequoia greet me as I walk down the path. Grounding myself, I open and close the gate of the labyrinth, as instructed. Entering with bare feet, I slowly begin the journey, feeling the presence and support of the many surrounding trees.

With each step, I sing the song that came to me during a tree ceremony in my backyard. "Ho Tree, Sacred Tree: I am here to honour you…I am here in gratitude… You give to us your all… I will remember you." Stepping into the centre of the labyrinth, I am surprised by a strong jolt of energy, rising from the Earth, electrifying my body. The strength of it nearly knocks me off my feet. Standing still to regain my composure,

I burst into laughter. Sensing an overwhelming acceptance by the trees, I am instructed to work on their behalf. Crying tears of joy, I am initiated into a Global Circle of Trees."

Engaging in Natural Communication

There are many ways in which you can explore natural communication. Deborah's story is a reflection of someone who has spent many years practising to reach the depth she has. If you've not got a lot of experience, then the easiest way is to start by asking yes/no questions and notice the reaction in your body and breath. This can help build up your confidence and make you feel more comfortable. I recommend asking about issues in your life with which you wish to receive greater clarity.

Once you have the confidence that you are actually engaging in communication, you can then explore open-ended questions. In order to translate the answers to these you need to be fully focused on your senses and be aware of which ones are being activated. For example, a memory might come to mind or you'll feel attracted to moving your body in a certain way. It's important to go with whatever comes up, even if you don't initially understand it.

Pay attention to where your eyes are drawn to and what sounds you hear. Maybe there will be a gust of wind or raindrops will start to fall. In the moment when you're engaged with natural communication, everything you notice with your senses is meaningful.

It can also be helpful to start a dialogue with yourself using your sense of language. This can make it easier for you to get your universal translator fully working. Ask a question and then give yourself the answer based on what you're sensing.

Remember, this is a completely subjective experience. Fundamentally, it doesn't matter whether the answers to your questions are, in fact, coming from the external nature around you or from within the inner nature within. What's important is that engaging with exercises like this helps bring clarity and insight to things that are happening in your life. Natural communication is less about improving your well-being and more about enhancing your life.

It enables you to explore creative ways to do things differently and create new ways of looking at challenges within your life.

What I recommend to my clients who use The Nature Process in its entirety and who are completely comfortable with exploring natural communication is to add another layer onto The Nature Process; when they do the full process, by asking at the end, "What's the next step that I need to take?" or "What do I need to know that will help me take better action with this?" Doing so helps you create a sense of empowerment and belief in taking action that enhances your life.

The answers to questions like these generally come through your sense of intuition, or your gut instinct, as a knowing or certainty about what to do. This can make the answers received easier to understand, especially if you've already worked on developing this sense individually.

It can also be helpful to journal about your experience with natural communication and reflect upon it to help bring further clarity. Allowing yourself to 'sleep on it' can also be helpful.

Natural Communication with Animals

Communicating with animals starts by understanding the body language of the animal you wish to communicate with. You also need to understand how human behaviour differs from the animal's behaviour. Many of our human ways to communicate friendliness can be interpreted as acts of dominance and aggression by animals, especially those who are considered prey. For example, eye contact is very important for us, yet direct eye contact with animals can be very intimidating and classed as a challenge for dominance.

Animals also have clear warning signs that show you're making them angry. If you don't know what these are, you can miss them. In the case of cats, biting and scratching are last resorts. If this happens to you, then you've not been listening to what the cat has been communicating.

One of the biggest blocks to communicating with animals is that we humanize them. Animals have the same senses as us but they do not think, act, and sense the same way we humans do. When we make the assumption that they do, we're not able to truly hear what they're communicating.

Should you wish to explore a more psychic sense of communication with animals find someone who is skilled in this form of communication and can help you learn more. Anna Breytenbach (www.animalspirit.org) is a South African animal communicator who is most well-known for her work with a black panther whose behaviour was very challenging. When Anna communicated with him she discovered that the panther didn't like its name Diablo and wished to be called Spirit instead. As soon as the panther's name was changed, he became a completely different animal. This story has been documented on film which you'll be able to find on YouTube.

NATURAL COMMUNICATION WITH TREES AND PLANTS

Trees and plants are the easiest place for you to start in terms of practising natural communication. They are everywhere. Unlike animals, they don't require you to invest large amounts of time and energy to ensure their well-being. However, they also have no body language, which means you need to ensure all your senses are developed to support your ability to connect.

What makes trees and plants the easiest place to start is that they don't have a well-developed sense of self like humans and animals. This allows them to act as a form of antennae to help us tune into our own natural communication.

To start communication, get out and go for a walk in the woods. Spend time getting to know the different trees around you. Notice how you feel when you are with different trees. This will help you get a sense of each tree.

As I mentioned in chapter three, trees and plants naturally produce phytoncides, which help us reduce stress and strengthen our immune system. This is part of their ability to connect with us. If it helps, imagine this connection between you and the tree taking place and notice what thoughts and feelings you have about the tree.

If hugging trees is too hippy for you, simply place your hands on the trunk or sit underneath the tree with your back to it. If you're brave enough, and once you have permission of course, you can climb them. This puts you fully into contact with their electromagnetic field and connects you in a way that hugging them doesn't.

What also makes trees and plants particularly interesting to practise natural communication with, is many people argue that plants and trees may actually be conscious and state they've received communication from them. Indeed, there is scientific evidence that highlights the intelligence of trees.

In Peter Wohlleben's books, *The Hidden Life of Trees,* he demonstrates how trees form social bonds, look after their family members, feel pain and communicate with each other when there's danger. Whether or not this means that trees and plants are conscious, is open to interpretation. There is currently not enough scientific evidence to conclude whether this sign of intelligence also demonstrates consciousness.

However, should you be particularly interested in developing your skills in communicating with trees and plants, then you need to check out the work of Dr Jim Conroy (www.treewhispering.com) who has developed tools and techniques that help you use your sense of intuition to know or feel impressions and receive communication and wisdom from trees. His book, *Tree Whispering: A nature lover's guide to touching, healing and communicating with trees, plants and all of nature* is a great place to start.

Natural Communication with Stones, Stars, and Water

Stones, stars and water are the most challenging for us to connect with. We know animals are alive as are trees and plants. However, the Western world sees stones, stars and water as non-living beings, which can get in the road of communicating.

If you're attracted to practising Natural Communication with stones and water, then the best way to start is by exploring them as much as possible through your fifty-four senses. Spend time playing with stones and water without any expectations of communication at first.

Physical contact with the stone or water you wish to communicate with is preferred, as this will enable you to connect more of your senses far easier than if there's a distance between you.

If you wish to communicate with stars, start by spending time outside looking at them. Get to know the ones that shine brightest in the sky and learn some constellations to help you identify more stars.

Stones, stars, and water make up the majority of the composition of the earth and the universe. Once you're able to connect with them, you're able to connect with the essence of the earth and the universe itself as weird and woo-woo as it sounds.

To be able to listen and truly understand what the earth and universe are communicating to you, will require you to interpret the communication you receive without letting the filters of your humanity distort it. There are no human characteristics in the earth and universe at all. The knowledge and wisdom inherent within the earth and the universe challenges most of humanity's fundamental beliefs about how we see ourselves and the world.

This type of communication is not for the faint-hearted. You need an extremely open mind. Remember, the earth is 4.6 billion years old while the universe is 13.7 billion years. As a being who lives on average eighty years, it can be hard to understand the growth and evolution of earth and the universe.

Read books and research the study of the cosmos to help you understand just how complex our entire existence is. Explore the past and question what you think you know about human history. We have lost so much knowledge over the centuries; we are still relying on theory and speculation as to the original purpose of Neolithic stone structures such as Stonehenge and other such standing stones. We still don't know what really exists out there among the stars and in other galaxies. The possibilities are limitless.

When you do sense that you've received communication from stones, stars and water, if appropriate do some investigation into the information you've received and see if it is backed up by any other sources. This can help give you greater confidence in the information you receive.

MERGE NATURAL COMMUNICATION INTO THE NATURE PROCESS

As part of The Nature Process, natural communication is the fourth step.

First, you go out into nature and enter into a state of natural presence.

Then, from your state of natural presence you expand your sensory awareness to your natural body.

Afterwards, you find an aspect of nature that activates your natural attraction in that moment.

From there, you start with the permission exercise and ask for consent to interact with and learn from whatever aspect of nature you're attracted to.

Two things may happen after you do.

First, you may find that you receive information back in return in the form of feelings and insights. If this happens, it tends to be a sign that you need to do no more in that moment than stay in a place of natural communication. Nature, both inner and outer, wishes to offer you guidance and insight that will help prepare you to go beyond reducing stress and anxiety and into a more creative mindset.

When this happens, sit and notice where your senses are led. I find the use of my eyes particularly helpful here in sensing what nature wants to tell me. I find myself literally unable to take my eyes off certain parts of nature and my gaze continues to return to the same place again and again. Also, pay attention to the thoughts, feelings, and sensations that arise within you at the same time. It can be helpful to move your sense of awareness continually back and forth between the natural world around you and the natural landscape within you.

It's important to take your time when this happens. Allow your universal translator to work so that you get some answers. If you feel attracted to, ask more questions and explore whatever you're working on until you sense complete clarity around the information you've been given.

Then go away and think about your experience. Do any necessary research, like I did with my encounter with Roachie, the cockroach. Allow yourself time to fully integrate the experience in the next few days.

Additionally, what may happen after you engage with natural communication is that you'll move into the next principle/step of The Nature Process; natural release. We'll be talking more about that in the next chapter.

If you are attracted to exploring your own capacity for natural communication further, then do the 'Deepen Your Ability for Natural Communication Exercise' on page 225.

Exercises to Practise in Nature

- Every time you see a part of nature you are attracted to when outside, ask permission before asking whether this part of nature has a message for you.
- Whenever you encounter an animal or insect, observe its body language. What can you learn from it?
- Observe an aspect of nature and see what metaphors about life you can get from it.
- Go to a wooded area and observe the relationships that exist among all the different parts of nature within it.
- Think about an area of your life that you find challenging and see what insights you can receive from nature that can help you gain insight on this challenge.

Key Points to Remember

- The earth can be considered a complex self-regulating organism, where the earth and its organisms act intelligently to keep the earth's entire ecosystem in a state of balance.
- We can understand this intelligent behaviour through sensory information received through our fifty-four senses such as in the case of Tilly Smith.

- As you receive sensory information from nature, your brain filters the information received through your existing knowledge, experiences and beliefs to translate it into something you can understand.
- How you understand natural communication and its purpose will depend on how you define 'you'.
- Asking permission to connect to nature is a way of setting a conscious boundary that enables you to recognise the difference between being in nature and connecting to nature.
- When asking permission, give yourself a minute to tune into the sensory information you're receiving to decipher whether the part of nature you're asking permission from becomes more attractive or not.
- Receiving consent can be quite subtle at times depending on the depth of your state of natural presence.
- Yes/no questions, open-ended questions, starting a dialogue with yourself and asking for guidance on what to do next are all suggestions to explore natural communication.
- When communicating with animals, understand how their body language differs from humans and don't assume they act like humans.
- When communicating with trees and plants, take time to explore the differences you notice between them and experiment with touching, hugging, sitting under and climbing trees.
- Spend time observing and interacting with stones, stars and water to get to understand them better.
- As part of The Nature Process, natural communication helps you receive guidance and insight from nature about issues in your life that are causing stress and anxiety, or as preparation for entering into natural release.

QUESTIONS FOR REFLECTION

- Do you think of the Earth as a living organism? Why? Why not?
- What are your beliefs about the natural communication that exists among all life on Earth?

* Have you ever had an experience where you felt nature was communicating with you? What happened and how did it make you feel?
* What does developing a relationship with nature mean to you?
* Do you think the Earth itself can communicate with us? Why? Why not?

CHAPTER 7

Natural Release

❧   ❧   ❧

There are moments when one feels free from one's own identification with
human limitations and inadequacies. At such moments, one imagines that
one stands on some spot of a small planet, gazing in amazement at the cold
yet profoundly moving beauty of the eternal, the unfathomable: life and
death flow into one, and there is neither evolution nor destiny; only being.

- ALBERT EINSTEIN

'BEING' IS A STATE OF complete balance as you stand fully in the essence of
who you are, free from the stories and conditioning of civilisation and culture.
You experience the truth of your existence fully in the present moment, as the
past and future falls away. In this moment you discover the power inherent
within you. The same power that has created all life on Earth: Nature. Its key
principles; evolution and growth.

You were born to evolve and grow. To experience more and understand
yourself better. To move beyond the identification with your perceived limitations and inadequacies and recognise the beauty of the eternal, both around
you and within. It's here that you find the peace and strength to move forward
and take action to create the life you want.

Natural release is the final principle/step of The Nature Process. It's the
essential part of the process that deepens the ability of your natural body to
harmonise its natural rebalancing properties with that of the Earth's. It's also

the part of the process that takes you even deeper into connection with the Earth and Nature. The more you engage in a natural release, the more you'll be able to tune into the way you were born to feel: alive, present, and whole.

While natural release is the final principle/step, each time you enter into a natural release it is the beginning of a deeper connection to nature and yourself. There is no ending and you'll continue to discover more and more about yourself that you never knew.

In this chapter, you'll explore why engaging the power of your heart can amplify your natural release, along with how your imagination can support this part of the process. I'll remind you why your breath is key in this part of the process before sharing an experience of my own to help you get a better sense of natural release and The Nature Process. We'll also go over why it's essential to take action after doing an entire session of The Nature Process and I'll share with you a simple way to integrate the experience into your psyche, and remind you of The Nature Process basic steps before offering suggestions to help you integrate The Nature Process into your daily life.

You'll know that you've mastered this principle/step of the process when you find yourself able to engage with The Nature Process without much conscious thought. It will feel natural and normal and you'll find yourself moving through the steps intuitively whenever your body needs to rebalance.

Your ability to sense and feel a connection between you and the rest of Nature will strengthen and you'll find yourself thinking of yourself more and more as part of a greater whole, rather than a separate being.

As I mentioned previously back in chapter two, natural release works on a sensory level, using the body's intelligence and connection to the earth to create new neural pathways within the brain that reduce the stress and anxiety created by worry and doubt and help bring you back to a state of balance with life.

Due to its sensory nature, and the support of the natural environment upon the body, you are able to experience the sensations of the body without getting caught up in the stories behind the physical sensations. Natural release is about allowing the intelligence of nature, combined with the intelligence of your body, to create a dynamic interplay of chemical reactions that work to create balance without any effort from you.

THE POWER OF YOUR HEART

When engaging with natural release, one of the most powerful ways for you to connect to the earth and nature is through your heart and feelings of love. When you bring your awareness to your heart and focus on a feeling of love, you are helping to activate your parasympathetic nervous system.

The parasympathetic nervous system is responsible for creating a feeling of calmness and connection. It does this through releasing opiates, which reduce pain, and oxytocin, which makes you feel close and connected – in this case to the earth and nature.

While your parasympathetic nervous system will already be activated, through entering a state of natural presence and tuning into the natural body, focusing specifically on the heart after establishing a connection with an aspect of nature deepens this response, thus triggering more production of opiates and oxytocin.

It's these chemicals that help bring you back into a state of balance and allow you to go deeper into your natural release. Put bluntly, you're literally drugging yourself to feel better! The only difference is that these chemicals are ones that are naturally produced by your body and specifically designed to counteract the effects of the chemicals, adrenaline and cortisol, which are released during a stress response.

When you experience feelings of contentment and connection to nature, you are able to stay within a Theta brainwave state and fully experience this connection. As a result, you are able to experience what Abraham Maslow, a North American psychologist who focused on how people could achieve their full potential, called peak experiences – "moments of highest happiness and fulfilment".

Using the power of your heart and focusing on this connection is a way in which you can help yourself have these peak experiences or experience what

Mihály Csíkszentmihályi, a Hungarian psychologist, calls flow, a milder form of peak experiences characterised by a feeling of total energy, engagement and enjoyment of an activity.

The way to engage the power of your heart through a natural release and create the possibility of a peak experience or state of flow is through a concept created by The Institute of HeartMath in Boulder Creek, California. They propose that the heart's electromagnetic field can be detected by other people and can impact another person's heart electromagnetic field from up to five feet away. HeartMath also suggests that the heart possesses its own brain which can be considered separate and distinct from our head brain. They propose that traditionally we thought the head brain controlled the heart but, in reality, it's actually a two-way system with both head and heart communicating with each other. Apparently, the electromagnetic frequency of the heart is approximately sixty times greater in amplitude than the brain. HeartMath proposes that our heart's electromagnetic field can interact with the earth's own electromagnetic field, thus creating a symbiotic relationship between humanity and the earth.

Now sadly, as of this writing, the research into electromagnetic fields by HeartMath lacks scientific validity and isn't peer-reviewed. However, as an idea of expressing our relationship to the earth it's fantastic. When I've used this concept with many of my clients they report feeling an energetic connection between themselves and the part of nature they're connecting with, that creates an additional feeling of support as they move through a natural release.

HARNESS THE POWER OF YOUR IMAGINATION

Imagination is more important than knowledge.

- ALBERT EINSTEIN

Back in chapter four, when I talked about the natural body, I mentioned how the brain doesn't know the difference between real or imaginary thoughts.

Brain studies show that simply by thinking about an action you are able to engage many of the cognitive processes within the brain that would be involved if it were a real action or event. In effect, you are training yourself to do something successfully. Furthermore, there are numerous studies, especially in the areas of sport, which show how imagining exercise can, in fact, increase the strength and flexibility of the body. But what does this have to do with natural release?

Throughout this book, I've been giving you an understanding of what happens within the body as you connect to nature. This allows you to ground your imagination in knowledge and then go beyond it, which is why the HeartMath exercise of imagining the electromagnetic frequency of the heart connecting with the Earth is so powerful.

The fact is, the heart does have an electromagnetic field. Whether or not it's actually powerful enough to truly connect with the Earth is irrelevant, if you are able to use the power of your imagination to create a felt sense within you that your heart is connected to the Earth. This connection, imagined or real, deepens the power of your natural release as you have your focus fully on connecting with nature and receiving the benefits of that connection, which then amplifies them.

As you learned in chapter 1, you know that connecting with and spending time in nature is beneficial for you. There's ample knowledge published in the form of scientific research that clearly demonstrates this. This knowledge then becomes the foundation for your imagination to soar and discover what else is possible.

The more you use your imagination when moving into natural release, the easier this part of the process becomes and it can even start to happen automatically. Imagine that every time you looked at the sky you felt a sense of peace and freedom without conscious thought. How would that impact your day? What if every time you looked at a mountain you felt a sense of excitement and adventure? How would that change the way you lived your life?

This is fundamentally what natural release is all about: creating psychological associations between your thoughts, feelings, sensations and the natural world. Rosemarie Anderson, a North American transpersonal psychologist, notes that this experience of feeling embedded in and connected to the Earth is prevalent in indigenous cultures. They are able to see patterns, symbols and visions within nature. We're all indigenous to the Earth. This is part of our birthright. All it requires is a little imagination to return home.

Use your imagination to visualize the electromagnetic field of your heart expanding out and connecting, not just to the part of nature you're working with through your natural attractions, but to all of the other parts of nature contained within this 'bubble'.

Imagine that the electromagnetic field of the Earth is merging into your heart's field and creating a two-way loop where the energy of the Earth flows into your heart, moving throughout your body, helping to release all stress and tension.

If you want, you can even imagine the energy of the Earth moving in through one hand and out the other, flowing through your body in the same way your heart pumps blood throughout the body. You could also imagine that the energy of the Earth is washing through you, taking all stress and anxiety away to be returned to the Earth and recycled.

Use Your Breath

Back in chapter two I mentioned how natural release can be the most challenging part of The Nature Process for some people, because they believe that they have to do something in order to bring themselves back into a state of balance. It's not about doing. It's about being.

Are you able to *be* present, open and receptive to the natural rebalancing power of nature and allow it to help bring you back into balance, without letting your human thoughts and stories get in the way?

Most of the time, you are not conscious of breathing. Yet even the simple act of breathing connects you on a basic level to the Earth. Without the oxygen in the Earth's atmosphere you wouldn't be able to exist. This connection exists whether you are aware of it or not.

The simple act of conscious breathing, while you engage in natural release, can support you tremendously. Breathing slowly and deeply helps trigger feelings of calmness and connection, as it activates your parasympathetic nervous system.

As you breathe, recognise the complex relationship that exists between all life in Earth. The trees produce oxygen which allowed the Earth to create you. You breathe out carbon dioxide, which the trees breathe in to help them grow. Breathe deeply and slowly allowing yourself to really feel the changes that occur within the body as you do. Imagine that every breath in offers a cleansing and healing and that you release all stress and anxiety as you exhale.

THE NATURE PROCESS: A REAL-TIME ACCOUNT

When I first taught The Nature Process group program, I created a video in which I took myself through a complete The Nature Process using the five principles as basic steps. It was quite uncomfortable and vulnerable for me to do so as it meant sharing my own process publicly. However, I wanted people to have a working example of The Nature Process in action. Hopefully by now, you'll already have an idea of how The Nature Process works from the additional stories shared by my clients within this second edition. Nevertheless, I still wanted to include this experience, though rather than using the basic transcript of the video, I have tidied it up and added an extra analysis to help give you even more clarity around The Nature Process in action.

When I did this exercise I was still living in Ibiza, although I knew that my time there was coming to an end. There was a lot of uncomfortable emotion arising from the thought of leaving the island and not knowing if I was going to return again. To do the exercise I went to a nearby wooded area and sat down on a stone pathway that meandered through the trees.

As I started speaking into the video recorder, my hand stroked the cat next to me. Two of my landlady's cats, called Biscuit and Hindu, had followed me all the way from the house, and down into the woods. I'd spent the last six months building my relationship with them through natural communication. They slept on my bed with me at night and followed me around like dogs.

A warm feeling entered my heart as I thought of the relationship I had with them. I was happy they were here with me as it helped me feel more comfortable with recording my own experience of The Nature Process.

I was leaving Ibiza in less than a week. It was clearly a transition. My room, with its double doors that opened straight into the garden, was going to be cleared out and my stuff packed away. I had three or four months of travelling ahead of me that involved writing the first edition of The Nature Process and developing another online course.

However, I wasn't excited. Instead I felt overwhelmed. There was a feeling of tension in my chest and my head hurt. Normally I love to go travelling. Yet in this moment, I felt a real sense of loss. I was packing up. Leaving. Moving on and not coming back.

I'd spent the last six months integrating myself into the area where I was living. I thought I'd be here for much longer than this. There were five cats, three dogs, a beautiful garden, and a wonderful sense of community. Somebody new had just moved in who had a seven-year-old kid. This was actually everything I've ever wanted in a place to stay.

Sadness welled up inside me. I suddenly thought of all the stuff I still had at my ex-partner's house in Galicia from a few years back. It was still in boxes that I haven't been back to collect. Leaving there was one of the hardest things I'd ever had to do. I loved Galicia and when my relationship with my partner ended, my relationship with Galicia ended too. I didn't even know if I would ever go back to Spain when I left.

This was my intention for working with The Nature Process. The sadness of leaving the land, people and culture I'd fallen in love with and not knowing when or if I would return. Connected to the present moment intertwined with memories of a past event I hadn't even realised until now that I was still holding onto.

Now that I'd discovered the root of my anxiety I started to move into a state of natural presence. I'd sat down on a lovely rock at the side of the path and the rock felt smooth under my legs. Behind me were lots of green bushes. There were more of the same bushes in front of me.

To the left of me was a small grove of pine trees with pine cones in them. The brown of the cones contrasted against the deep green of the needles. The air was still around me with no wind. Suddenly a little bird moved in the branches of one of the trees, fluttering about from branch to branch. The air was filled with the sound of birdsong and everywhere I looked there was green all around. In the distance, I noticed a dead tree which stood straight like a soldier stretching up into the blue sky. Behind the tree were hills, stretching out endlessly. Biscuit, the ginger tom, was lying stretched out on the ground next to me purring softly. Hindu, the black cat, had disappeared into the bushes behind me, rustling them as she went.

There were some dry, brown flowers on the bush that looked as if they were dying because of the heat. As I looked around, I noticed the green and brown of the earth contrasting dramatically with the blue of the sky. A small sycamore leaf swirled down slowly to the ground as my awareness returned to the movement of the birds in the tree. The sky was a lovely pale blue with the light of the sun reflecting off the white candy floss clouds. The contrast was incredible and when the light of the sun faded from the clouds they turned into darker grey wisps. The pressure of the rock against my bum started to feel uncomfortable and I had dirt on my hands from stroking the ground as I felt the earth beneath my fingers. Suddenly, the ginger cat came over to me and started to lick my fingers with his raspy tongue and rubbed himself around my legs.

How long you spend moving into a state of natural presence depends on how you are feeling. If you are relaxed and calm it may take you five minutes. If you're really stressed or upset, it may take you twenty minutes or more. I'd sat there for about seven minutes deepening my state of natural presence until I felt my mind go quite and time seemed to disappear. The beauty of the environment around me created a sense of openness and I felt ready to move into my natural body.

I thought about moving. It felt like my whole body was swollen. I had a slight nauseous sensation in my stomach and it felt like something was stuck in my throat. My chest was tight and heavy. I felt like I wanted to cough and my throat tightened. I could feel an ache in my head as I tried to think about how my upcoming move was connected to my time in Galicia.

Having identified the sensations caused within the body I returned my awareness to the natural environment around me. The contrasting colours of the bright green leaves against the darker backdrop of the hills caught my eyes. I could feel myself starting to move into natural attractions. I was present to both the nature around me and the nature within. There was still a tight yukky feeling running up and down my chest area as I looked around to find something I was attracted to. The green colour was beautiful but I didn't feel compelled to go deeper with it.

As I sat there, I became even more conscious of the fact that underneath me was a wonderful big rock with some moss attached to it. I liked the feeling of my feet underneath the rock. I loved running my fingers over it and feeling its smoothness. All I could think about was the rock and I knew then I'd found my natural attraction. Tears filled my eyes and the cat bit me again as if to offer confirmation.

I completed the attraction sentence: I really like this rock because it's strong and stable. It's powerful and present. It's also connected to everywhere else in the world because it's part of the earth.

I then turned the sentence around: I really like myself because I am strong, stable, powerful and present. I am connected to everywhere else in the world because I am part of the earth. Even though I am leaving Ibiza, a part of me will still be here.

A fly buzzed past my face. After my brother died I started seeing flies everywhere. It's now a running saying in my family that if there's a fly it's my brother joining us. I interpreted that as a sign of support. More tears filled my eyes, a clear sign that something was shifting within the natural body.

I couldn't stop touching the rock and knew it was time to ask permission. As I explained that I don't do formalized statements like, "Can I have permission to connect with you?" I started laughing because the moment I'd spoked the question to the camera I got the sensation of a response that I translated as, "Why, yes you can!" I continued laughing and could feel some of the heaviness within my body lifting. This was how I knew I'd received consent.

More tears filled my eyes as I felt myself powerfully connected to the rock. I knew I was about to move into natural release. I brought my awareness to my heart and the nausea increased as I felt like I wanted to burp. I tend to burp a lot when I'm releasing stress and anxiety. The connection to the rock continued to deepen. I imagined I sensed the energetic field of my heart emanating out and connecting with the rock. I closed my eyes so I could sense this better. It felt as if there was energy being drawn up from the rock through my hands and legs into my heart.

The ginger tom came up, rubbed against my legs and nipped at me again. I imagined I could sense the energy of the rock moving through my natural body. I repeatedly yawned and suddenly I farted. Things were definitely shifting! My stomach started to rumble as if it were a washing machine. The tightness in my chest increased and I could feel a tighter pain at the back of my head.

I could hear the black cat meowing. It felt as if both animals were there supporting me. The thought of this made me very emotional and I focused on my breath as the sensations in my body continued to shift. I felt more tears in my eyes and as expected, I started to burp. I moved my shoulders, loosening the tension I could feel in them. My nose started to run and I could feel the changes happening within the natural body. The tightness in my chest was loosening although the band of tightness around my head still remained.

I opened my eyes. Two women walked towards me along the path. I closed my eyes and the black cat meowed again. Opening my eyes, I said hello to the women before closing them again. This is one of the things I love about The Nature Process. Nobody has any idea what you're doing. To those ladies, it just looked as if I was recording a video.

I didn't expect anyone to walk past me as I was doing this, but I felt happy that I was able to continue practising The Nature Process as they walked past and while the camera was rolling. The tightness in my chest shifted and I let out another large burp. My chest felt soft. Bringing myself back into balance like this felt so gentle. My nose was still running and I wiped it away with my hand.

I was still conscious of the tightness in my head. There was a sensation of pressure and as I sat there I realised this pressure had been there for the last few days, slowly building up. I hadn't even noticed until now! I let out another large burp and my stomach jiggled. I burped again even louder than before. In that moment, the sun shone brighter as if to acknowledge the intensity of this natural release. I started to feel lighter as I continued burping, surprised at how much tension was still within the body. I burped again!

The pain in my head numbed and I felt a sense of opening there. I breathed in and noticed a wheeze arising from my lungs. I breathed through my nose and the wheeze was gone. I breathed through my mouth and the wheeze was there. It felt as if there was something trapped in the lungs. I burped again!

Both cats came out and sat next to me. I felt like I was finished, but a sudden tightness in the chest showed me I wasn't. Another burp. I looked at the cats and smiled. They were so adorable.

Suddenly a wave of clarity hit me. I didn't need to be sad to leave. In truth, I wasn't really leaving. A part of me would remain behind in spirit. I'd always be connected to this place, just like the rock. Ibiza was my home. In fact, the whole world was my home. All that was happening was that I was going to see another part of my family in Scotland and continue to write, launch programs and travel to see many other parts of my home.

Excitement bubbled up inside me. I'd been so focused on what I thought I was leaving behind that I'd forgotten about all the great things that were about to happen. Lightness filled me. All the tightness, heaviness and pressure was gone. Even the wheeze from my lungs had softened and changed. I felt happy and knew that my natural release was complete. I felt good. There was a sense of peace within me.

I knew exactly what I was going to do next. I was going to go back to my room, pack my suitcase and tidy all my personal belongings away. This was how I would celebrate the transition that was happening in my life. I could feel my sense of metamorphosis building as 'Traveller Tabi", who only has a backpack with her laptop and clothes, started to emerge. That felt so exciting. I was energized and ready to move forward.

There was a big smile on my face as I embraced the paradox I'd discovered by doing The Nature Process. I was already on an adventure and I was already home. I was leaving nothing behind and yet going nowhere. A smile flashed across my face and I wanted to dance. I felt so much better than I had all day.

This entire process took me twenty-eight minutes in total. It's something you can do in the morning, on your lunchbreak, or in the evening before bed, without it affecting too much of your day.

I hope that by sharing it here with you it helps you to gain additional understanding of how simple The Nature Process can be and that it fills you with excitement to continue to explore it for yourself.

TAKE ACTION

As you can see from my own real-time account, I identified an action step to do following my experience of The Nature Process. This is key as it helps you to move forward and embody the insights you've experienced after having a natural release.

Behaviour change is an integral part of boosting your well-being and enhancing your life. While using the principles/steps of The Nature Process is great, without taking different action to what you were doing before, the benefits of connecting to nature through The Nature Process become nothing more than a band aid placed over a pus-filled wound. It has a temporary beneficial effect but it doesn't deal with the root of the issue.

The point of The Nature Process is to help you create sustainable change within your life. Sustainable in this context means a change that will continue in your life and enhance the quality of it. Being stressed and anxious isn't sustainable. It ultimately destroys you and your well-being. If you use The Nature Process to reduce your stress and anxiety without addressing the underlying cause of it, you're missing the point. Remember, the essence of nature is growth and evolution.

The Nature Process helps you access your creativity and the ability to think in a different way. The principles/steps practised regularly can't help but inspire action. I've seen this again and again in my clients who have changed careers, gone back to university, moved cities and countries, committed to their dreams, found new relationships, started businesses and non-profits, developed better relationships with their loved ones, had children, and even decided to become The Nature Process Facilitator or Coach because of the impact The Nature Process has had on their life. All because connecting to nature has enabled them to think differently and be inspired to take action.

Now, behaviour change is a complicated thing because we are part of a system that conditions how we think and act. It's very rare that our behaviour happens independently of the system we are born into. This is why developing your natural attractions and learning to trust them are so important. You may find yourself gaining an insight that feels really good to you but is also quite scary as it challenges some of the societal stories you grew up with. For example, if your family places high value on a steady, stable career that earns you lots of money, then realising that you're attracted to lower paid or voluntary work, that aims to make a real difference to society, may bring up some conflicting feelings. You will be able to work through those conflicting feelings through using The Nature Process.

Sometimes the action you feel inspired to take doesn't seem to directly connect to what's happening in your life. However, you are a complete being with all aspects of your life interacting and impacting every other part. One of my favourite stories from one of The Nature Process clients is the woman who used The Nature Process to help her conceive twins through IVF. On the day she was due to receive her last treatment my client went to a local park and took herself through The Nature Process into a natural release. The action she was inspired to take was to tidy up the litter in the surrounding area. Now, there's no direct link between picking up litter and conceiving and I'd be mad to suggest otherwise. What this action did though, was to allow her to enter into a state where her body was receptive and ready for the treatment. My client told me that she had no doubt that she would conceive that day and she was right.

What might have been seen as magic hundreds of years ago, was nothing more than my client learning how to listen to her natural body and ensure she was able to release any stress that was stopping her reproductive system from working properly. It wasn't the fact that she picked up the litter on the day of her treatment that helped her conceive. It was the fact that she'd been practising The Nature Process regularly in the months beforehand and learning how to reduce her stress and anxiety around conceiving. Picking up the litter merely helped her to access the same relaxed feelings she'd been tapping into previously.

Natural Systems Thinking Process (NSTP)

It can take a couple of days for your experience with The Nature Process to fully integrate within you. The reason is that what you experience while in the Theta brainwave state of natural presence stays in the Theta brainwave state. As you move out of this state into either an Alpha state (relaxed but alert) or the Beta state (your normal, everyday brainwave state) you are unable to access the information you've received.

It's the same process involved with dreams. As you wake up and get caught up in the busyness of your daily life you tend to forget what you dreamt about. Sometimes fragments of the dream will work their way into your consciousness and you get a flash of recall.

The Natural Systems Thinking Process (NSTP) was originally developed by Dr Mike J. Cohen as a way to help people integrate their experiences in nature into their daily life. I've adapted the questions, incorporating elements of coaching into them, so that you are able not only to integrate your experience, but also get insight about what your next steps are as you deepen your connection to nature, boost your well-being and enhance your life. These questions are an integral part of The Nature Process Facilitator training and I often use them with my private clients too.

I recommend doing them immediately after you've gone through The Nature Process, as the experience is more vivid in your memory. Then, after a couple of days, go back and read over what you've written and see if you have any additional insights that have taken a few days to move into your conscious awareness.

1. How did you do the exercise, and what happened when you did it?
2. On a scale of 1-10 (1 = very poor 5 = average 10 = extremely great) how good did you feel before starting as per the instructions?
3. On a scale of 1-10 (1 = very poor 5 = average 10 = extremely great) how good did you feel after doing this exercise?
4. What were the three most important things you learned whilst doing the exercise?
5. Finish this sentence in three different ways (e.g. I feel the wind in my hair and I feel refreshed): I am a person who gets good feelings when ___.
6. Does this exercise enhance your sense of self-worth? Your trustfulness of nature?
7. How would you feel if this experience was taken away from you?
8. Did you have any negative signals (feelings, memories) during the exercise?
9. Do you have any fears, concerns, or reservations about moving forward?
10. What one or two keywords symbolise this experience for you?
11. What short power sentence conveys the contribution this exercise makes to your growth?
12. Who could you share this experience with?

If you're not attracted to journaling about your experience, you can also use audio and video to capture the present moment. The challenge with using technology is that it too emits electromagnetic frequencies. If you aren't fully grounded into a Theta brainwave state, then you can actually knock yourself out of it and weaken the power of The Nature Process. If you are going to do this, make sure that you create some distance between you and whatever equipment you choose to use.

You may also want to ground your experience into a physical movement to help you fully embody the experience. Once you have the sensation of feeling good and complete around your experience, focus on the feeling. Ask yourself what movement would best represent the way you feel in the moment. Some people have done hand waves, a shoulder shrug, a hand gesture or even just a small movement with part of their body. Once you have your movement repeat it a few times. This connects the movement to the way you feel. Then at any time you can make this movement and remind yourself of your experience and the way you felt at the time. It's no substitute for being out in nature, though it's a great tool to use whenever you can't get outside for whatever reason.

THE NATURE PROCESS BASIC STEPS

As I've stated again and again, The Nature Process is a set of principles/steps. As you develop confidence in using The Nature Process you'll discover there is no right or wrong way to do it. The more you engage with nature, the more you'll find that you will have your own way of working with The Nature Process that is unique to you.

Making The Nature Process your own requires a deep level of trust. You have to be able to trust that you can enter a state of natural presence at will, that your natural body knows exactly how to release stress and anxiety without your human thoughts and stories getting in the way. You also have to trust that you already know how to follow your natural attractions and that, deep down, you already know how to do The Nature Process.

However, if you want to experience The Nature Process as a set of basic steps, I've outlined the structure below for you to follow.

1. Set your intention for what you want to experience/learn with the support of The Nature Process. You'll refer to this intention throughout this series of steps. Give yourself a minute to become clear on this and observe any physical sensations within the body as you do.
2. Find a natural environment, whether indoors or out, that you want to use to help you enter a state of natural presence. Give yourself

five or ten minutes exploring your surroundings with the fifty-four senses.

3. Turn your sense of awareness inwards to your body and become aware of the thoughts, feelings, and sensations that arise within your natural body as you reflect on your intention for this experience. Do the body awareness exercise and mentally scan your body. Give yourself a few minutes to really tune into the body's intelligence.

4. Use your fifty-four senses to find a part of nature that you are attracted to. Spend a minute exploring this natural attraction with only your senses. Then ask yourself why you find this part of nature attractive before reframing the sentence to why you find yourself attractive in the same way. Take a moment and reflect upon how this statement could relate to your intention for this experience.

5. Use the permission exercise from natural communication to discover whether it's ok for you to fully connect with this part of nature. Give yourself a minute to receive the answer, observing any thoughts, feelings, and sensations that arise as you do.

6. Bring yourself back into balance with a natural release, allowing your body to move and do whatever feels good. Imagine the power of nature flowing through you, refreshing and revitalising you as your body returns to a state of balance and harmony.

7. Ask yourself, "What's the next thing I need to do to move forward?" Give yourself a few minutes to listen for any guidance from your inner nature. Listen to it, no matter how strange or confusing it seems. Once you feel complete offer thanks to the part of nature that you have been connecting with and return to your daily life.

8. Schedule some time to complete the NSTP process and reflect upon your experience.

If at any point, you feel that you are forcing any part of the process, stop. I've had clients who have gone out with the intention of doing The Nature Process basic steps and instead discovered that what they have needed the most is to experience and stay in a state of natural presence and natural body.

As I've said to them, this comes back to trust. Let go of any expectations of how you think the process should and will work for you. Stay open to the experience and let go of any judgment. You will get the exact experience you need, even if it's not what you expected. Once I've explored my client's experience with them, they tend to end up agreeing with this and laughing at how their human stories were getting in the way of what was actually a beautiful experience.

INTEGRATING THE NATURE PROCESS INTO YOUR DAILY LIFE

The purpose of The Nature Process is that it's easy to integrate into your daily life without much disruption to your routine. Today, the majority of us live in towns and cities. While getting "back to nature" and exploring the wilderness is a wonderful idea, in practise it's not that easy when you have the daily demands of work, family and finances, etc. Finding time to spend a whole day in nature can be a challenge. I teach this and I still struggle to pull myself away from the laptop and get outside at times!

The key to making The Nature Process a part of your daily life is to keep it simple. Start by putting nature pictures as your screensaver on your phone and computer. Then, consider getting a plant or two for your house or workplace if you don't have some already. Leave the house five minutes earlier so that you can stop, breathe and explore the nature that's present around you with your senses before you continue on during the day. Go to a window and spend time exploring the nature that you can see from it. Find a nearby park where you can go and have a walk during your lunchbreak. Count the number of trees you see as you travel. Explore a different route home and travel slower to see what nature you can observe and explore, stopping only if you feel attracted to. When it's dark, stand outside for five minutes and observe the night sky. At the weekends, plan a walk to a nearby nature spot with your family or friends. These simple actions will help you develop your natural presence and inspire you to explore more of The Nature Process just because it feels good to do so.

If you're attracted to explore natural release further, then go and do the 'Experiencing Natural Release Exercise' on page 233.

Exercises to Practise in Nature

* Explore the different thoughts, feelings, and sensations that arise as you experiment with putting your hands on different parts of nature and then notice what sensations you experience when you remove them.
* Find a part of nature that attracts you and imagine what it would be like to be it. How does it move? Where does it get its nutrients from? How does it interact with the rest of the natural world?
* Experiment with different ways of breathing – deep and slow, short and fast, pausing between breaths, etc. - and notice what thoughts, feelings, and sensations arise as your breathing changes.
* Go to one of your favourite natural spots and reflect upon what this setting does to keep itself in balance and discover if there's anything you can do to help support this balance.

Key Points to Remember

* Use your heart and feelings of love as a way to help activate your parasympathetic nervous system and create a feeling of calmness and connection that supports you to move into natural release.
* Imagine the electromagnetic field of the heart expanding and connecting to the Earth so that there is an energy flow between you and the part of nature you were naturally attracted to working with.
* Focus on your breath, recognising that every time you breathe in oxygen you are breathing in a gift from the trees while every time you breathe out you are exhaling a gift for the trees.

- Natural Release, as a part of The Nature Process, is a simple way of consciously focusing on the relationship that exists between you and the natural world and using it to help you cope with the challenges of daily life.

- After you've completed a natural release, take a moment and listen to your inner nature about what the next step you need to take to move forward is and then do it. This helps you embody your experience.

- You can also help integrate your experience of The Nature Process by using the Natural Systems Thinking Process (NSTP) to help you reflect about what happened when you connected to nature.

- The basic structure of The Nature Process follows the following steps:
    a. Set your intention for your time in nature
    b. Move into a state of natural presence
    c. Discover the sensations in your natural body related to your attention
    d. Find your natural attraction in nature and what you can learn about yourself from it
    e. Get permission to move into natural communication with this part of nature
    f. Allow yourself to experience natural release
    g. Get clear on the next step you need to take to boost your well-being and enhance your life

- Explore how to experience all or some of The Nature Process in your daily life so it becomes easy and effortless to make it part of your routine.

QUESTIONS FOR REFLECTION

- What do you believe about the power of the heart?
- How often do you use your imagination to explore what you want in life?

- What does the act of breathing mean to you?
- How often do you feel balanced and whole?
- What can you do to experience more nature in your daily life?
- What are you attracted to doing to help you integrate your nature experiences into your daily life?

CHAPTER 8

Get Out of Your Own Way

❧ ❧ ❧

The true value of a human being is determined primarily by the measure and the sense in which he has attained to liberation from the self.

- ALBERT EINSTEIN

WHAT WILL STOP YOU FROM fully engaging with The Nature Process are the stories and beliefs you possess that have moved your natural attractions from nature to culture. We first explored the impact of cultural stories in the chapter on natural attractions. This chapter offers an in-depth exploration of the ways in which you can prevent yourself from getting caught up in some of the key pitfalls that people encounter when connecting deeply with nature, along with exercises that can help you explore these pitfalls.

While we like to think that we are fully in control of our lives and exercising free will at all times, that's not strictly true.

Our identity is made up of thousands upon thousands of stories and beliefs that we've had ingrained into us since we were born. We experience more thoughts than we are consciously aware of. These thoughts drive our behaviour whether we are aware of the thoughts or not.

As an example, research shows that despite our thinking we have conscious control over the movements of our body, the body is already in the process of moving before the thought to move consciously registers in our awareness. As the Zen quote says, "Relax, nothing is under control!"

Another example is learning to walk. As a young child, you needed to put all your attention and focus upon learning the skills of walking. It took numerous attempts to learn how to pull yourself up, balance on two legs and co-ordinate your motor skills to walk even a short distance. Now, unless you suffer from a disability, you do it automatically and without conscious thought.

Resistance is actually the tension created by using your conscious awareness to create new thought patterns and behaviours. It takes time and repetitive action to make changes to your life that will enhance your well-being. You don't get six pack abs from doing sit ups once. You don't learn to play the piano from one lesson. You don't deeply connect to nature from going outdoors once. Research shows that when we are in a Beta brainwave state (your everyday level of brain activity) it takes thousands of attempts to change behaviour. When you're in a Theta brainwave state (as you are in the state of natural presence) behaviour change can be achieved in only one or two attempts. This is why it's key to be able to identify a Theta brainwave state and access it at will.

Fear is a symptom of a stress response, as we discussed in the chapter on natural body. It's also a sign that you are disconnecting from your own inner nature. The first thing you need to do if you start to experience resistance, is to explore where your fear is coming from.

With regards to the stories and beliefs we hold about ourselves and the world around us, we can become so attached to them that we believe they are part of who we are – whether they are supporting us or not. This has a negative effect upon, not only our health and well-being, but also impacts any changes we try to make in our lives.

SUGGESTED EXERCISE:
Go outside and pick up a rock that's small enough to fit in one hand, but still heavy. Start walking. As you continue walking notice how you and your body start adapting to carrying it. Tap into your natural body and notice the physical changes.

Then, bring your awareness to the surrounding area in which you're walking and start to explore it with your senses.

Notice how the stone will start to get more comfortable in your hand and that you may even forget that you are carrying it.

Let go of the stone. Notice the difference in the body as you do.

Reflect on how this relates to holding onto stories and beliefs about who you are.

BE AWARE OF YOUR DISTRACTION BEHAVIOURS

In our modern, busy world there are so many distractions, and it's easy to get caught up in them. I eat, breathe and sleep nature, literally as well as metaphorically. Yet even I still find myself getting distracted and putting off going outside to experience any part of The Nature Process. I might drink a little bit too much wine, or spend time surfing the internet wondering what on earth I was looking for again. That's the moment I put everything down and go to nature.

When we engage in unconscious behaviour that is counter-productive to what we want to achieve in life, then there's a good chance that we're engaging in distraction behaviour. This is a form of coping that helps numb our capacity to feel stress and anxiety without actually doing anything to help reduce it.

It's important to recognise that there's nothing wrong with distraction behaviours. What's important is to recognise them for what they are. If we start to judge our actions because they are inconsistent to what we want to do and start saying that we should be doing something different, all that happens is we create even more stress and anxiety.

Acknowledge that you are engaging in distraction behaviours. Some common ones are watching too much TV, eating too much unhealthy food, spending too much time on the computer, or drinking too much.

The problem with engaging in distraction behaviours, without acknowledging that you're doing it, is that you'll start justifying to yourself why you're not going outside and doing any part of The Nature Process. If you're truly not interested in going outside, you'll be able to acknowledge that you're just not attracted to it. However, if you're not going outside because it's too cold, or raining, or too hot, or you've got more important things to do, then that's distraction.

Once you've acknowledged that you are distracting yourself, accept the behaviour and make it ok. From here you can start to explore the reasons why you may be distracting yourself. Once you understand the reasons, you can then start to take different action by creating a plan.

This is nothing more than giving yourself time and space to reflect on when you engage in distraction behaviours and what else may be happening when you do so. By giving yourself this time and space you're then able to think of an alternative action to do instead. When you think of an alternative action when you are relaxed and calm it means that this action will be better than one decided in the heat of the moment. It also allows you to prepare yourself to do things differently.

SUGGESTED EXERCISE:
Go for a walk outside and reflect upon the following questions:

* What distraction behaviours do you typically engage in?
* When do you most commonly engage in these behaviours?
* How do you feel when you are engaging in these behaviours?
* What would be a more attractive activity to engage in?
* How can you plan to do this activity so that you would be less likely to engage in distraction behaviours?

ACKNOWLEDGE YOUR EMOTIONS

Something else that can mean you're getting in your own way when you start to practise the principles/steps of The Nature Process is by disconnecting from how you really feel. Typically, we humans want to feel happy and find it challenging to engage with our more difficult emotions, especially when they trigger feelings of stress and anxiety. As a result, we can engage in defence mechanisms, which are largely unconscious.

One common way in which we can refuse to acknowledge our emotions is through denying that we feel that way. We pretend to be happy when deep down we're not. We don't let others see that they have frustrated us or annoyed us and pretend that everything's fine. The problem with this is that the body's natural wisdom knows that something is wrong but can't do anything to rebalance itself. Alexander Lowen, who developed a psychotherapeutic body technique called bioenergetics, stated that he could read a person's emotional history through how they carried the body. When you deny how you feel, your body holds onto the emotional energy.

Another common way around acknowledging our emotions is through projecting them onto other people. We may call other people rude and angry, yet don't see the rudeness and anger within ourselves. We may call others liars and cheats because we don't want to acknowledge those behaviours within ourselves and how we feel about this. Again, our body knows the truth.

We also have to be clear when we empathise with others, that we are not assuming they're feeling something due to emotions that we ourselves haven't acknowledged. Instead of accurately interpreting how the other person is feeling, we are tapping into how we ourselves would feel in that situation. While we do possess mirror neurons in our brain which allow us to experience what someone else is going through, it is possible that our own previous experiences can get in the way of this empathizing.

You'll know that you're not owning your own emotions if you get defensive and feel the need to let other people know how you feel, often interrupting them as you do. This has been the driving factor behind a lot of the environmental activism movement in the past, though thankfully this is changing.

When you don't own your emotions, you have no hope of changing them. Once you own how you feel, then you can let it go. That's why The Nature Process is so powerful. It allows you to do this by acknowledging the stress and anxiety created by the stories and beliefs that you have, then creates the space for you to acknowledge and release them, creating a more empowering story and emotional state.

Suggested Exercise:

Get a piece of paper and draw a line writing the word 'birth' at the left-hand side of the line and your current age at the right-hand side of the line. Think back over your life and draw a horizontal line for any major life events at the approximate age it happened. These life events can be good or bad.

For each life event reflect on, or journal, the following questions:

* What physical sensations do you notice in the body when you think of this life event?
* What phrases come to mind when you think of this life event?
* Do the physical sensations and phrases reflect a sense of peace and acceptance about this life event?
* Is there anything about this event that you wish to explore further by using The Nature Process?

Finally, give yourself some extra time to reflect on, or journal these additional questions:

* How do you feel about humanity's current relationship with the Earth?
* Is there anything you wish to take to nature and explore further to receive clarity and insight on?

Explore Your Beliefs About Nature

We all have hidden beliefs about nature. Many of them aren't even our own. They've been culturally ingrained into us over the last two thousand plus years, creating a story of nature as something humans have the right to control and use for their own gain.

This story goes right back to the first chapter of the Bible. Genesis 1:28 says:

"And God blessed them, and God said unto them, be fruitful, and multiply, and replenish the earth, and subdue it: and have dominion over the fish of the sea, and over the fowl of the air, and over every living thing that moveth upon the earth."

This belief has driven our modern western Christian society forward, giving us God's permission to basically do what we want to the earth in the belief that, not only is it our right, but God will save us from our actions in the afterlife.

Throughout history, this belief has been reinforced again and again. In the sixteenth century, Sir Francis Bacon argued that the only way to gain objective scientific knowledge was to separate ourselves from nature and to "conquer and subdue" it. Incidentally, he also referred to nature as a "common harlot," thus helping to create the idea that nature and women were linked.

Bacon developed his ideas right in the middle of the witch trials that spread across Europe between the fifteenth and the eighteenth centuries. As I mentioned in the chapter on natural attractions, this was a period of time when thousands of victims—primarily women—were accused of witchcraft and burned at the stake. Many of them were natural healers, women who lived alone with cats, or women who were outspoken and disobedient.

Rene Descartes, the man responsible for creating mind/body dualism as mentioned in chapter one, claimed that the goal of mind/body dualism was to "make ourselves masters and possessors of nature."

John Locke, the English philosopher and physician, who was one of the most influential thinkers of the Enlightenment, told us that, "Land that is left wholly to nature, is called as indeed it is, waste."

Whether you like it or not, these beliefs have been floating around influencing you since you were a child. Think about the other things you've been told about nature. It's dirty and unclean. It's dangerous and scary. It's uncomfortable and hard to survive in.

These stories can influence how we engage and interact with nature. If you've not explored what you think about nature, it's possible that these unconscious stories can impact your ability to engage fully with the principles/steps of The Nature Process.

In the first chapter of this book I encouraged you to start exploring your beliefs about nature. I am mentioning it again here to reinforce the power of questioning what you really think about the natural world. When you are able to go beyond your human stories, both positive and negative, you will discover a deeper relationship to nature than you thought possible.

SUGGESTED EXERCISE:
Go for a walk outside and reflect upon the following questions:

* When you think of nature what ten words come to mind?
* What are some of the cultural stories about nature that you grew up with?

BE AWARE OF HOW YOU TALK ABOUT THE ENVIRONMENT

When talking about nature, there's empowered language and there's disempowered language. I mentioned earlier in the chapter about how much of the environmental activist movement is tied into trying to guilt and shame us into making changes. This is further supported by the language that's used by many in the environmental movement. We talk about saving the planet and protecting it. We say that it's a fragile planet and is in peril.

This language actually blocks you from being able to connect deeply to nature and develop a relationship with it. If you view nature and the planet as something that's weak and at risk, then you don't consider it your equal. Furthermore, as part of nature yourself you're also viewing yourself as weak too. How then are you able to reduce your stress and anxiety by unconsciously considering yourself weak? And if you view nature as something that's at risk, how then can you truly engage with it and receive the benefits of doing so?

One of the reasons that I grounded natural communication in chapter six into James Lovelock's Gaia hypothesis, is to help you see just how adept the planet is at keeping itself in balance and has been able to do so for billions of years. The planet knows more about what it's doing than we do. To pretend any different is to commit the cardinal sin of being human: that of assuming we know best.

If we humans were truly bringing the planet completely out of balance, nature would have wiped us out by now. If we continue our destructive behaviour, then that's probably what's going to happen. The planet is not going to get caught up in guilt and shame over whether or not we survive. Those emotions belong firmly in the realm of humans.

When we scale the planet existence of 4.6 billion years into forty-six years, it's said that humans have been around for approximately four hours with the industrial revolution starting only a minute ago. This point is usually made along with the example that in that minute we've destroyed over fifty percent of the Earth's forests. But let's consider this from the Earth's perspective. It's been four hours since humans evolved on Earth and it's only been a minute since we've started behaving in a way that doesn't support life on Earth. In that minute the Earth's own self-regulating system has already kicked in. It's melting ice caps to raise the sea level. Should the Earth's temperature increase by the four degrees predicted by our current rate of carbon emissions, many of the major cities of the world will be underwater. We are experiencing more extreme weather events. The ocean is acidifying. Our ability to produce food is being affected. Oxygen production is decreasing. The Earth isn't weak and fragile. It's a seriously hardcore motherf***er that's determined to bring itself back into balance and destroy the "virus" that's affecting its health and well-being. In another four hours, it'll be completely recovered.

It's our own fear over the thought of being wiped out that drives so many of our actions towards the environment. Remember, fear is a sign that we are disconnected from nature and that we need to reconnect. Any action we take towards saving or protecting the environment from this place of fear is actually going to have the opposite effect.

For example, in the documentary, *Confessions of an Eco-terrorist*, they talk about the annual seal culls in Canada. It's proposed that the amount of money made from people flocking to the area to protest the seal cull, and get their pictures taken with the cute baby seals, actually makes it worthwhile to con-tinue the cull. Now, I don't know if this is true or not, but what I do know is that we need to clearly question our motives before taking any action to ensure that we are acting for the highest good of all involved.

We also need to acknowledge how our own understanding of the way nature works may be limited. This is something that James Lovelock, who initially developed the Gaia hypothesis, did. He was one of the alarmists who predicted that the earth would be destroyed by human activity by now. Yet his perspective has changed dramatically. In a UK TV interview in April 2014 he turned around and actually heavily criticized the United Nations Intergovernmental Panel on Climate Change (IPCC) as relying on guesses as to what is really happening on earth right now.

Scientists state that we are in the age of the sixth great extinction, brought on by human behaviour. This is when there's a widespread and rapid decrease of the amount of life on earth. The last time this happened was 65 million years ago, with the extinction of the dinosaurs. Their death made room for mammals to become the dominant class on earth and for us to exist as we now do today.

The thing is that when we look at the evolution of the Earth itself, we discover that each time there was a great extinction event on Earth, life then evolved dramatically afterwards. Is it possible that what we call extinction really is the start of an evolutionary process that our human perspective strug-gles to see?

Suggested Exercise:

Write about the environment for one minute non-stop. Don't edit what you write or stop and think about it. Allow whatever comes to mind to be expressed.

Read what you've written and identify any language that you consider to be disempowering. Rewrite the sentence in a way that feels empowering and inspires you to deepen your connection even more.

MAKE PEACE WITH CLIMATE CHANGE

In the last section I touched upon the impacts of climate change. This section is about acknowledging the feelings you may have about that. It's something that's not talked about freely in our society. What do you do with the feelings of grief that you have about humanity's current behaviour towards the earth?

This is something that I've personally spent years working on. The pain of seeing how we are destroying life can be unbearable. Yet every day I find more and more evidence that shows how humanity is taking action and changing its behaviour. If you're struggling to find inspiration, then you need to listen to *Sustainable: The Podcast* (www.earthself.org/sustainable-the-podcast). Hosted by myself, it features inspirational interviews with people who are leading the way to creating a sustainable world for all.

Yet when change seems to be taking so long (from our human perspective) it can be hard to stay positive. It can also be hard to find people who want to listen to the pain and grief you feel over the destruction of the Earth.

I didn't know who to speak to about this, so I went outside and spoke to the Earth itself. While this might sound like a strange idea, indigenous cultures connected to the Earth have being doing this all along.

Tell the Earth of the grief you feel over the damage that's happening to it. Tell the Earth how much you love and appreciate it. Tell the Earth you don't want to let it die. Allow yourself to cry. Use The Nature Process and discover what's on the other side of your grief. Feel the power of a being that's existed for 4.6 billion years and see what it has to tell you about climate change.

Climate change is not necessarily a bad thing. That's a human judgment. Change can be used as a catalyst for growth and transformation. What would be "bad" is if we didn't use climate change as an opportunity to create a world that is truly sustainable for all life.

The following exercise is pretty intensive. It's something that will take you a few weeks to complete and will require you to use The Nature Process as part of it. However, if you're struggling with grief about climate change it will definitely help.

S<small>UGGESTED</small> E<small>XERCISE</small>:
Explore the following questions through journaling. Remember there are no right or wrong answers, only your answers.

- What do you feel about climate change?
- When you read about the destruction of the planet what do you want to do?
- How do you feel about the idea that nothing seems to be happening quick enough in terms of taking real action to stop the impact of climate change?
- Who do you feel is to blame for this?
- How do you want to feel about climate change?
- What would you like to do to make a difference?
- What actions do you take in your daily life that support how you feel about climate change?
- Who do you have in your life that you can share your feelings with and feel supported?
- How do you currently deal with the emotions you feel around climate change?
- How effective is the way you're dealing with emotions?
- What issues in particular are causing you the most stress and anxiety and how can you use The Nature Process to help with this?
- What aspects of climate change are you most passionate about and why?
- What action can you take that will make a difference with these issues?
- How can you make sure that you don't end up tired, burnt out and stressed from taking action?
- How can you acknowledge that the small things you do add up to make a big impact?

- How has taking action against climate change made you a better person?
- What has changed in your life as a result of your commitment to taking action against climate change?
- What changes are you seeing in the world as a result of action being taken against climate change?
- How can you be grateful for this?
- What can you do to stay positive when you hear more news about the negative impacts of climate change?
- How can you celebrate the action that you and others are taking?

Be Discerning About "Green" Marketing

Green marketing refers to products or services that claim to be better for the environment. With the increasing awareness of the impact of global warming and climate change, products that are good for the environment represent a market worth over £4 billion per year worldwide. This market is known as LOHAS (lifestyles of health and sustainability), a term coined by Paul Ray and Sherry Anderson, co-authors of *The Cultural Creatives: How 50 million people are changing the world*. If you are passionate about environmental and social justice, care about human rights, believe in fair trade and sustainable practices and have an interest in personal or spiritual development, then you're considered part of this market!

With the rise of green marketing comes greenwashing. This is marketing of a product or company in such a way that it promotes being environmentally friendly, when in reality it isn't. Examples of this are when a company spends more money promoting itself as environmentally friendly than actually engaging in environmentally sound practices, or creating a product name that suggests it's more natural than it actually is.

This can make it very hard for you as a consumer to know exactly what products and services are in fact "green." It requires you going beyond the marketing to research more about the products and services you're considering. Don't take anything at face value.

According to the Underwriters Laboratories 2010 report on greenwashing, ninety-five percent of consumer products that claimed to be green committed at least one of the seven sins of greenwashing.

The seven sins are:

1. Sin of the hidden trade-off – suggesting a product is green without addressing all factors of its production and only focusing on one small part of its production.
2. Sin of no proof – making an environmental claim without third party evidence to back up the claim.
3. Sin of vagueness – using a term that's so broad or vague it is likely to be misunderstood by the consumer.
4. Sin of worshipping false labels – a product that gives the impression, through images or words, of a third-party endorsement when none actually exists.
5. Sin of irrelevance – stating an environmental claim that is unhelpful or unimportant for consumers searching for an environmentally-friendly product.
6. Sin of lesser of two evils – a claim that might be true about the product, that has the potential to distract the consumer from the greater environmental impacts of the category the product belongs to as a whole.
7. Sin of fibbing – a claim that is not true.

Take Ecover as an example. It's a Belgium based company that manufactures ecologically sound products. Yet in June 2014, Ecover admitted that they were using ingredients derived from "synthetically modified organisms" which are the next wave of GMOs to enter our marketplace. Synthetic biology has been classed as "extreme genetic engineering." How does that fit into being ecologically sound? Does that change your perception of the company?

Another area where "green" marketing is prevalent is the beauty industry. There are wonderful products marketed as natural and soft and gentle on your skin. Yet when you actually look at the ingredients, they're manufactured using chemicals that have been connected to causing cancer or are not as natural as they advertise.

Even our food has been taken over by "green" marketing. If you go to any health food shop you'll see a bewildering array of foods that you've never heard of, all packaged up as the next super food designed to bring your body back into balance and counteract the effects of the toxic environment we now live in. Yet science doesn't back up the claims of superfoods and suggests that it's nothing more than an effective marketing technique.

Now, all of this might seem as if I've digressed slightly from talking about The Nature Process. I've not. If you buy into the "green" marketing, you buy into a disconnect from nature that will not allow you to experience the full power of The Nature Process, and furthermore may cause you to discount your experiences because they run contradictory to what you hear through marketing and media.

The power you have as a consumer is far more than you think. We still live in a world where money speaks louder than nature. Use your money as a force of good for the planet. Companies will follow your lead. If you don't buy products that are harmful to the Earth, they won't make them. It really is as simple as that.

Suggested Exercise:
Find out more about greenwashing and research the companies that are doing the most to help support the Earth and create a sustainable world for everyone. Then buy your products from them.

Let Outer Nature Reflect Your Inner Nature

Nature offers us a mirror with which we're able to see ourselves clearly. You have a choice in which parts of yourself you choose to examine. To let go of stress and anxiety and improve your well-being and your life, it's essential that you tap into the strength and power within nature.

Actively seek out parts of nature that inspire you. Then take action to create more of that in your life. Our brains naturally remember the unpleasant things more than the good ones. If you reinforce this by focusing on the pain and destruction of nature, then you're focusing on your own pain and destruction too.

Not only are you focusing on your disconnect from nature and the ways in which you are not connected to your own inner nature, but you're allowing your body to stay in a stress response, which, as you discovered in the chapter on natural body, isn't a good state to be in. Remember, your senses of pain, distress or fear are signs that you're disconnecting from nature.

You won't reduce stress and anxiety by focusing on things that cause you more stress and anxiety. Not even in the natural world. Always look for what makes you feel good. Doing so helps reframe your perspective and deepens your connection to nature so that you can harness its benefits.

If you follow The Nature Process as I've outlined here in the book, you will not experience pain, distress, and fear in nature. If you do, then it's imperative that you shift and connect to something that makes you feel good. That's the essence of natural attractions.

This is something you will have to practise. We are not trained by our society to naturally move towards things that make us feel good. We're trained to make the most of a bad situation. That's why so many of us who have bought into what society tells us we should do with our lives, achieve the goals society has set up but then still feel unfulfilled and unsatisfied with our lives.

Become fulfilled and satisfied through your connection to the natural world and then watch the impact of this on all other areas of your life. As you recognise how good it feels to be connected to nature – both around you and inside you - you won't be able to do anything else but continue to follow your natural attractions and do what feels good more and more of the time.

SUGGESTED EXERCISE:
Buy a small notebook and start a daily fulfilment diary. Each day write down the things you did that gave you a feeling of satisfaction, no matter how

small. At the end of each month read back over the entries and note the re-curring things you did that made you feel fulfilled and satisfied. Then, once you've identified them, create a plan to do more of them. At the end of three months, read back over all the entries and reflect upon how satisfied and fulfilled you feel with your life. If you feel that there's still room for improve-ment, think about what area of your life doesn't fulfil or satisfy you and then create a plan of action. Review the plan in your next monthly reflection and look at how you can continue to improve it. Do this for a minimum of six months.

BE SCEPTICAL

Dr Michael J. Cohen of Project NatureConnect, who developed the work around the fifty-four senses, natural attractions, and the permission exercise that form the basis for The Nature Process, has a great expression: "I'll trust science when it figures out how to turn grass into milk."

Don't put all your trust into science. While it's great for helping us un-derstand the world that we live in better, it doesn't know everything. Our scientific models fail to capture the full complexity of the world in which we live in and tend to focus on one part of the system rather than studying it as a whole. They are also based upon assumptions of how the world works that are fundamentally unprovable, which can influence the researcher's conclusions.

Furthermore, science can have a habit of making you forget just how mys-terious and magical nature is. As my man, Einstein, said:

"There are only two ways to live your life. One is as though nothing is a miracle. The other is as though everything is a miracle."

If you are not viewing your life as a miracle while you go through The Nature Process, then it's a sign you're not fully engaging with it. I promise you, what's contained in this book will take you on a journey into nature that you've never experienced before.

It's possible that as you go further into The Nature Process, you might start discounting your natural attractions. You may start to limit what you think is possible and not allow yourself to fully explore where you can go with nature.

The thing is, you can go as deep into nature as you allow yourself to. In the introduction, I offered you the opportunity to swallow the red pill, enter the rabbit hole, and see how far it'll take you into the earth. Think of Alice's disbelief as she entered Wonderland and how curious she found it. As you consciously connect with nature you'll experience the same thing.

When you engage in natural communication with nature, you get insights that may seem a little bizarre. These insights will test your understanding of both yourself and the world. They're supposed to.

Take a moment and think about it. I have conversations with bugs, as I've told you about in this book! Do you know how bizarre that is for me? As I worked on this chapter I had a flying beetle land on my keyboard and crawl around it while a moth has danced around my head before landing on my leg. It's taken a huge stretch of my imagination to accept that there was conversation going on between us. In fact, while I have an idea of what they were communicating, I still need some time to fully process that.

It's just like the whole Roachie story. I mean, seriously. I carried a cockroach in my luggage to release it back into the wild when I arrived in France! Who on earth does that?

You have no idea what's possible when you fully connect to nature in a conscious manner. This book is only the beginning. I've focused on consciously connecting to nature for nearly thirteen years and have a deeper understanding of it than most people I meet. Yet I know I'm just at the tip of the iceberg in what's possible for me to learn from nature, both about myself and the world as I keep doing The Nature Process.

I trust nature. I let go and let my imagination run free as I engage in The Nature Process because I know that it's only through this that I can keep on stepping up into my natural power.

Whatever you get when you consciously connect with nature through The Nature Process is right, even if you initially interpret it wrong. Trust it. Go with it. Keep at this. Develop your imagination so that it's so powerful you never doubt the information you receive. Even if it takes you a while to properly translate it!

Suggested Exercise:

Keep a sceptical yet open-mind when reading scientific articles and non-scientific articles, as well as when practising The Nature Process. Ask yourself, "How do they/I know this is true?" Research and learn more about the topics/ your experience. Pay attention to the arguments and viewpoints that differ. Consider the different perspectives before arriving at a conclusion. Stay open to changing your perspective and understanding of both science as well as your personal experiences in nature.

Learn How to Stay Connected

Our natural state of being with nature is a state of connection. To be in a state of disconnect from nature is a learned experience. If you find yourself getting frustrated with any part of The Nature Process, ask yourself what you are doing in that moment to keep yourself in a state of disconnect.

Many times, when this happens you'll find that you are not fully engaging your natural presence, so your Theta brainwave state is not stable. You're then letting your mind get in the way and judge what you're experiencing or interpret it incorrectly due to some of the concepts I've mentioned earlier. Remember there is no right or wrong in nature, there is only nature.

If you're not able to stay connected to nature even when your mind questions it, you've not gone deep enough into your natural presence. Ideally you need to use your natural presence every day, even if it's just for five minutes as you stare out of the kitchen window while preparing dinner.

You'll find that it actually requires more effort to stay disconnected that it does to remain connected. Frequently, when people feel disconnected from nature it's because they've chosen to focus on the three senses (pain, distress, fear) that are signals for us to reconnect. Don't be one of these people.

Even if it takes you a few minutes of feeling helpless and powerless before you reconnect to nature, that's ok. You're way ahead of most of the other people out in the world.

The more that you notice when you are disconnecting yourself from nature, then the more you'll be able to bring yourself back into the connection, until The Nature Process is such a part of your life that you don't have to think about it. You just follow Nike's example and "Do it."

Suggested Exercise:
Check in with yourself every morning and evening and ask yourself how connected to nature you feel on a scale of 1-10 with one being not at all and ten being totally connected.

Key Points to Remember

 * You are not in control of your thoughts and behaviour as much as you believe. The family and societal stories you learned as a child influence your behaviour. Become aware of how they impact your life.
 * Learn to recognise your distraction behaviours and explore why you are engaging in them.
 * Become aware of how you really feel and recognise that it's ok to feel like that.
 * Discover the stories you have about nature that you may not have recognised until now.
 * Explore the language you use when you talk about nature and make sure it reflects the true power of nature.
 * Understand how you really feel about climate change and work through any challenging feelings.
 * Learn when marketing and the media are lying to you about the impact of their products on the environment or on your body.

- Use nature as a mirror to reflect back to you your greatest strengths and not your weaknesses.
- Keep an open mind when faced with facts/experiences and explore their validity for yourself.
- Keep working on developing a connection to nature that is present at all times and becomes part of your daily life.

CHAPTER 9

What Happens When You Connect Deeply to Nature

When I examine myself and my methods of thought I come
to the conclusion that the gift of fantasy has meant more to
me than my talent for absorbing positive knowledge.

- ALBERT EINSTEIN

As you've been reading this book, I hope you committed to doing the exercises and really experience the power of The Nature Process. It's one thing to know something intellectually but it's another thing to fully embody the knowledge. I keep on repeating myself with this but it's important you understand this. Experiencing and embodying something takes your understanding to a whole new level and without it, The Nature Process is nothing more than an interesting tool that you're not really getting a lot out of.

When I first started my coach training I was intimidated by the many names and books people would mention as having read. I quickly realised that many of these people were reading the books but not implementing things from them. Publishing statistics on self-help books show that eighty percent of people who buy the books are repeat buyers, which suggests that they're not helping.

I know The Nature Process makes a difference in your life. My clients have told me. The fact that there's an entire body of existing research that shows the benefits of interacting with nature, already highlights the validity of this process.

If you haven't, now is the time to go back and start doing the exercises outlined in this book. Doing so will make The Nature Process real and tangible for you in a way that reading this book won't. This book is merely a tool to help you open your mind enough, to go beyond the cultural stories we have about nature, discover what it really means to be connected to nature and use that connection to boost your well-being and enhance your life.

What you get from The Nature Process depends on how much you practise the exercises in the book. The clients of mine that have received the most benefit from doing The Nature Process are those who practise it regularly. Clients report that, even though they have always been drawn to spending time in nature, The Nature Process has shown them that they've only begun to scratch the surface of what's possible. They receive valuable lessons from observing nature and applying its wisdom to their life. The Nature Process becomes a tool that they return to again and again. For some, The Nature Process even becomes a form of prayer. My clients comment on how alive and powerful they feel. The Nature Process has helped them heal past wounds, prepare themselves for new relationships, new jobs and new additions to the family. As a result, they spend even more time outdoors. Some clients say how connecting to nature has changed their world completely. Even those clients who already considered themselves deeply connected to nature, found themselves going deeper into this connection and considering it one of the most profound journeys of their life.

WHAT EINSTEIN, JESUS AND BUDDHA HAVE IN COMMON

Throughout this book, I've used quotes by Einstein as he, for me, is one of the greatest thinkers of the twentieth century. I once met someone who knew Einstein when she was a child (how cool is that?). He was a friend of the family of her best friend in childhood. Her memories of him were of a sweet, caring man who played the violin very well and kept turning up late because he had got lost in the gardens, literally smelling the flowers, on his way over. That story has connected me more to Einstein than anything else. When combined with the quotes throughout this book it gives me a sense of a man whose understanding was far beyond the worldview of his time.

The thing is though, a love and respect of nature isn't enough. You need to have a connection to nature. Hitler is a great example of this. In *Mein Kampf*, Hitler stated that for everything, nature was the best teacher. He explained that if people tried to work against nature it would lead to their downfall and that humans could never become the masters of nature. However, it's quite clear that Hitler was not connected to nature in any form. His senses were so out of balance that his fundamental disconnection to nature led to the deaths of more than 5.5 million Jews, and millions of other people because he couldn't understand and embody the inherent truth within nature, that we are all one.

Two brilliant, yet anecdotal, examples of people who were truly connected to nature and demonstrate what's possible when you are, are Jesus and Buddha. According to the bible, Jesus spent forty days and forty nights in the desert going through his own nature process before beginning his public ministry. Buddha reached enlightenment after sitting under a Bodhi tree, going through his own nature process after searching for years to end his suffering. And in the last moments before reaching enlightenment, Buddha was asked by the Demon Mara, to tell him who was witness to this claim of enlightenment. Buddha touched the Earth and the Earth acknowledged itself as witness. Both Jesus and Buddha have left a lasting legacy of love and compassion for all beings on Earth that still profoundly affects millions today. Who knows what's possible for you as you do The Nature Process!

Once you understand the principles /steps of The Nature Process, you'll be able to play with them and adapt the process. I've said this many times throughout the book. You don't need to follow the five principles/steps in order all the time. You can mix them up and experiment. That's where the fun really starts. You'll find that it connects to many other experiences you've had, along with other activities you're interested in. For example, if you're into yoga, then how do you incorporate that into The Nature Process? What about running? Or diving? Or writing? Or making music? Or having fun with your friends? The possibilities are endless. The only limits are the limits of your imagination.

Give Yourself in Trust

The verb commit means to 'give yourself in trust'. This is a key component of The Nature Process. To be able to create The Nature Process, write this book, and go beyond it, I've done a lot of unusual things in my life as I've deepened my own connection to nature. None of this would have been possible if I hadn't trusted.

I've spent hours altering my state of consciousness while clicking my fingers so that I could train myself to shift my consciousness at will. Great skill but highly impractical.

I've climbed rocks and trees and practised jumping off them. Spent hours standing in the ocean staring at the horizon. Walked for miles both under the sun and the moon. Sat in woods for hours on end. Camped out at night in the middle of the woods by myself. Just recently I've even undergone a five-day wilderness survival training course – and even eaten a fried woodlouse.

I've spent hours sitting in a room with the windows open in winter just to feel more connected to nature and allow animals into my room. I've allowed cats to continue to bring ticks into my bedroom just so I could study them and see what I could learn from them. Lizards, geckos, mice, and mosquitoes have been my bedroom companions. I studied them all to see what I could learn from them.

I've tried *ayahuasca*, which is a plant medicine from the Amazon, known for creating altered states of consciousness that promote healing. Although I had an interesting experience with the plant, the altered state of consciousness was exactly the same as what I experience when I go for a powerful walk in nature using the principles of The Nature Process.

I've danced under full moons and imagined the stars are my dance partners. I've spent hours in a deep trance receiving weird and wonderful communication from the natural world around me. I've done all this so that you don't have to.

To reach the level of understanding I have about connecting with nature and using it to help you improve your well-being and enhance your life, I've spent years studying and experimenting with this. A lot of the time I had no clue what I was doing. Thanks to this book, you do. More importantly you'll be able to shave years off your journey to connecting with nature if you want. It's my goal that you find it easier to trust in Nature because of the information contained within this book and challenge yourself to explore how deep you can go, how much you can boost your well-being and enhance your life

Thanks to The Nature Process, I've also run 10k obstacle races, covering myself in mud in the process. Something I've always wanted to do but never thought possible. Due to the chronic ill health I've suffered from, I've always been conscious of my body. When you're in so much pain, it's hard not to be. Asthma and eczema have challenged me my whole life. At times, they've severely limited what my body is capable of doing, and nearly killed me a few times.

As a result, I learned to view my body as weak. I had to be careful of what I did with it. If the weather was cold and damp I couldn't go outside. It might make me ill. If I did too much exercise it'd trigger my asthma and eczema. So I stopped exercising. I despised my body for this perceived weakness. I used food as a tool of punishment against it. The guilt and shame that came along with this paralyzed me for years before I finally turned to nature for support.

The last flare-up I had of my eczema was five years ago. As I mentioned in chapter one, eighty-five percent of my body was covered with red, itchy, inflamed skin. I sought advice from the leading dermatologist in Spain. His advice made my skin worse. When he told me to get out of the way and let him treat me, I left and never went back. Instead I started listening to my body and letting it tell me what it needed to do to heal. My body was so badly out of balance that it took years to work through the underlying causes of my eczema and rebalance my body, but I did it.

Now I'm doing the same with my asthma. Before my eczema flare-up I hardly ever needed inhalers. On the odd occasion that my asthma did flare up, I could breathe through it without medication. I lost that, along with my confidence to do so, the more that the side effects of eczema took my body out of balance. Recently I did some breath work to help me manage it better. During one of these sessions I realised just how much I'd hated my lungs for not working properly. There was deep sadness around this to be released. Now I realise just how powerful my lungs are. I've tortured them with mindless smoking, disrespected them with bad food choices, put them in toxic environments, and still they've fought to keep me alive.

A month after publishing the first edition of this book, I ended up in hospital for five days with an asthma attack. It was an intense healing moment. Since then, my asthma has slowly improved. Within a few months of being in hospital my lung capacity expanded beyond what even my doctor thought I was capable of. I'm back to reducing my medication and my lungs feel better than ever.

Today I'm starting to see my body as a miracle. I'm in awe of just how amazing it is. For the first time in my life I'm attracted to caring for my body as if it were a temple and to see just how magnificent it can be if I truly take care of it. It may have taken me over thirty years to reach this understanding, but I have the rest of my life to put it into practise and discover just what this body is capable of. It's still a learning experience. Even so, I'm the fittest I've ever been – physically, mentally, emotionally and spiritually.

My life keeps getting better and better. I've noticed that there's a direct correlation between how much time I spend connecting to nature and how awesome my life seems to be.

No More Hiding

For a long time, I've hidden the insights I've received from nature deep inside. I first started 'nature processing' when I was around five years old. I didn't know what I was doing at the time; all I knew is that when I tried to explain or talk about this, people didn't understand. The fact that people are now interested and able to grasp what I'm talking about is, actually quite bemusing to me. All my life I've judged and ridiculed myself for the beliefs and experiences I've had, yet now I find that they are more valuable than I ever knew. I thought I was the weird one, that there was something wrong with me. Yet what I've known my whole life is what people have been trying to discover for years. Who would have thought you could learn so much by merely going outside for a walk, climbing a tree, or wading through a river?

I've lived in this nature-connected world for so long that I'd forgotten just how extraordinary it is and how easy it is to access it at will. At times, I've taken nature for granted. I don't want you to do the same.

We are nature. We are one. Our minds, grounded in nature, are the most powerful tools we have at our disposal. We are our own free energy source and can move mountains with our minds, if only we let go of the stories that hold us back from doing so.

I don't want you to take my word for it. I want you to get out into nature and experience this for yourself. If you've made it this far in the book, you already have a connection to nature. It might be strong. It might be weak. It doesn't matter. You start where you are. The only place you can go is deeper. Everyone's journey is their own. There is no right or wrong way. There is only your way. Trust in nature and it will lead you where you need to go.

You know the path you need to take with The Nature Process. Now it's time to walk it. When you do, you'll discover that you're able to free your mind from fear, doubt and disbelief. You'll be able to see beyond the stories that keep you trapped in a state of pretend powerlessness, and take clear action to boost your well-being and enhance your life with nature's support.

What's more, is that as you continue to experience a deeper connection to Nature it's also possible that you'll experience a shift in your understanding of how you experience your relationship with the Earth.

This is something that's not only happened with me but I've also seen it happen with many of the people I've work with. Using The Nature Process regularly has the potential to help you develop what I call the Earth Self.

THE EMERGENCE OF THE EARTH SELF

The Earth Self is the full body recognition that you are part of the Earth and that the Earth and everything in the planet are actually one living organism. The body belongs to the Earth Self, which is why the natural body is key to The Nature Process.

Many of us are living our human experience trying to connect to a higher power, whether you call it Nature, God, Source, Spirit, Allah or whatever your choice of name for it is. We stand on the Earth in our human form and look up into the cosmos seeking answers, telling ourselves that we come from the stars. The truth is we come from the Earth. Our human form is the result of Nature working with the Earth through evolution.

If we want to find the answers to life, they can only be found by looking down into the Earth and realizing that we are part of it. As we connect to nature through the physical manifestation of the Earth's environment, we are able to ground into the body and experience not only what it is to be truly human, but also what it is to be one with the world around us.

The idea of the Earth Self may take a little getting used to. What I term Earth Self also has another label: ecological identity. Mitchell Thomashow, author of the book *Ecological Identity* says:

Ecological Identity refers to all the different ways people construe themselves in relationships to the earth as manifested in personality, values, actions, and sense of self. Nature becomes an object of identification. For the individual, this has extraordinary conceptual ramifications. The interpretation of life experience transcends social and cultural interactions. It also includes a person's connection to nature, perception of the ecosystem, and direct experience of nature. (p.3)

What this means is, that as you develop your own Earth Self through deepening your connection to Nature with The Nature Process, how you see yourself, how you behave, what you find important, and the actions you take change. This experience is not limited to the society or culture you grew up into. It's something that has the potential to unite us all as one.

Furthermore, research suggests that people who develop a sense of ecological identity possess strong values, have a high level of ethical standards, don't worry about themselves, are able to co-operate well with others and demonstrate great leadership potential. Now, at this point in the history of humanity, we need people like this more than ever.

The evolutionary biologist, Julien Huxley argued that, thanks to evolution, the universe is becoming conscious of itself and its potential through some human beings. Let's forget about the universe for a second and think only about the planet in which we live. The Earth is becoming conscious of itself as we develop our Earth Self.

There's no point in reaching for the stars if we are destroying the planet that created us. If you remember back to chapter one, a fundamental tenant of ecopsychology is that not only is the Earth a living organism, but that humans and the Earth are interconnected. Boosting your well-being and enhancing your life means boosting the well-being and enhancing the life of the Earth. The truth is that people and planet are one and the same thing.

EARTH AND HUMAN AS ONE

Life on planet Earth is currently undergoing a major transition. We have already entered the sixth mass extinction event in the Earth's known history where a large number of species die in a short period of time.

Collectively, as a species we are slowly waking up to the knowledge that our behaviour is negatively impacting the Earth. Humans are just one of 8.7 million species on Earth, with many of these still unknown to us. Just like each one of these species, humans are as dependent on the Earth's ecosystem as is any other creature.

As part of life on Earth we have evolved to be a species that functions best when we interact fully with our surrounding environment. Not only are we dependent on the Earth for food but the trees and plants around us produce the oxygen needed for us to breathe. These trees also produce chemicals that boost our immune system.

Research continues to show that we experience better health the more time we spend outdoors. Our ability to deal with stress improves. We experience more well-being with emotions such as depression, anger, and aggression reducing as we interact with the natural world around us.

Even our brain functions differently when we are outside. The part of our brain that is responsible for negative thoughts switches off when we spend at least ninety minutes walking outside in a natural area.

All this research shows that humans are unable to function independently from the rest of life on Earth. Yet despite being the most adaptable mammal that has ever evolved on earth, we are currently engaged in behaviour that is destroying the environment upon which we depend. In the process, we are also destroying ourselves.

Janine Benyus, author of Biomimicry, argues that right now human beings are acting as a type one species within an ecosystem. Type one species are opportunists that focus on growth and output that, once they consume all available resources, move on to another area to do the same.

Benyus argues that if we are to evolve as a species on Earth we need to become a type three species. Type three species have a deep relationship to the place that they inhabit and so live in a state of balance, using no more resources than they put back.

To do this means that we need to change the very way in which we interact with the Earth. Developing our Earth Self, or ecological identity, is key to that. The institute that Benyus went on to found, called Biomimicry 3.8, states that it's only when we humans learn to recognise the Earth and its ecosystem as models and mentors for the species that the species will develop the right motivation and perspective to survive and thrive on Earth.

This is the true power of The Nature Process. First, you learn how to deepen your connection to nature for your own well-being. Then, as a result of experiencing how nature can support you to enhance your life, you end up taking better care of the Earth as a result. It really is a win-win situation for us and for all life on Earth.

THE STAGES OF EARTH SELF DEVELOPMENT

If you've been working through the exercises in the book, you'll probably find that you've already been experiencing some of the stages of development of the Earth Self. In all truth, you've probably already experienced some of them even before you picked up this book – whether you've known it or not.

The following stages was developed from, not only my own personal understanding, but also from observing this within my clients. I've also observed this through speaking with and studying the texts of people who have had similar experiences.

The first stage of developing the Earth Self is to identify your Human Self with the Earth. This starts with the intellectual understanding that we are all connected and moves into an embodied awareness that you and the Earth are the same. As our human understanding of the Earth and humanity's role within it expands thanks to scientific and technological advances this is becoming easier for more and more people to understand and experience.

The second stage of developing the Earth Self is to experience a shift in consciousness when out in Nature. This is exactly what Natural Presence does when it takes you into the Theta brainwave state. The mind chatter you normally experience becomes quiet and you start to feel a connection to something more than your individual human self.

The third stage is to recognise the earth, not just as a living organism, but as a sentient living organism and to experience communication with it. So far with The Nature Process, I've been preparing you for this by helping you to understand what it feels like to communicate with another aspect of nature. It's important to note here that there is no scientific evidence that supports the idea that the Earth is a sentient living organism. However, what I'm referring to here is the human experience of feeling that the Earth is a living sentient being. How you feel about the Earth, and how you experience your relationship with the Earth, is what's important here - not the scientific evidence.

The fourth stage is to have an experiential understanding of sharing consciousness with another aspect of nature. This is an experience where you don't just feel a connection to and an appreciation of nature but you feel that you actually become one with another part of nature. Again, whether this is scientifically accurate or possible is irrelevant. People do experience this, even if it's only through their imagination. It's about acknowledging this as a valid experience and accepting the experience as real for you.

The fifth stage is to embody the Earth by pulling the Earth into you so that you become the Earth. Most people experience this stage through various meditative practices, which is why the in-depth exercises associated with each chapter are written as meditative exercise. To successfully achieve this, you need to drop all labels about Mother Earth so that you can tap into the power. This is why I encouraged you to do this from the start. When you label something, it becomes a concept rather than an experience. The label you then attach to an object stops you from experiencing it further – especially if there are societal and cultural stories around it.

The sixth stage is the awareness that you are the result of 4.6billion years of evolution. As life on Earth has continued to grow and develop, you have been the result. The fact that you are here, now, is thanks to the life-supporting systems of the Earth. It's the embodied awareness that without the Earth you wouldn't exist. You wouldn't be able to have all the human hopes, wishes and dreams you have without the Earth's existence. It's the knowledge that the only way you can reach your full potential is through the support of and the reliance upon the Earth that gives you life.

These six experiences keep repeating until they become fully integrated in the last stage, that of the fully developed Earth Self. This is where you perceive no separation between you and the earth. Everything - the good and the bad - on Earth is experienced as part of you. From this place of deep connection and unity you are then able to let the Earth speak through the actions that you take. At this stage your thoughts and actions support continued life on Earth for all living beings.

This is not something that happens overnight. It's a gradual process that comes from spending more and more time outside. What's also key here is that if you're experiencing stress, anxiety, depression, or trauma then embodying Earth Self is incredibly challenging. Before you can start to develop the Earth Self you first need to be whole and healthy.

This is something that Abraham Maslow, the North American psychologist I mentioned back in chapter seven, identified and represented in his hierarchy of needs. What made Maslow different in his psychological approach was that he studied notable individuals who he termed as self-actualising, or having reached their full potential. Rather than look at what was wrong with humanity, he wanted to discover what was right so that we could collectively learn and grow from this.

From studying over one hundred extraordinary people, Maslow developed a hierarchy of needs that explained what people needed to be capable of self-actualising.

At the bottom level of the hierarchy are our physiological needs such as air, water, food, shelter and clothing. Without these essential needs, the body is incapable of surviving.

Next comes our safety needs. These include not just our health and well-being but also our personal and financial security along with safety nets to protect us against accidents and misfortune.

After our physiological and safety needs are fulfilled we then look to fulfil our love and belonging needs. This is our ability to form and maintain emotionally meaningful relationships through family, friendship and intimacy. This need is so strong that it has the potential to override the two previous needs and can result in unhealthy and destructive attachments to people and groups.

We then move onto developing our esteem needs. There are two areas within this. The first focuses on receiving recognition from others and deriving a sense of esteem from them. The second part is being able to derive a sense of esteem from within and to give ourselves recognition. It's only then that we are able to self-actualise and reach our full potential.

If you go back to the researched benefits of spending time in nature highlighted in chapter one, you'll discover that spending time in nature has the potential to help us satisfy all these needs and enable us individually and collectively to move towards self-actualisation.

It's at this stage of self-actualisation where most peak experiences occur. As I mentioned back in chapter seven, peak experiences are heightened moments of awareness around an experience that create a sense of awe and wonder whereby people feel at one with the universe. These experiences help drive people forward to reach their full potential. These are in essence what happens when you are able to access a deep theta brain wave state.

What's key about Maslow's work on peak experiences is that most of them happen outside in the natural world. When you look at the framework for developing the Earth Self, it becomes clear that peak experiences are actually stage two of developing the Earth Self, where you experience a different state of awareness and connection while out in Nature.

Without these peak experiences, or a deep state of Natural Presence, it is challenging to develop the Earth Self and become a person with strong values and ethics who is concerned with the well-being of all life on Earth.

Furthermore, at the end of his life, Maslow identified plateau experiences, which were where an individual could access peak experiences at will, or even live permanently from that place. These plateau experiences lost the intensity of peak experiences but retained the deep connection to the universe. Again, looking at the framework for developing the Earth Self, this is stage seven, whereby you've had so many experiences that you then begin to live fully from this place of deep connection and oneness with the Earth.

What It's Like to Experience the Earth Self

I remember connecting to the Earth through visualising an array of roots coming out from my own feet, and going towards to core of the Earth. Through the support of Natural Presence and Tabi's energy on the recording, I started to feel the 'pulse' of the Earth in sync with my own heartbeat. It was quite a surreal moment. It was the moment which made me realise in depth that Earth was alive and it was breathing too! At the same time,

I was humbled by the vastness of the Earth and how supportive it was to me. It was like a huge envelope which just took me in. I experienced a sense of heaviness and a sensation of being stuck in the earth while I was in my human body. In that moment, my human thoughts stopped. In fact, I could not experience human thoughts in that state of consciousness. I ended up doing that same exercise many times and wanted to relive that experience. They were the moments of a deeper connection with nature beyond the Natural Presence through the Human Self.

This short piece was written by Claire Zhu, one of The Nature Process trainee coaches after she experienced a deepening of the Earth Self through continuing to work with The Nature Process. While this experience may seem a bit 'far-out', what I hypothesise is that Claire was able to put herself into such a deep meditative state that her brainwave frequency matched with that of the Earth's electromagnetic field. A similar experience happened to Sami Aaron, Director of Training and Development with The Nature Process, who wrote this reflective piece after one of her own experiences as she developed the Earth Self:

There's a moment in deep meditation when you become aware that you're not breathing.

You're not out of breath, or holding your breath, or struggling for breath; you just notice that tendrils of oxygen are gently flowing through your body; no nostrils or lungs required.

The earth breathes in the same way. I can see it.

I was on a meditation retreat, day four of silence. I had tripped over a step earlier in the morning, in a hurry to get to the meditation hall and out of the cold, and I twisted both ankles. I didn't think I was injured, but after the meditation session my feet started to ache and one ankle was swollen.

As I headed back to my room to assess the damage, each step made me wince, so I had to slow my pace.

With a gentle smirk, the thought came to me that maybe I fell so that I would slow down. Smirking - because it seems like a 5-day silent retreat would have been slow enough! But there was this sense, just then, that I needed to go even slower. Although I slowed my pace even more, my foot and ankle still complained. There was a feeling that kept repeating from inside me - go slower. NO ... slower. Really ... slower ... slow down more ... I can't type it slowly enough to express this intentional, deliberate stepping back from time.

My thoughts were being drawn into a mesmerisation with the details and nuances of everything I saw and touched.

As the cement pathway changed to a wooden walkway, all my focus shifted to the sensation of the wood beneath my feet. There was a surprising and delightful awareness that the feel of the wood was so much more natural than the concrete; each footstep felt as if the wood gave way; that it received, almost welcomed, my weight; realigned its structure to accommodate my injury. After a few moments, I realised I had stopped walking altogether.

I glanced up momentarily and was cognizant of the movement of people and birds around me but their presence was fuzzy, as if out of my range of perception.

As I stood still, this inner voice urged me to slow down even more. But I was already stopped; how could I go slower? Yet it caressed me ... slower yet... softer ... it beckoned me ... settle your thoughts to a deeper level than you ever imagined was possible.

Just as I began to align my new-found senses to the depth of this stillness, I glanced up to the brick pathway ahead and saw that the path, and the earth beneath it, and the sand on either side, undulated.

It was a gentle, almost imperceptible heaving as if a great breath of life had expanded up into the ground from beneath the surface; from somewhere deeper than I ever knew existed. It was an inspiration from nature.

And then, at the top of the in-breath, it paused. Paused for so long that it made me wonder if I had imagined the whole thing. But I waited for it, settled into its rhythm and finally, with relief - an exhalation, a release of the inspiration as the ground gently settled back down to where it had always been.

It happened again, off to my right and soon to the left of the path. I became aware that different areas of the ground breathed at their own pace, in their own rhythm and it was so ... soooooo ... (take a breath here before continuing) soooooooooooooooo ... slow.

My own breath was too fast. I tried to adjust it to the pace of the breath of the earth but I couldn't do it. Its rhythm didn't match the beat of my body; it felt as if my physical being wasn't capable of breathing that slowly no matter how much I willed it.

I was embraced by undulating ground everywhere I gazed. Gently moving my head or refocusing my sight was too fast, almost startling; I had to pause with intention and instruct myself, my awareness, to reconnect with the stillness each time before I could see it. Or was it that I had to just be open and receptive before it could be seen by me? My everyday eyes go looking for things to perceive; this was the opposite; the motion was already, always there; I had to be in its space and in its time in order to receive it.

There were no bells or confetti strewn with this discovery. No great sense of being awash in a shower of divine love. It was just me, in my earmuffs and gloves and sore ankles, standing still - a zoned-out meditator moving more slowly than just being stopped. A time-perception slowness. A deeper realm slowness. A pervasive breathing stillness. Seeing the whole world and being breathed with it.

Most humans can't see it because we move too quickly. Our eyes and thoughts and breath move so rapidly it leaves no space for this awareness of the ever-present, rhythmic life that emanates from the depths of our earth.

Is an elephant able to see a hummingbird?
Does the hummingbird know the elephant breathes?

Experiences like these remind us that there's a different way of living life – a way of living that helps us create balance and harmony, not just in our own life but in the lives of all others who inhabit the Earth.

They help us see the world in a different way and once you do there's no going back. You know something more is possible. You start to take action, no matter how small, that helps us all create a world that works for all life on Earth

It's going to take all of us, fully connected to nature, living and working in harmony with the rhythm of the Earth to create this. Each one of us holds a part of the Earth's dream, whether it's to have technology that works with Nature, education that encourages the exploration of nature – both inner and outer, financial systems that make the cost of nature visible, a means of production that supports life instead of destroying it, a healthcare system that truly allows us to thrive, a food distribution process that ends poverty or meaningful employment that allows us to support our families and the Earth.

The list is endless. No matter how big or small your dream is it's valuable and so desperately needed in this world. Connecting to nature to improve your well-being and ultimately developing your Earth Self will help you achieve it.

If you're ready to start experiencing the Earth Self for yourself then the following exercise is designed to help you take your connection to nature and go deeper into relationship with the Earth. If not, then go back and keep exploring The Nature Process. Your Earth Self will develop anyway of its own accord the more you keep connecting to Nature and the deeper you can go with a state of Natural Presence. If you are attracted to, do the 'Discover the Earth Self Exercise' on page 239.

YOUR MARCHING ORDERS

At the beginning of this book I asked you whether you wanted to take the red pill or the blue one. By continuing to read this book – and put what you've learned into practise – you've chosen the red one.

In the film *The Matrix*, after Neo takes the red pill and wakes up, he asks Morpheus why his eyes hurt. Morpheus replies that it's because he's never used them before. It's same with your senses. Your fifty-four senses have been dulled from the moment you were born. We don't live in a culture that supports us to become fully human. Yet.

Like Neo, you're on a mission. It's a mission to discover what's possible when you deepen your connection to nature. Remember, nature refers to both the natural world around you and your inner nature too.

Connecting to nature is not just about taking care of the world around you. It's about learning to love, honour and respect yourself first.

This is not an easy journey for any of us. However, The Nature Process will help support you on it.

What you need to do now is to continue to deepen and explore your relationship with nature. You don't know where it will take you if you don't.

Keep doing the exercises in the book. Explore your fifty-four senses and deepen your natural presence. Connect to your natural body and discover what it is saying. Find out who you truly are and live life through your natural attractions. Spend time in natural communication and see what nature teaches you. Practise a natural release and let your stress and anxiety go.

This book contains everything you need to know about how to deepen your connection to nature so that you can bring the benefits of doing so into your daily life. People tell me that they take this book with them when they go hiking. Others say they return to it again and again, each time finding something new that helps them deepen their understanding.

A connection with nature is a fundamental human need. In today's world, we need it now, more than ever. What you've learned within this book has the power to change your well-being far more than you could ever imagine. Nature is simple, easy – and right outside. So go, get outside. Discover the power and potential of your natural self and watch what happens to your well-being as you do.

RE-ACTIVATE YOUR FIFTY-FOUR SENSES EXERCISE

❧   ❧   ❧

THIS EXERCISE IS DESIGNED TO help you reactivate and rebalance your fifty-four senses so that you can deepen your ability to be in a state of Natural Presence and become more present, engaged, and grounded in life.

It's important to note that senses are developed differently in each person. As you go through this exercise you may experience more with some senses and less with others. This is ok. It's nothing to worry about.

It's also important to remember that reactivating and rebalancing your fifty-four senses is something that you need to return to again and again. The clients that have had the most powerful experiences with the fifty-four senses are the ones who have practiced developing them on a regular basis.

Think of it like exercise. You wouldn't expect to do a few sit-ups once and end up with a taught, toned stomach. It's the same with the senses.

While it's more powerful to do this exercise outside in a natural environment you can also do the exercise indoors with some plants, a picture of nature, or even tapping into a memory of one of your favourite times spend outside. I've had had clients use all of these techniques with great results.

What's key when you do this exercise is that you are in a place where you are safe, comfortable, relaxed, and warm.

If possible, do this exercise standing with this book in your hand. Read each section and give yourself a minute to experience each sense.

Start by re-activating your sense of mind and consciousness. Become fully aware of your surroundings. Don't focus on anything in particular. Allow the awareness to build that you are right here, right now, in this moment.

Next, re-activate your sense of relaxation and sleep. Can you notice your brainwave state? Combine your sense of mind with your sense of relaxation and sleep. What brainwave state do you think you're experiencing right now?

Now, take a deep breath in through your nose. Re-activate your sense of hunger for air. Breathe out. Notice if you feel hungry or thirsty as you continue to take deep breaths in and out.

On the next in breath through your nose, re-activate your sense of smell. What smells do you notice in the air as you inhale? When you exhale does the air smell different?

Next time breathe in through the mouth. As you inhale re-activate your sense of taste. What does the air taste like as you inhale? When you exhale does the air taste different?

Re-activate your sense of feeling and touch by bringing your sense of mind and consciousness to the sensations of your feet on the ground. How do your feet feel against the ground?

Re-activate your sense of weight and balance by slowly lifting one foot, lowering, then lifting the other off the ground, then lowering. How easy is it for you to balance on one foot?

Continue doing this while you re-activate your sense of motion. How does your body feel as you move it?

Re-activate your sense of temperature and notice how warm or cold the air feels on your bare skin. How does it contrast to your clothing-covered skin?

Re-activate your sense of pressure and notice how the wind and air feel as they move around your body. Can you notice any pressure changes as you continue to move your body?

Stop moving. Re-activate your sense of light and sight and observe your surroundings. What do you notice about them?

Re-activate your sense of space and proximity to sense the space around you. Let your eyes rest on something that attracts you. How far or near is this object from you?

Re-activate your sense of colour and explore the different colours in your space. Look closely at colours of the same shade. What differences do you notice between them?

Focus on one colour. Re-activate your sense of mood and identity from colour. What does this colour represent to you? Do you like this colour?

Close your eyes. Re-activate your sense of seeing without eyes. Turn your head and notice any difference in light. Can you sense where the light is coming from? How are you able to sense this?

Bring your sense of mind to your body. Re-activate your sense of and pain. Know that you are safe and supported by Nature. Become aware of anything that is currently painful in your body. How does this make you feel?

Re-activate your sense of physical place with an awareness of the land around you. Look at the position of the sun/moon/stars. What do you notice? If you're indoors, do you have an awareness of the land surrounding the building you're in?

Re-activate your humidity sense and feel the moisture in the air as you breathe in and out. How does it feel?

Re-activate your sense of weather. What do you notice? If you're indoors, what can you sense from looking out of the window?

Look closer at the landscape/environment around you. Re-activate your sense of form and design. What do you notice about the space you are in? How does it make you feel?

Re-activate your sense of season. How does this time of year make you feel?

Re-activate your sense of emotional place, community and belonging. How do you feel living where you do?

Re-activate your horticultural sense that allows you to cultivate crops in a way that lets you live from the Earth. How often do you use this sense? How does that make you feel?

Re-activate your sense to hunt or gather food. How does it feel to eat the food you do? How does the Earth provide the food that you eat?

Re-activate your aesthetic sense and observe the beauty that exists in this present moment. What are three beautiful things that you notice around you? How do they make you feel?

Re-activate your sense of pleasure and laughter. What brings you pleasure? What makes you laugh? How often do you have fun?

Move your sense of awareness into your body. Re-activate your hormonal sense. For women, feel where you are in your cycle. How does your menstrual cycle (or lack of it) make you feel? For men, feel the steadiness of your hormones. How much testosterone do you have in your body? How does that make you feel?

Feel how this impacts your urge to procreate as you activate this sense. How often do you have sex? How often do you want to have sex? How skilled are you at raising children?

Re-activate your sense of self. What are the things you like about yourself? What are the things you dislike? What makes you different from other people?

Re-activate your psychic capacities. Can you sense the life forces of the natural world around you: animals, plants, rocks, water, the earth itself, nature? If not, how does this make you feel? If yes, how does this make you feel?

Re-activate your sense of electromagnetic fields outside the body. Can you feel the electromagnetic frequency of the Earth? Are there any other electromagnetic fields around you that you can sense?

Imagine the energy of Nature's life force surrounding you. Re-activate your sense of pupation. Let the energy cocoon you and support you to transform. How does it feel to be enveloped in the energy of nature?

Know you are safe in the energy of nature. Re-activate your sense of fear. What scares you the most in life? Know this is another sign of disconnect from nature. Let this sense slowly draw you back into nature as nature dissolves your fear. How do you feel as your fear fades away?

Feel your sense of self dissolving as you continue to imagine the energy of nature surrounding you. How does it feel to imagine yourself and nature merging into one?

Re-activate your sense of stress and surrender. Allow yourself to move deeper into the energy of nature. How does it feel to surrender to the energy of nature?

Imagine the energy of nature moving through you. Re-activate your electromagnetic sense and feel this power move through your nervous system and brain. Do you notice any changes in your body?

Re-activate your spiritual sense. Let love and ecstasy fill your being. How easy is this? How does it feel?

Go deeper into the love and ecstasy. Re-activate your sense of unity and enter fully into a state of oneness with all beings. How does it feel to know that you are interconnected with every other being in the universe?

Let yourself drift away from this unity. Re-activate your sense of mental/spiritual distress. How does that feel? Feel the disconnect and know that Nature is calling you to return to unity. How does it feel to know that you can return to a state of unity?

Re-activate your sense of humility and appreciation as you experience this connection. How does your connection to nature feel?

Re-activate your sense of language and articulation. What one word expresses your experience?

Re-activate your sense of intuition. Let Nature offer you guidance for your next step in life. What's the one thing you need to do next in life? What's the first thought that comes to mind?

Re-activate your sense of reason and memory to anchor this guidance into the essence of your being. Is there a movement you can make with your body to help you remember the information you received?

Re-activate your sense of astral time and journey into the future. What will your future be like if you act on the guidance received? What will your future be like if you don't act on the guidance received?

Re-activate your sense of gravity and feel yourself grounded down in the Earth. How does it feel to be connected and grounded in the Earth?

Feel the wisdom of this 4.6billion year old being. Re-activate your sense of survival through joining a more established organism. Recognise yourself as more than human, as an earth being. How does it feel to know you are part of the Earth?

Re-activate your awareness of the rotation of the earth as it spins and dances throughout the universe. Can you feel the earth move?

Re-activate your territorial sense. Earth is your home. You are an Earth being. How do you feel about the Earth?

Re-activate your colonizing sense. Feel compassion for all of the earth's living beings. How does it feel to know that we are all part of the same planet?

Re-activate your capacity to hypnotize other beings. Feel the presence and charisma fill your being. How does this feel?

Re-activate your sense of excretion. How does your bladder feel? Empty? Full? Feel a desire to eliminate all the waste from your body that stops you from caring for the earth in the way you choose.

Re-activate your sense of hearing and become aware of the sounds, or silence, that surround you. What can you hear?

Re-activate your sense of awareness of your own visibility/invisibility as you stand present fully back in your body. Do you feel visible to other people? Or do you feel invisible?

Re-activate your sense of time and rhythm. Let it match the ebb and flow of your breath. Can you sense time passing? What is the rhythm of your breathing?

Refocus on your sense of relaxation and sleep. Pay attention to your brain-wave state. As you observe your sense of mind and combine this sense, what state of consciousness are you currently experiencing now? Is it any different to your brainwave state at the start of this exercise?

Give yourself five minutes to reflect on this experience. What did you gain from doing it? What senses would you like to explore further? What senses felt comfortable to you? What senses didn't you feel comfortable with?

If you find this exercise challenging to do reading from the book, you can access a variation of this created as a guided meditation at: http://www.the-natureprocess.co/54sensesmeditation

EXPAND YOUR AWARENESS OF THE NATURAL BODY EXERCISE

❊　❊　❊

THIS SECOND EXERCISE IS DESIGNED to help you ground into a state of natural presence and deepen your capacity to be in the natural body. This will help you become aware of the minute physiological changes that occur through stress and anxiety so that you can take action to rebalance yourself and maintain a state of productivity, creativity and flow.

As with all the exercises in this book, this is not an exercise that you can do once and expect to master the state of natural body. It's something that you need to do again and again. Once you have a basic understanding of this exercise you'll be able to adapt it and incorporate it into any existing physical movement routine you already have.

As before, while it's more powerful to do this exercise outside in a natural environment, you can also do the exercise indoors with some plants, a picture of nature, or even tapping into a memory of one of your favourite times spent outside. Remember, it's key to be in a place where you feel safe, comfortable, relaxed, and warm.

With this exercise, we're also starting to introduce elements of natural body that will help support you when it comes to the chapter on natural release. You can do this exercise standing, sitting, or lying down.

Take a few deep breaths in and out, feeling your stomach rise with each inhalation.

If you're outside, keep your eyes open and start to explore your surrounding environment using as many of your senses as possible.

If you're indoors, close your eyes and bring forth a memory of a favourite time or place outdoors in nature.

Count from one to fifty-four, imagining that you are opening up all of your fifty-four senses. Don't worry about remembering what the senses are right now. Each time you count a number, allow yourself to notice something different about the natural environmental around you, whether real or from your imagination. How do you feel after you activate each sense?

Once you've activated all fifty-four senses, take a moment and observe any thoughts, feelings or sensations that arise.

Reflect on the following questions individually for about a minute per question:

* How does it feel to be connected to nature?
* How can you tell you are in a state of natural presence?
* What is it about the natural environment around you, or in your imagination, that appeals to you?
* What one thing in the natural environment attracts you the most and why?
* Could you ask this aspect of nature to support you?
* How does it feel to have nature supporting you?

Now, think of a situation that you're currently experiencing within your life that is challenging you or that you find difficult to deal with.

Allow yourself to really focus on this situation, observing the thoughts and feelings that you have about it without judgment.

Acknowledge that all thoughts and feelings you are experiencing are valid and okay – no matter what they are.

Now, focus on the body. What physical sensations do you observe as you continue to think about this situation?

Take your time and really focus on these physical sensations going into as much detail as possible. Give yourself at least a minute to explore each of the following questions:

- Do you feel hot or cold when you think about this situation?
- What sensations do you notice in your feet, if any?
- What sensations do you notice in your legs and thighs?
- Check your hips, stomach and buttocks for any further sensations.
- Whenever you notice a sensation ask yourself how does it feel.
- What sensations do you notice in your back, shoulders, and neck?
- What sensations do you notice in your arms and hands?
- How do your face and head feel?

All the sensations you've observed are your body's response to the situation you're thinking of.

- What is your body telling you?
- How does that make you feel?

Keep observing all the different sensations that you're experiencing without judgment.

Trust your body. Trust what you are experiencing. Know that you are safe and supported by the natural world around you.

Bring your sense of awareness back to your fifty-four senses. Re-activate them again by counting to fifty-four again. Don't worry about remembering what the senses are. Again, each time you count a number, allow yourself to notice something different about the natural environment around you, whether real or from your imagination. How does each sense feel now as you re-activate it?

Once you've re-activated all fifty-four senses, take a moment and observe any thoughts, feelings or sensations that arise. How does your body feel compared to before?

Bring your awareness back to the situation you were thinking of earlier. What thoughts and feelings are you experiencing now?

How have the physical sensations changed within the body?

Now, ask your body to help return you to a state of balance and harmony.

Ask your body what it needs to do.

Does it need to move or be still?

Be quiet or be noisy?

Does it need to cry or scream?

Stretch itself or curl up into a ball?

What does the body need to do to release any stress and tension it's holding onto around this situation?

Trust your body and allow it to move in the way it wants.

Trust yourself.

Know that there is no right or wrong way to do this. There is only your way.

Engage with the body, allowing it to move, shift, stretch until you feel calm and at peace with the situation you've been thinking about.

Give yourself some time to rest and relax after this exercise. If you want, journal/draw about your experience. Remember to drink some water afterwards too.

RE-ACTIVATE AND RE-ENERGISE YOUR
NATURAL ATTRACTIONS EXERCISE

❊　❊　❊

THE EXERCISE IN THIS CHAPTER is designed to allow you to discover the power of experiencing natural attractions in nature and explore how they can impact your natural body when you connect and explore them in relation to a problem or challenge you're currently facing.

As with the other exercises, while it's more powerful to do this outside in a natural environment you can also do the exercise indoors with some plants, a picture of nature, or even tapping into a memory of one of your favourite times spent outside. Remember, it's key to be in a place where you feel safe, comfortable, relaxed, and warm. You can do this exercise standing, sitting, or lying down.

Close your eyes.

Take a deep breath in. And then out.

Continue taking a few more deep breaths in and out.

Become aware of your feet in contact with the ground. Imagine this is a connection to the Earth itself.

Become aware of your sense of interconnectedness as you recognise that your body is part of the Earth. As the Earth, your body is also part of nature.

Right now, you are safe. You are secure. You are supported.

Think of a challenge/opportunity for growth that you are currently facing in your life right now. Give yourself a minute to explore the thoughts, feelings, and sensations that arise within the body as you focus on this problem or challenge. Let the thoughts, feelings, and sensations arise without judgment.

There are no right or wrong thoughts, feelings, or sensations. Focus on exploring and experiencing.

If you're outside, open your eyes. If you're doing this exercise indoors, keep your eyes closed and bring into your awareness a memory of a time spent in nature. You're now going to bring yourself into a state of natural presence by re-activating your fifty-four senses.

We're going to use one or two words as a way to tap into the senses. As you say the word, either silently or out loud, focus on a part of nature. Give yourself a few seconds to explore the thoughts, feelings, and sensations that arise in the body after you acknowledge the sense.

Light.
Sun Sense.
Colour.
Mood.
Invisibility.
Radiation.
Temperature.
Season.
Gravity.
Pressure.
Protection.
Hearing.
Balance.
Touch.
Smell.
Motion.
Space.
Rotation.
Taste.
Food.
Appetite.

Hormones.
Humidity.
Pleasure.
Play.
Love.
Fear.
Landscape.
Time.
Distress.
Energy field.
Community.
Weather.
Language.
Compassion.
Self.
Horticultural.
Territory.
Humility.
Reason.
Mind.
Form.
Joy.
Beauty.
Intuition.
Relaxation.
Future.
Psychic.
Charisma.
Capitulation.
Metamorphosis.
Surrender.
Interconnectedness.

Now that you are grounded in a state of natural presence, take a minute and again notice any thoughts, feelings, or sensations that are arising in the body.

Think back to the challenge or opportunity for growth in your life that you decided to work with. Keep your senses open. What thoughts, feelings and sensations arise within you as you do?

Remember you are safe. You are supported by the Earth and Nature flows through you reminding you of your own power.

How have the thoughts feelings and sensations shifted since you started this exercise? Close your eyes, take a minute and notice what emerges.

Open your eyes. Allow yourself to focus fully on the natural environment around you. What part of Nature calls out to you and attracts your attention?

What do your eyes keep returning to again and again? What thoughts, feelings and sensations arise within the body?

Focus on this part of nature. Give yourself a minute to explore it with as many senses as possible.

Now, complete this natural attractions statement:

"I'm attracted to [this part of nature] because…"

Give yourself a minute. What thoughts, feelings, and sensations do you notice within the body?

Now, change the sentence around:

"I'm attracted to myself because…"

Don't worry about whether it makes sense logically. Give yourself a minute to explore how this statement feels, observing any thoughts, feelings, and sensations that arise in the body as you do.

Close your eyes. Take a few deep breaths in and out as you feel your feet on the ground.

Open your eyes and find another part of nature that attracts you.

Focus on this part of nature. Give yourself a minute to explore it with as many senses as possible.

Complete the natural attractions statement:

"I'm attracted to [this part of nature] because…"

Give yourself a minute. What thoughts, feelings, and sensations do you notice within the body?

Change the sentence around:

"I'm attracted to myself because…"

Don't worry about whether it makes sense logically. Give yourself a minute to explore how this statement feels, observing any thoughts, feelings, and sensations that arise in the body as you do.

Now, bring into your awareness the challenge/opportunity for growth that you were thinking about at the start of this exercise. What can these two statements of what's attractive about yourself help you discover about yourself that can help with the challenge/opportunity you face? Give yourself a few minutes to reflect.

How have the thoughts, feelings, or sensations that arose within the body changed since you started this exercise? Give yourself a few minutes to reflect.

Take a few deep breaths in and out.

Feel the pressure of your feet on the ground.

Continue doing this until you feel ready to continue the rest of your day.

DEEPEN YOUR ABILITY FOR NATURAL COMMUNICATION EXERCISE

❧   ❧   ❧

THE EXERCISE IN THIS CHAPTER is designed to allow you to experience entering a state of natural presence and moving into your natural body simultaneously before finding a natural attraction in nature and then entering into natural communication with it. It will help you practise asking for consent and explore the possibility of receiving insights from nature.

Like the other exercises, while it's more powerful to do this outside in a natural environment, you can also do the exercise indoors with some plants, a picture of nature, or even tapping into a memory of one of your favourite times spent outside. Remember, it's key to be in a place where you feel safe, comfortable, relaxed, and warm. You can do this exercise standing, sitting, or lying down.

Make yourself comfortable wherever you are.

Take a deep breath in. And then out.

Repeat this a few times noticing any changes in your state of natural presence.

Close your eyes.

Continue to take deep breaths in. And then out.

Open your eyes.

Become aware of your sense of light. What do you notice in nature? And how does that feel within the body?

Close your eyes. Become aware of your sense of seeing without the eyes. What do you notice? And what sensations do you experience within the body?

Open your eyes. Become aware of your sense of colour. What colour stands out the most for you? What do you notice happening in your body now?

Become aware of your sense of mood attached to colours. What emotion comes to mind when you look at the colour from the last sense? How does that feel within the body?

Become aware of your sense of visibility and invisibility. What is visible in the surrounding landscape? What is invisible even though you know it's there? What physical sensations are you experiencing within the body?

Become aware of your sense of temperature. How is the temperature where you are? How does that temperature feel compared to the temperature of your body?

Become aware of your sense of season. What season is it and how can you tell? What sensations do you notice in your body as you do this?

Become aware of your sense of electromagnetic energy. Are there any sources of electromagnetic energy near you? How does your body feel?

Become aware of your sense of hearing. What sounds do you notice the most? What physical sensations does this sound create within your body?

Become aware of your sense of pressure. What signs of pressure are you aware of? Can you feel any pressure within or around your body?

Become aware of your sense of gravity. How does gravity help maintain the natural world around you? How are you aware of gravity affecting your body?

Become aware of your sense of protection. What signs of protection can you see around you? How does it feel within your body when you think of being protected by nature?

Become aware of your sense of touch. What can you touch that's close to you? What thoughts, feelings, and sensations arise within the body when you do?

Become aware of your sense of balance. What signs of balance can you see around you? How does balance feel within the body?

Become aware of your sense of space. How close/far are you from the natural world around you? How does that feel within your body?

Become aware of the Earth's rotation. How can you tell the Earth is rotating? What sensations do you notice in the body at the thought of the Earth's rotation?

Become aware of your sense of motion. What movement can you sense around you? What movement can you sense within the body?

Become aware of your sense of smell. What smells can you sense in the air? How do they make your body feel?

Become aware of your sense of taste. What can you taste in the air around you? How does this make your body feel?

Become aware of your sense of appetite. What food or water sources can you sense around you? How does your body respond to these?

Become aware of your urge to gather and hunt food. Is there anything edible you could gather or hunt? What sensations do you notice in the body at the thought of doing so?

Become aware of your sense of humidity. How much humidity is in the air around you? How does the body feel with it?

Become aware of your sense of hormones. What parts of nature around you are excreting hormones? What hormones can you sense within the body?

Become aware of your sense of pleasure. What part of nature around you brings you the most pleasure? How does that feel within the body?

Become aware of your sense of love. What do you love about being outside? What thoughts, feelings, and sensations arise in the body as you sense this?

Become aware of your sense of fear. What are you afraid of in the environment around you. How do you feel?

Become aware of your sense of play. What signs of play can you sense in the environment around you? What sensations in the body do you notice as you sense this?

Become aware of your sense of distress. What, if anything, upsets you about the environment surrounding you? How does that feel?

Become aware of your sense of landscape. What do you notice about the landscape around you? How does that make you feel?

Become aware of your sense of time. How can you sense time passing where you are? What thoughts, feelings and sensations arise in the body that reflect this passing of time?

Become aware of your sense of energy within the body. What examples of energy can you sense in the environment around you? What sensations do you notice in the body as you sense this?

Become aware of your sense of weather. What can you sense about the weather? How does this weather make you feel?

Become aware of your sense of community. What signs of community can you sense in the environment around you? What thoughts, feelings, and sensations do you notice in the body?

Become aware of your sense of self. Does this sense of self extend to the environment or stay within the body? How does that feel?

Become aware of your sense of territory. What examples of territory can you sense around you? How does this make you feel?

Become aware of your sense of compassion. How is compassion expressed in the environment around you? What thoughts, feelings, and sensations arise in the body as you explore this?

Become aware of your sense of language. What signs of language can you sense around you? How does that make you feel?

Become aware of your sense of humility. What reflects humility in the environment around you? What sensations do you notice in the body?

Become aware of your sense of form and design. What do you sense about the form and design of the environment around you? How does that make you feel?

Become aware of your sense of reason. What part of nature around you reflects logic? What thoughts, feelings, and sensations arise in the body?

Become aware of your sense of intuition. What can you intuitively sense about the environment around you? How does that make you feel?

Become aware of your sense of mind. How is this reflected in the environment around you? What sensations arise in the body as you tune into your sense of mind?

Become aware of your sense of beauty. What is the most beautiful part of the environment around you? How does that make you feel?

Become aware of your sense of stress. What part of nature around you looks stressed? What signs of stress do you sense within the body?

Become aware of your sense of past, present and future. What did the landscape around you look like in the past and what will it look like in the future? How does this make you feel?

Become aware of your psychic sense. How is this reflected in the environment around you? What thoughts, feelings, and sensations arise in the body as you observe this?

Become aware of your sense of relaxation. What part of nature appears most relaxed to you? What sensations in your body show you are relaxed?

Become aware of your sense of metamorphosis. What part of the environment around you looks as if it's going through a transformation? What thoughts, feelings, and sensations arise in the body as you sense this?

Become aware of your sense of survival. What part of the environment around you looks as if it's struggling to survive? What sensations in the body do you notice as you observe this?

Become aware of your spiritual sense. How is this reflected in the environment around you? How does the body feel when you think of this?

Become aware of your sense of interconnectedness. What connections can you sense in the environment around you? What thoughts, feelings, and sensations arise in the body as you sense these?

Look around the natural landscape. What part of nature stands out the most? Give yourself a minute to explore it through your senses.

What do you like most about this part of nature and why?

Turn this sentence around and make it about yourself. What thoughts, feelings, and sensations do you notice as you say this?

Now, ask permission to connect with this part of nature. Give yourself a minute to explore if you feel you have consent – or not.

If you feel that you've received consent, pay attention to the thoughts, feelings, and sensations that arise within you. Give yourself a minute to explore them.

Offer thanks to this part of nature for the experience you've just had. How does it feel to offer thanks?

Now, find another part of nature that stands out. Give yourself a minute to explore it through your senses.

What do you like most about this part of nature and why?

Turn this sentence around and make it about yourself. What thoughts, feelings, and sensations do you notice as you say this?

Now, ask permission to connect with this part of nature. Give yourself a minute to explore if you feel you have consent – or not.

If you feel that you've received consent, pay attention to the thoughts, feelings, and sensations that arise within you. Give yourself a minute to explore them.

Offer thanks to this part of nature for the experience you've just had. How does it feel again to offer thanks?

Find a third part of nature that stands out and attracts you. Give yourself a minute to explore it through your senses.

What do you like most about this part of nature and why?

Turn this sentence around and make it about yourself. What thoughts, feelings, and sensations do you notice as you say this?

Now, ask permission to connect with this part of nature. Give yourself a minute to explore if you feel you have consent – or not.

If you feel that you've received consent, pay attention to the thoughts, feelings, and sensations that arise within you. Give yourself a minute to explore them.

This time, ask if this part of nature has a message for you. Ask a yes/no question. How do you sense whether you have received a yes or no answer? What thoughts, feelings, and sensations arise within you? Give yourself a minute to explore this.

Open your sense of mind and see if you can understand what this part of nature is communicating to you. What senses do you notice are particularly active? What thoughts, feelings, and sensations arise within you? How are they connected to what you're observing on a sensory level? Give yourself a few minutes to explore this.

Offer thanks to this part of nature for the experience you've just had. How does it feel once again to offer thanks?

Close your eyes.

Become aware of your breath. Take a deep breath in. And then out. Repeat this until you feel ready to open your eyes.

EXPERIENCING NATURAL
RELEASE EXERCISE

❧　❧　❧

THE EXERCISE IN THIS CHAPTER is designed to allow you to combine the fifty-four senses along with the power of the heart and imagination to help you experience your own natural release and discover the action you can take to help you integrate it into your daily life.

As with the other exercises, while it's more powerful to do this outside in a natural environment, you can also do the exercise indoors with some plants, a picture of nature, or even tapping into a memory of one of your favourite times spent outside. Remember, it's key to be in a place where you feel safe, comfortable, relaxed, and warm. You can do this exercise standing, sitting, or lying down.

Take a deep breath in. And then out.

Become aware of the natural environment around you, whether real or through your sense of memory.

Give yourself ten seconds to explore each of the fifty-four senses. Notice what you observe in nature and any thoughts, feelings, and sensations that arise as you do.

Light.
Colour.
Seeing without eyes.
Emotions attached to colour.
Temperature.

Season.
Visibility.
Hearing
Gravity.
Radiation.
Pressure.
Energy of the body.
Balance.
Protection.
Space.
Touch.
Smell.
The movement of the Earth rotating.
Taste.
Movement.
Humidity.
Pleasure.
Food.
Hormones.
Appetite.
Play.
Fear.
Love.
Weather.
Landscape.
Worry.
Time.
Community.
Self.
Energy fields.
Weather.
Language.
Territory.

Compassion.

Humility.

Horticulture.

Mind.

Form.

Reason.

Interconnectedness.

Beauty.

Past, present and future.

Intuition.

Relaxation.

Psychic.

Charisma.

Surrender.

Metamorphosis.

Survival.

Joy.

On a scale of 1-10, with one being not at all and ten being completely, assess your level of natural presence. If it's still lower than six, give yourself another five minutes to deepen your natural presence.

Turn your awareness inwards to your natural body.

What uncomfortable thoughts, feelings, and sensations do you notice within the body?

Give yourself a few minutes to tune into the body's intelligence and let it tell you what it needs to release during this exercise.

Bring your awareness back to the natural environment around you. What part of nature attracted you the most right now?

Why does it attract you?

What thoughts, feelings, and sensations arise as you acknowledge that you possess the very same qualities as this part of nature?

Give yourself a minute to ask permission to connect with this part of nature. What thoughts, feelings, and sensations arise as you do?

How do you know you've received consent?

Put your hand on your heart and take a few deep breaths in and out.

Now, imagine a translucent field expanding from your heart every time you take another breath in.

Continue allowing the field to expand from your heart until you sense it connecting to the part of nature you got permission to connect with.

Observe the thoughts, feelings, and sensations that arise within your body as you do this.

Focus on creating a feeling of calmness and contentment as you continue to imagine your heart field fully merging with the energy field of whatever part of nature you're connecting with.

If you can, and feel attracted to, make physical contact with the part of nature you're working with.

Now, bring your attention back towards your natural body and observe the physical sensations that are arising as you do.

Focus on your sense of light. What does the body need to release?

Now focus on your sense of colour. What does the body need to release?

Sense of seeing with eyes. What does the body want to release?

Emotions attached to colour. How does the body release?

Temperature. What physical sensations do you notice in the body?

Season. How does the body feel different?

Visibility. What is the body doing to release now?

Hearing.

Gravity.

Radiation. What's happening in the body now?

Pressure.

Energy of the body.

Balance. How is the body releasing?

Protection.

Space.

Touch. What thoughts, feelings, and sensations continue to arise?

Smell.

The movement of the Earth rotating.

Taste. How does the body want to move?

Movement.

Humidity.

Pleasure.

Food. What sensations are you experiencing now?

Hormones.

Appetite.

Play.

Fear. Is there any fear within the body still?

Love.

Weather.

Landscape.

Worry. What does the body do to continue to release?

Time.

Community.

Self.

Energy fields. Can you still imagine the connection of the heart's field with nature?

Weather.

Language.

Territory.

Compassion. What changes are you observing within the body?

Humility.

Horticulture.

Mind. What thoughts arise within the body?

Form.

Reason.

Interconnectedness. How connected to nature do you feel right now?

Beauty.

Past, present and future.

Intuition. What does the body want to do to finish its natural release?

Relaxation.

Psychic.

Charisma. What thoughts, feelings, and sensations are arising in the body?

Surrender. How has your body surrendered to the power of nature?

Metamorphosis. What feels different within the body from before you started this exercise?

Survival. What does the body want to do now?

Joy. How does the body feel now it's completed a natural release?

Ask yourself what action you need to take next. Give yourself a few minutes to gain clarity on the answer, paying attention to any thoughts, feelings, and sensations that arise as you do.

Offer thanks to the part of nature that supported you today.

Take a deep breath in. And then out.

Feel the pressure of your feet on the ground.

Keep doing this until you feel ready to go on with your day.

DISCOVER THE EARTH SELF EXERCISE

※　※　※

FIND A PLACE WHERE YOU feel safe, warm and comfortable. You can be standing, sitting or lying down. Most importantly, you need to be in a place where you feel connected to the Earth. You can do this exercise indoors or out, making sure you have a view of a natural landscape with an expanse of sky. Give yourself at least an hour to complete this exercise. Be aware that it may take a few practises with this exercise to go really deep and it's not an exercise to do unless you've practised the rest of The Nature Process first, as it assumes you have an ease and familiarity with its principles/steps.

Take a few deep breaths in and out.

Start to enter a state of natural presence by exploring the surrounding areas with your senses. Observe what thoughts, feelings, and sensations emerge as you start to activate each sense to fully connect it to your sense of mind.

Close your eyes. Imagine your sense of mind as a being in the centre of a circle with fifty-three other beings surrounding it. Notice how you feel.

Allow each being to introduce itself to the sense of mind. Imagine, as each sensory being introduces itself, that a beam of light emerges from the centre of this being and connects to the sense of mind being in the centre. Give yourself a few seconds to allow this connection to emerge.

Welcome the sense of light and allow it to connect to the sense of mind.

Welcome the sense of seeing without the eyes. Two beams of light connected.

Welcome the sense of colour. Three beams of light connected.

Welcome the sense of mood and emotions attached to colour. Four beams of light connected.

Welcome the sense of visibility. Five beams of light connected.

Welcome the sense of radiation. Six beams of light connected.

Welcome the sense of temperature. Seven beams of light connected.

Welcome the sense of season. Eight beams of light connected.

Welcome the sense of electromagnetic fields. Nine beams of light connected.

Welcome the sense of hearing. Ten beams of light connected.

Welcome the sense of pressure. Eleven beams of light connected.

Welcome the sense of gravity. Twelve beams of light connected.

Welcome the sense of protection. Thirteen beams of light connected.

Welcome the sense of touch. Fourteen beams of light connected.

Welcome the sense of balance. Fifteen beams of light connected.

Welcome the sense of Space. Sixteen beams of light connected.

Welcome the sense of the Earth's rotation. Seventeen beams of light connected.

Welcome the sense of motion. Eighteen beams of light connected.

Welcome the sense of smell. Nineteen beams of light connected.

Welcome the sense of taste. Twenty beams of light connected.

Welcome the sense of appetite and thirst. Twenty-one beams of light connected.

Welcome the sense of gathering food. Twenty-two beams of light connected.

Welcome the sense of humidity. Twenty-three beams of light connected.

Welcome the sense of pheromones. Twenty-four beams of light connected.

Welcome the sense of pain. Twenty-five beams of light connected.

Welcome the sense of distress. Twenty-six beams of light connected.

Welcome the sense of fear. Twenty-seven beams of light connected.

Welcome the sense of love. Twenty-eight beams of light connected.

Welcome the sense of play. Twenty-nine beams of light connected.

Welcome the sense of landscape. Thirty beams of light connected.

Welcome the sense of time. Thirty-one beams of light connected.

Welcome the sense of energy fields. Thirty-two beams of light connected.
Welcome the sense of weather. Thirty-three beams of light connected.
Welcome the sense of community. Thirty-four beams of light connected.
Welcome the sense of self. Thirty-five beams of light connected.
Welcome the sense of territory. Thirty-six beams of light connected.
Welcome the sense of compassion. Thirty-seven beams of light connected.
Welcome the sense of growing plants. Thirty-eight beams of light connected.
Welcome the sense of language. Thirty-nine beams of light connected.
Welcome the sense of humility. Forty beams of light connected.
Welcome the sense of form. Forty-one beams of light connected.
Welcome the sense of reason. Forty-two beams of light connected.
Welcome the sense of intuition. Forty-three beams of light connected.
Welcome the sense of beauty. Forty-four beams of light connected.
Welcome the sense of psychic capacities. Forty-five beams of light connected.
Welcome the sense of astral time. Forty-six beams of light connected.
Welcome the sense of charisma. Forty-seven beams of light connected.
Welcome the sense of relaxation. Forty-eight beams of light connected.
Welcome the sense of metamorphosis. Forty-nine beams of light connected.
Welcome the sense of surrender. Fifty beams of light connected.
Welcome the sense of survival. Fifty-one beams of light connected.
Welcome the sense of joy. Fifty-two beams of light connected.
Welcome the sense of interconnectedness. Fifty-three beams of light connected.

Imagine that all the sensory beings are now connected to the sense of mind in the centre of the circle. Notice any thoughts, feelings, or sensations that emerge as you do. Observe your state of natural presence. How does it feel?

Open your eyes and look at the environment around you. From this place, sense into the interconnected web of senses, into the truth of who you are. You are not just your human self. Everything you see is part of you. The Earth is part of you.

Connect your sense of consciousness to your sense of need for air. Breath in and out. Focus on the pressure of the air as it enters and leaves your lungs.

Bring your sense of sight and colour to the sky in all its expansiveness. Allow your gaze to soften. Activate your sense of electromagnetic fields and allow your sense of movement to detect a subtle translucent shimmer across the sky. Don't force yourself or worry if you can't see it. You've spent years not seeing it. Be patient. Can you sense it with any of your other senses?

Keep breathing. Keep focusing on the sensations that are being activated within your body. Keep your gaze soft. Once you sense the field, observe how it dances and changes.

Acknowledge that this is a shift in consciousness, a deeper sense of presence, a deeper sense of connection. How does this feel?

This electromagnetic field comes from the Earth. The sky is part of the Earth even though it may seem separate. Take a moment and ask for permission to connect. Not with the sky, but with the Earth itself, even as you stare at the sky. How do you know you've received permission? Pay attention to the thoughts, feelings and sensations that arise as you do.

Whether you have gained permission or not, take a moment and say silently or out loud to the Earth:

I acknowledge you as a living sentient being.
I acknowledge you as kin.

What thoughts, feelings, and sensations arise as you do?

Now ask the Earth if it has a message for you. Let the Earth communicate to you through your 54 senses. Commit. Give yourself in trust. Allow whatever response you get to flow through you.

Bring your sense of consciousness back to the sky. Now ask to connect with the Sky. What thoughts, feelings and sensations arise as you do?

With every breath in, breathe the sky into your body. Allow it to fill you. Focus on the experience you're having with all 54 senses. Don't get stuck on one. Allow them to dance and play with each other. What do you notice as you do?

Extend your consciousness from your sense of self to your sense of sky. Experience yourself standing connected to the sky, feet on the earth and eyes to the sky. Sense yourself as the sky, surrounding the earth, looking down at yourself, so small and tiny on the earth. Feel the connection as you merge into one.

Through this connection, sense how the sky envelops the whole earth. Even as you sense your feet grounded and connected to the earth, and you sense yourself surrounding the earth, draw the earth through this connection into you. Every breath that you take in, allow the earth to expand within you, so that there is no separation, that you become both your Human Self and the Earth Self.

Feel the power and wisdom of 4.5 billion years of life and intelligence. Don't try to understand this. Just feel it. Contained within you.

4.5 billion years of life and intelligence to create the body that you inhabit today, to create your Human Self.

4.5 billion years of dreaming, growing, expanding to be here today, in this moment and witness the Earth Self through your Human Self.

This moment has been 4.5 billion years in the making so that you can experience yourself as you are today. What thoughts, feelings, and sensations do you observe? Can you sense whether they come from your Human Self or the Earth Self?

This is just the beginning. It's the beginning of you embracing both your Human Self and the Earth Self.

You are safe. There is nothing to fear. Your Human Self does not disappear. It expands to include the Earth Self.

Feel the Earth Self within you. How does it feel?

Imagine the Earth Self standing in the centre of the circle along with your sense of mind. Connect the Earth Self to each of your senses so that you experience the Earth Self again and again.

Welcome the sense of light and allow it to connect to the sense of mind.

Welcome the sense of seeing without the eyes. Two beams of light connected.

Welcome the sense of colour. Three beams of light connected.

Welcome the sense of mood and emotions attached to colour. Four beams of light connected.

Welcome the sense of visibility. Five beams of light connected.

Welcome the sense of radiation. Six beams of light connected.

Welcome the sense of temperature. Seven beams of light connected.

Welcome the sense of season. Eight beams of light connected.

Welcome the sense of electromagnetic fields. Nine beams of light connected.

Welcome the sense of hearing. Ten beams of light connected.

Welcome the sense of pressure. Eleven beams of light connected.

Welcome the sense of gravity. Twelve beams of light connected.

Welcome the sense of protection. Thirteen beams of light connected.

Welcome the sense of touch. Fourteen beams of light connected.

Welcome the sense of balance. Fifteen beams of light connected.

Welcome the sense of Space. Sixteen beams of light connected.

Welcome the sense of the Earth's rotation. Seventeen beams of light connected.

Welcome the sense of motion. Eighteen beams of light connected.

Welcome the sense of smell. Nineteen beams of light connected.

Welcome the sense of taste. Twenty beams of light connected.

Welcome the sense of appetite and thirst. Twenty-one beams of light connected.

Welcome the sense of gathering food. Twenty-two beams of light connected.

Welcome the sense of humidity. Twenty-three beams of light connected.

Welcome the sense of pheromones. Twenty-four beams of light connected.

Welcome the sense of pain. Twenty-five beams of light connected.

Welcome the sense of distress. Twenty-six beams of light connected.

Welcome the sense of fear. Twenty-seven beams of light connected.

Welcome the sense of love. Twenty-eight beams of light connected.

Welcome the sense of play. Twenty-nine beams of light connected.

Welcome the sense of landscape. Thirty beams of light connected.

Welcome the sense of time. Thirty-one beams of light connected.

Welcome the sense of energy fields. Thirty-two beams of light connected.

Welcome the sense of weather. Thirty-three beams of light connected.

Welcome the sense of community. Thirty-four beams of light connected.

Welcome the sense of self. Thirty-five beams of light connected.

Welcome the sense of territory. Thirty-six beams of light connected.

Welcome the sense of compassion. Thirty-seven beams of light connected.

Welcome the sense of growing plants. Thirty-eight beams of light connected.

Welcome the sense of language. Thirty-nine beams of light connected.

Welcome the sense of humility. Forty beams of light connected.

Welcome the sense of form. Forty-one beams of light connected.

Welcome the sense of reason. Forty-two beams of light connected.

Welcome the sense of intuition. Forty-three beams of light connected.

Welcome the sense of beauty. Forty-four beams of light connected.

Welcome the sense of psychic capacities. Forty-five beams of light connected.

Welcome the sense of astral time. Forty-six beams of light connected.

Welcome the sense of charisma. Forty-seven beams of light connected.

Welcome the sense of relaxation. Forty-eight beams of light connected.

Welcome the sense of metamorphosis. Forty-nine beams of light connected.

Welcome the sense of surrender. Fifty beams of light connected.

Welcome the sense of survival. Fifty-one beams of light connected.

Welcome the sense of ecstasy. Fifty-two beams of light connected.

Welcome the sense of unity. Fifty-three beams of light connected.

Imagine that all of your senses now belong to the Earth Self. Notice any thoughts, feelings, or sensations that emerge as you do. What differences do you observe between your Human Self and the Earth Self?

Take some deep breaths in and out. Give yourself a little time to sit quietly and reflect on your experience with this exercise.

❧   ❧   ❧

CHAPTER I

Abram, David. *Becoming Animal: An Earthly Cosmology.* New York, Pantheon Books, 2010.

Cox, Brian, and J. R. Forshaw. *The Quantum Universe: (and Why Anything That Can Happen, Does).* Boston, Da Capo Press, 2012.

Getty, Adele. *Goddess: Mother of Living Nature.* New York, NY, Thames and Hudson, 1990.

Louv, Richard. *Vitamin N: The Essential Guide to a Nature-Rich Life.* Chapel Hill, NC, Algonquin Books of Chapel Hill, 2016.

Marshall, Paul. *Mystical Encounters with the Natural World: Experiences and Explanations.* Oxford, Oxford University Press, 2005.

McPhee, John. *The Control of Nature.* New York, Farrar, Straus, Giroux, 1989.

Merchant, Carolyn. *The Death of Nature: Women, Ecology, and the Scientific Revolution.* San Francisco, Harper & Row, 1980.

Parenti, Christian, and Jason W. Moore. *Anthropocene or Capitalocene?: Nature, History, and the Crisis of Capitalism.* Oakland, CA, PM Press, 2016.

Sandifer, Paul A. et al. "Exploring Connections among Nature, Biodiversity, Ecosystem Services, and Human Health and Well-Being: Opportunities to Enhance Health and Biodiversity Conservation." *Ecosystem Services*, vol. 12, 2015, pp. 1–15.

Selhub, Eva M., and Alan C. Logan. *Your Brain on Nature: The Science of Nature's Influence on Your Health, Happiness and Vitality*. Mississauga, Ont., John Wiley &Amp; Sons Canada, 2012.

Swan, James A., and Roberta Swan. *Bound to the Earth*. New York, Avon Books, 1994.

Wilson, Edward O. *On Human Nature*. Cambridge, Harvard University Press, 1978.

Winter, Deborah Du Nann. *Ecological Psychology: Healing the Split between Planet and Self.* New York, HarperCollins College Publishers, 1996.

CHAPTER 2

Cohen, Michael J. *Reconnecting with Nature: Finding Wellness through Restoring Your Bond with the Earth*. Corvallis, Or., Ecopress, 1997.

Cohen, Michael J. *The Web of Life Imperative: A Primer of Organic Psychology: The Science of Greening Human Services, Education, and Alternative Medicine, Humanities, Politics and Spirituality*. Victoria, B.C., Trafford, 2003.

Cohen, Michael J. *Educating, Counseling and Healing with Nature: The Science of Natural Attraction Ecology: How to Create Moments That Let Earth Teach*. Friday Harbor, WA, Institute of Global Education, 2008.

CHAPTER 3

Abram, David. *The Spell of the Sensuous: Perception and Language in a More-than-Human World*. New York, Pantheon Books, 1996.

Ackerman, Diane. *A Natural History of the Senses*. New York, Random House, 1990.

Brooks, Jon. "26 Superhuman Benefits of Meditation." *Comfort Pit*, 2016, comfortpit.com/superhuman-benefits-of-meditation/.

Buhner, Stephen Harrod. *Plant Intelligence and the Imaginal Realm: beyond the Doors of Perception into the Dreaming Earth*. Rochester, VT, Bear &Amp; Company, 2014.

Fehmi, Les, and Jim Robbins. *The Open-Focus Brain: Harnessing the Power of Attention to Heal Mind and Body*. Boston, Trumpeter Books, 2007.

Miller, Richard Alan, and Iona Miller. "New Physics-Schumann's Resonances and Human Psychobiology (Extended Version)." *O.A.K.*, 2003, www.nw-botanicals.org/oak/newphysics/schumann/schumann.htm.

Mitsutake, G. et al. "Does Schumann Resonance Affect Our Blood Pressure?" *Biomedicine &Amp; Pharmacotherapy*, vol. 59, 2005.

Murchie, Guy. *The Seven Mysteries of Life: An Exploration in Science & Philosophy*. Boston, Houghton Mifflin, 1978.

Nadkarni, N. "Life Science in Prison." *Nalini Nadkarni: Life Science in Prison | TED Talk | TED.com*, 2010, www.ted.com/talks/nalini_nadkarni_life_science_in_prison.

Sewall, Laura. *Sight and Sensibility: the Ecopsychology of Perception*. New York, J.P. Tarcher/Putnam, 1999.

Wise, Anna. *The High-Performance Mind: Mastering Brainwaves for Insight, Healing, and Creativity*. New York, Putnam, 1995.

Ulrich, R. "View through a Window May Influence Recovery from Surgery." *Science*, vol. 224, no. 4647, 1984, pp. 420–421.

CHAPTER 4

Claxton, Guy. *Intelligence in the Flesh: Why Your Mind Needs Your Body Much More than It Thinks*. New Haven, Yale University Press, 2015.

Dorotik, Claire. *On the Back of a Horse: Harnessing the Healing Power of the Human-Equine Bond*. Bloomington, IN, IUniverse Inc., 2011.

Hallberg, Leif. *Walking the Way of the Horse: Exploring the Power of the Horse-Human Relationship*. New York, IUniverse, 2008.

Levine, Peter A. *Waking the Tiger: Healing Trauma: The Innate Capacity to Transform Overwhelming Experiences*. Berkeley, CA, North Atlantic Books, 1997.

Levine, Peter A. *In an Unspoken Voice: How the Body Releases Trauma and Restores Goodness*. Berkeley, North Atlantic Books, 2010.

Lowen, Alexander. *Bioenergetics*. New York, Coward, McCann & Geoghegan, 1975.

Lowen, Alexander. *The Language of the Body: Physical Dynamics of Character Structure*. Alachua, FL, Bioenergetics Press, 2006.

Maté, Gabor. *When the Body Says No: Understanding the Stress-Disease Connection.* Hoboken, NJ, J. Wiley, 2003.

Nummenmaa, L. et al. "Bodily Maps of Emotions." *Proceedings of the National Academy of Sciences*, vol. 111, no. 2, 2013, pp. 646–651.

Sapolsky, Robert M. *Why Zebra's Don't Get Ulcers.* New York, St. Martin's Press 2004.

Van der Kolk, Bessel. *The Body Keeps the Score: Brain, Mind, and Body in the Healing of Trauma.* New York, Viking, 2014.

CHAPTER 5

Camazine, Scott et al. *Self-Organization in Biological Systems.* Princeton, New Jersey, Princeton University Press, 2001.

Meadows, Donella H., and Diana Wright. *Thinking in Systems: A Primer.* White River Junction, VT, Chelsea Green Pub., 2008.

Powell, Simon G. *Darwin's Unfinished Business: The Self-Organizing Intelligence of Nature.* Rochester, VT, Park Street Press, 2012.

Sagan, Carl. *Cosmos.* New York, Random House, 1980.

Sahtouris, Elisabet. *Earthdance: Living Systems in Evolution.* Lincoln, NE, IUniverse.com, Inc., 2000.

Tyson, Neil deGrasse., and Donald Goldsmith. *Origins: Fourteen Billion Years of Cosmic Evolution.* New York, W.W. Norton & Co., 2004.

Chapter 6

Andrews, Ted. *Animal-Speak: The Spiritual & Magical Powers of Creatures Great & Small.* St. Paul, MN, U.S.A., Llewellyn Publications, 1993.

Buhner, Stephen Harrod. *The Secret Teachings of Plants: The Intelligence of the Heart in the Direct Perception of Nature.* Rochester, VT, Bear & Co., 2004.

Lovelock, James. *Gaia, a New Look at Life on Earth.* Oxford, Oxford University Press, 1979.

Mancuso, Stefano et al. *Brilliant Green: The Surprising History and Science of Plant Intelligence.* Washington, Island Press, 2015.

Miller, Peter. *The Smart Swarm: How Understanding Flocks, Schools, and Colonies Can Make Us Better at Communicating, Decision Making, and Getting Things Done.* New York: Avery, 2010.

Reddy, Jini. *Wild Times: Extraordinary Experiences Connecting with Nature in Britain.* Buckinghamshire, UK, Bradt Travel Guides, 2016.

Smith, Penelope. *Animal Talk: A Guide to Communicating with and Understanding Animals.* Point Reyes Station, CA, Pegasus, 1984.

Tompkins, Peter, and Christopher Bird. *The Secret Life of Plants.* New York, Harper & Row, 1973.

Tudge, Colin. *The Secret Life of Trees.* London, Allen Lane, 2005.

Williams, Marta. *Learning Their Language: Intuitive Communication with Animals and Nature.* Novato, CA, New World Library, 2003.

Wohlleben, Peter. *The Hidden Life of Trees: What They Feel, How They Communicate – Discoveries from a Secret World.* Canada, Greystone Books, 2016

CHAPTER 7

Anderson, Rosemarie, and William Braud. *Transforming Self and Others through Research: Transpersonal Research Methods and Skills for the Human Sciences and Humanities.* Albany, State University of New York Press, 2011.

Biaggioni, I. et al. *Primer on the Autonomic Nervous System.* Elsevier Science, 2012.

Childre, Doc, and Howard Martin. The HeartMath Solution: The Institute of HeartMath's Revolutionary Program for Engaging the Power of the Heart's Intelligence. New York, HarperOne, 2000.

Csikszentmihalyi, Mihaly. *Flow: The Psychology of Optimal Experience.* New York, Harper & Row, 1990.

Farhi, Donna. *The Breathing Book: Good Health and Vitality through Essential Breath Work.* New York, Henry Holt, 1996.

Gawain, Shakti. *Creative Visualisation: Use the Power of Your Imagination to Create What You Want in Your Life.* San Rafael (Calif.), New World, 1995.

CHAPTER 8

Corbett, Julia B. *Communicating Nature: How We Create and Understand Environmental Messages.* Washington, DC, Island Press, 2006.

Eisenstein, Charles. *The Ascent of Humanity: Civilisation and the Human Sense of Self.* Berkeley, CA, Evolver Editions, 2013.

Goleman, Daniel. *Emotional Intelligence: Why It Can Matter More than IQ: & Working with Emotional Intelligence.* London, Bloomsbury, 2004.

Hesz, Alex, and Bambos Neophytou. *Guilt Trip: from Fear to Guilt on the Green Bandwagon.* Chichester, U.K., Wiley, 2010.

Hood, Bruce M. *The Self Illusion: Why There Is No 'You' inside Your Head.* London, Constable, 2012.

Louv, Richard. *The Nature Principle: Human Restoration and the End of Nature-Deficit Disorder.* Chapel Hill, NC, Algonquin Books of Chapel Hill, 2011.

Pearse, Guy. *Greenwash: Big Brands and Carbon Scams.* Collingwood, Vic., Black Inc., 2012.

Silverstone, Matthew. *Blinded by Science.* Great Britain, Lloyd's World Publishing, 2011.

CHAPTER 9

Benyus, Janine M. *Biomimicry: Innovation Inspired by Nature.* New York, Morrow, 1997.

Gruel, N. "The Plateau Experience: An Exploration of Its Origins, Characteristics, and Potential." *The Journal of Transpersonal Psychology,* vol. 47, no. 1, 2015, pp. 44–63.

Huxley, Julian. *New Bottles for New Wine, Essays.* New York: Harper, 1957. Print.

Macy, Joanna. *World as Lover, World as Self: Courage for Global Justice and Ecological Renewal.* Berkeley, CA, Parallax Press, 2007.

Maslow, Abraham H. *Religions, Values, and Peak-Experiences.* Columbus, Ohio State University Press, 1964.

Maslow, Abraham H. *The Further Reaches of Human Nature.* Harmondsworth, Penguin, 1973.

Maslow, Abraham H. *Toward a Psychology of Being.* New York, J. Wiley & Sons, 1999.

Thomashow, Mitchell. *Ecological Identity: Becoming a Reflective Environmentalist.* Cambridge, MA: MIT, 1995. Print.

❧   ❧   ❧

The Nature Process Workshops and Seminars

We offer dynamic and engaging nature experiences that allow people to deepen their connection to nature and improve their well-being.

Our coaches and facilitators offer customised training and seminars based upon your needs that range from one hour seminars to three-day training events.

Please contact us to discuss your requirements at: nature@thenaturepro-cess.co.

The Nature Process Facilitator Training

We also offer training to enable people to become The Nature Process Facilitators so that they can help their organisation or local community deepen their connection to nature and improve their well-being.

The sixty-hour training can either be delivered online or in person.

Online, the training is a thirteen week, sixty-hour training comprising of twelve live coaching calls with forty-eight hours of practical nature activities and preparation to ensure you have the necessary skills to successfully facilitate The Nature Process.

If done in-person, the training program is delivered over five weekends.

To check out our facilitator training program go to: www.thenaturepro-cess.co/training

NOURISHING OUR ROOTS

※　※　※

TREESISTERS (WWW.TREESISTERS.ORG) IS A NON-PROFIT organisation whose mission is to help reforest the tropics within ten years by calling forth the unique gifts, generosity and leadership of women everywhere and focusing it towards this goal.

Thanks to you buying this book, we are able to plant five trees through our partnership with TreeSisters and help restore the mangrove forests in Madagascar.

According to TreeSisters: The tropical forests are more than 'the lungs' of our world - they are rain creators, weather stabilizers, air cleansers and conditioners for the whole planet. They are our major carbon sinks - absorbing excess atmospheric carbon that otherwise acidifies our oceans. They are the most biodiverse places on Earth in regions housing the poorest populations facing the worst extremes of climate change - and they need help. We cannot live without them and if we try, we'll lose. It's 'tree-time' - now.

For more information go to: www.treesisters.org/about/our-trees

ABOUT TABI JAYNE

❧   ❧   ❧

TABI IS A APPLIED PSYCHOLOGIST, coach and consultant who has spent the last six years synthesising coaching, eco-psychology (the benefits of a human-nature relationship) and biomimicry (how learning from nature can provide solutions to challenging human problems) into a unique approach that allows business people and organizations to achieve higher levels of performance and sustainability through Bringing nature into the core of their business.

Tabi also has a BSc. (hons) in Psychology, a MSc. in Applied Ecopsychology, is a member of the British Psychological Society, a Fellow with the Royal Society for the encouragement of Arts, Manufactures and Commerce (RSA), a certified professional coach with the International Coach Academy (ICA) and an accredited coach and trainer with the International Association of Coaches, Therapists, and Mentors (IACTM). She is currently studying for her second masters in consciousness, spirituality and transpersonal psychology.

Her connection to nature has been developed and inspired by the very same landscape that inspired John Muir in Scotland, the wild green mountains of Galicia, and various other landscapes in Europe and North America.

Over the last seven years Tabi has divided her time between Scotland and Spain and has spent much time travelling in Europe and the U.S. When she's not obsessing over how to bring nature to people and organisations you'll find her strength training, climbing trees, wading through rivers, running up hills, talking to herself in Spanish and figuring out how to maintain the title of "Best Auntie in the Universe" as awarded to her by her eldest and youngest niece.

ACKNOWLEDGEMENTS

❧ ❧ ❧

First and foremost, I want to thank myself for sticking with this second edition, even when I was pulling my hair out, banging my head off the desk and entertaining fantasies of printing the whole book out, then burning it on a bonfire in the middle of the woods as I danced around it.

Second, I want to thank nature for inspiring me and attracting me to create something that has inspired and attracted so many others. I am constantly in awe of the power nature, both within us and around us, holds.

Third, I want to thank Lyn Man and Sami Aaron. Lyn has patiently listened to the tortured anguish of a writer and calmly supported not only the development of this second edition but also of The Nature Process itself. Sami offered passionate feedback and editing on this second edition as she also supported the growth of The Nature Process itself. In fact, if it weren't for Sami's continued championing of a second edition of the book you wouldn't be reading this now!

Thanks also to goes to Sheila Holmwood for her detailed editing of language and grammar that prevented this book from being the love-child of British and American English as well as to the talented designer who created such a fantastic book cover.

I also want to thank Maitari Simone and Claire Zhu for their dedication and commitment to The Nature Process. Without their enthusiasm and belief, The Nature Process wouldn't be where it is today.

Also, the current group of The Nature Process facilitators need to be acknowledged. Without the continued energy and support of Kate Fismer,

Polly Burns, Betty Hames and Danuta Karpinksa as they master The Nature Process to share with others, I wouldn't have the drive to keep going.

Thank you again to every single person around the world who has bought The Nature Process book or taken part in one of The Nature Process courses. You are my inspiration.

Last but not least, the biggest thank you ever to my mummy and sister who have put up with a frustrated, grumpy cow on many an occasion throughout the re-writing of this edition.

Made in the USA
Lexington, KY
26 April 2017